CONCEPTS IN COMMUNICATION
INFORMATICS & LIBRARIANSHIP
(CICIL)

For a list of titles in this series,
see pp. 314-16 at the end of the book.

WOMEN'S EDUCATION IN INDIA

*Concepts in Communication
Informatics & Librarianship-13*

General Editor: S.P. AGRAWAL

WOMEN'S EDUCATION IN INDIA

**Historical Review, Present Status and Perspective Plan with Statistical Indicators
and
Index to Scholarly Writings in Indian Educational Journals Since Independence**

S.P. AGRAWAL
J.C. AGGARWAL

CONCEPT PUBLISHING COMPANY, NEW DELHI 110059

ISBN 81-7022-318-0

First Published 1992
Reprinted 1994

© Authors
S.P. **Agrawal** (*b*. 1929)
J.C. **Aggarwal** (*b*. 1928)

Published and Printed by
Ashok Kumar Mittal
Concept Publishing Company
A/15-16, Commercial Block, Mohan Garden
NEW DELHI-110059 (India)

Lasertypeset by
Microtech Advance Printing Systems (Pvt.) Ltd.
H-13, Bali Nagar
NEW DELHI-110015.

GENERAL EDITOR'S INTRODUCTION

THE EARLY beginnings of renaissance of the Indian womanhood can be seen in a Pandita Ramabai or an Anandibai venturing to go abroad for education, and the humble but heroic efforts of social reformers, like Karve.

After independence, we now see separate arts colleges for women, institutions imparting instruction in home science, in applied sciences, and polytechnics too. Equipped educationally, women find employment avenues and have fruitful careers in such diverse fields like administration, advertising, aeronautics, business and commerce, fashion technology and textiles designing, and what have you. But perhaps all this reflects more of an urban situation. In the wide remote hinterland of small towns and villages, women feel the shackles of ancient customs and old traditions stronger than that of modernity from city.

The progress of women's education as charted in this CICIL publication is not unimpressive and yet it reminds us that we have miles to go.

S.P. AGRAWAL

CONTENTS

PART II
STATISTICAL INDICATORS

PART III
INDEX TO SCHOLARLY WRITINGS IN INDIAN EDUCATIONAL JOURNALS AND NEWSPAPERS SINCE INDEPENDENCE

PART IV
SELECT BIBLIOGRAPHIES ON WOMEN'S EDUCATION AND ALLIED TOPICS

PART I

HISTORICAL REVIEW PRESENT STATUS AND PERSPECTIVE PLAN

1

QUOTES FROM ANCIENT SCRIPTURES AND WRITINGS OF MODERN THINKERS

ANCIENT SCRIPTURES

"As I have given this word (i.e., the four Vedas) which is the word of salvation for all beings — Brahmanas, Ksatriyas, Vaisyas, Sudras, women, servants, aye, even the lowest of the low, so should you all do, i.e., teach and preach the *Veda*."

यथेमां वाचं कल्याणीमावदानि जनेभ्यः ।

ब्रह्मराजन्माभ्याँ शूद्राय चार्याय च स्वाय चारणाम ॥ यजर्वेद ३६.२

Just as boys acquire sound knowledge and culture by the practice of *Brahmacarya* and then marry girls of their own choice, who are young, well-educated, loving and of like temperament, so should a girl practise *Brahmacarya*, study the *Veda* and other sciences and thereby perfect her knowledge, refine her character, give her hand to a man of her own choice, who is young learned and loving.

ब्रह्मचर्येण कन्या युवानं विन्दते पतिम ॥ अथर्ववेद ११.१६.३.१८

Panini gives a reference to residents at the schools in what were called *chatrisala*.* Women also occupied the exalted position of teachers and were called *acaryani*,** a counter-example of *acarya*.

---

*   छाघ्यादयः शालायाम् । पा० ६.२.८६

**   इन्द्र वरुण भव शर्वरुद्रमूड हिमारण्य यव यवनमातुलाचार्याणामानुक् । पा० ४.१.४९

"O Learned Lady! All life is dependant on you, because you impart education to all.

त्वे विश्वा सरस्वती । ऋग्वेद २.४१.१७

According to Vedas, women should have opportunity to attain knowledge of Vedas from all the four corners.

ब्रह्मापंर युज्यतां ब्रह्म पूर्व ब्रह्मान्ततो
मध्यतो ब्रह्म सर्वत : । अथर्ववेद १४.१.६४

In Vedas, woman has been called *updeshtri* of knowledge and this indicates women as teachers.

चोदयन्ती सूनृतानां चेतन्ती सुमतीनामू । ऋग्वेद १.३.११

अहमग्रा विवाचनी । ऋग्वेद १०.१५६.२

तवं विदथमावदासि । ऋग्वेद ८.५.२६

Women have also been described as administrators, judges and one who stood for truthfulness.

अहं वदामि नेत् त्वं सभायामह त्वं वद । अथर्ववेद ७.३६.४

वेधा ऋतस्य । ऋग्वेद १०.८६.१०

From the point of view of reverence due, a teacher is tenfold superior to mere lecturer, a father a hundredfold to teacher, and a mother a thousandfold to father.

उपाध्यायाद् दशाचार्यः आचार्याणां शतं पिता ।
पितुर्दशशतं माता गौरवेणातिस्विय्ते ॥

-- वसिष्ठ धर्मसूत्र १३.४८;
मनुस्मृति २.१४५

Where women are respected, there the gods delight, and where they are not, there all work and efforts come to naught. There is no hope of rise for that family or country where they live in sadness.

यत्र नार्यस्तु पूज्यन्ते रमन्ते तत्र देवताः ।

-- मनुस्मृति

What can the fire not burn
What cannot merge into the ocean
What can the weaker sex not achieve
And what can escape death.

काह न पावकु जारि सक का न समुद्र समाइ
का न करै अबला प्रबल केहि जग कालु न खाइ ।

-- श्रीरामचरितमानस- अयोध्याकाण्ड-४७

Atreyi's reply that 'In this region several savant sages like Agastya, etc., reside. I am coming from the ashram of Valmiki to study vedas from them.' clearly indicates women's educational pursuits in ancient India.

आत्रेयी --

अस्मिन्नगस्त्यप्रमुखा : प्रदेशे भूयासां उदगीयविदो वसन्ति ।
तेभ्योडधिगन्तुं निगमान्तविद्यां वाल्मीकि पाश्र्वादिह पर्यटामि ।।

उत्तररामचरितमानस २.३

MODERN THINKERS

In ancient India, Gargi and other ladies — jewels among women — were highly educated and perfect scholars of the Veda. This is clearly written in the *Shatpatha Brahmana*.

Now if the husband be well-educated and the wife ignorant or vice versa, there will be constant state of warfare in the house. Besides, if women were not to study, where will the teachers for girls' schools come from? Nor could ever the affairs of the State, the administration of justice and the duties of married life, that are required of both husband and wife (such as keeping each other happy, the wife having the supreme control over all household matters) be carried on properly without thorough education (of men and women).

— Swami Dayananda (1825-1883),
Satyarth Prakasha

If you do not raise the women who are living embodiment of the Divine Mother, don't think that you have any other way to rise.

All nations have attained greatness, by paying proper respects to the women. That country and that nation which does not respect the women have never become great, nor will ever be in future.

You will find in the Vedic and Upanishadic age Maitreyi, Gargi and other ladies of revered memory have taken the place of Rishis. In an assembly of a thousand Brahmanas who were all erudite in the Vedas Gargi boldly challenged Yajnavalkya in a discussion about Brahman.

— Swami Vivekananda (1863-1902)
(*The Complete Works of Swami Vivekananda*, Vol. VII)

The union of man and woman will represent a perfect co-operation in the building up of human history on equal terms in every department of life.

— Rabindranath Tagore (1861-1941)

As for women's education I am not sure whether it should be different from men's and when it should begin. But I am strongly of opinion that women should have the same facilities as men and even special facilities where necessary.

A WOMAN LIKE MAN NEEDS EDUCATION

The question of the education of children cannot be solved unless efforts are made simultaneously to solve the women's education. And I have no hesitation in saying that as long as we do not have real mother teachers who can successfully impart true education to our children they will remain uneducated even though they may be going to schools.

She must have special knowledge of the management of the home, care of children, their education, etc.

— M.K.Gandhi 1869-1948
True Education

Indeed, if the education is to have its maximum result, it must begin even before birth. The part of education which the mother has to go through is to see that her thoughts are always beautiful and pure, her feelings always noble and fine, her material surroundings as harmonious as possible and full of a great simplicity.

— Aurobindo (1872-1950)

Truly no argument is required in defence of women's education. For my part, I have always been strongly of the opinion that while it may be possible to neglect men's education it is not possible to neglect women's education. The reasons are obvious. If you educate the women, probably men will be affected thereby, and in any event children will be affected.

— Jawaharlal Nehru (1889-1964)

. . . . Our civilisation became arrested and one of the main signs of that decay of our civilisation is the subjection of women"

(Speech at the laying of the Foundation
Stone of Sri Sarada College,
Salem, 6 January, 1963)

. . . . The position of women in any society is a true index of its cultural and spiritual level. Men, who are responsible for many of the views about women, have woven fantastic stories about the latter's glamour and instability, and their inferiority to men as well as their mystery and sanctity."

(Introduction)
— *Great Women of India*, 1953.

. . . . The climate of opinion has to change and women themselves have to exert their utmost to improve their mental stature."

(Speech at the laying of the Foundation Stone of Mahila Mandal,
Bikaner, 31 October, 1951)
— Dr. Sarvepalli Radhakrishnan (1888-1975)

2

WOMEN'S EDUCATION IN INDIA THROUGH THE AGES

Before 200 B.C.

Women were eligible for the study of the Vedas and the performance of sacrifices. *Upanayana*, the Vedic initiation of girls had been as common as that of boys. There were women scholars who remained unmarried for a long time devoting themselves to higher studies. Dr. Ramsarup Rasikesh* has mentioned the names of eight learned women who composed *mantras* for the Vedas. They were : Vishvavara Atreyi, Apala Atreyi, Indrani, Kakshivati Ghosh, Surya Savitri, Dakshina Prajapati, Vak Ambhirini, and Ratri Bhardwaj. [1]

It is said that Rigvedic collection contained hymns composed by different poetesses. Maitreyi was deeply interested in the problems of philosophy and Gargi was a great dialectician and philosopher of religion and philosophy. Many of the women made teaching their profession. There were boarding houses for girl students probably under the superintendence of women teachers. Several ladies in Buddhist families used to lead a life of celibacy in pursuit of religion and philosophy.

Maitreyi when proposed to settle down some property on her by her husband, Yajnavalkya, at the time of his retirement in old age from worldly life turned to him and asked whether even the possession of this whole earth, full of wealth would make her immortal and added,"What should I do with that by which I cannot become immortal?"

Vakil and Natarajan observe "one may well ask whether the history of any other country in the world can give any such instance of a woman's insatiable love of knowledge."

Such learned women were generally known as Brahmavadini

---

1. * *Aryan Heritage*, Vol. 5, October 1988.

(women who had attained knowledge of Brahman — the Supreme Being). Other names by which they were known were Mantranid (knowing the Mantras, i.e., the Vedas) and Pandita (learned). For instance, Kausalya mother of Rama, and Tara, wife of Bali, are described as Mantranid in the Ramayana, and Draupadi as Pandita in the Mahabharata.

Gargi, Maitreyi, Atreyi, Kausalya, Tara and Draupadi are not the only instances of highly learned women of ancient times. Several others have been immortalised in Sanskrit literature."

Girls were free to go through the Upanayana ceremony, wear the sacred thread, live a life of celibacy. They were free to study the Vedas, Vedangas and other subjects studied during those days along with their brother pupils.

According to Bhavabhuti, the author of *Uttar Rama Charita*, Atreyi studied the vedanta with Rama's sons Lava and Kush in Valmiki's Ashrama.

Atharva Veda declared that a maiden was not entitled to marry until after she had completed her student life.

There are instances when women were so advanced in learning that they challenged men of acknowledged learning in public discussions on philosophical and metaphysical subjects. *Brihadaranyaka Upanishad* gives an instance of Gargi who challenged Yajnavalkya in the court of Janaka, King of Videha and at the end made him defeat with the words "O Gargi, do not ask me too much." K.S. Vakil and S.Natarajan have quoted this instance in *Education in India.*

Quoting from *Atharva Veda*, Dr. Veda Mitra has stated in *Education in Ancient India* that "just as boys acquire sound knowledge and culture by the practice of 'Brahmacarya' and then marry girls of their own choice, who are young, well educated, loving and of like temperament so should a girl practise 'Brahmacarya', study the Veda and other sciences and thereby perfect her knowledge, refine her character, give her hand to a man of her own choice, who is young, learned and loving."

According to A. S. Altekar (*Position of Women in Hindu Civilisation*) in the Vedic period "in the higher sections of society the sacred initiation (Upanayana) of girls was common and they used to go through a regular course of education. Some attained distinction in the realm of theology and philosophy and a considerable number of women used to follow the teaching career."

Altekar goes on to say, "the general freedom and better status enjoyed by women in Vedic period was largely due to men being engrossed in the work of conquest and consolidation. Women used to take an active part in agriculture, and in the manufacture of cloth, bows and arrows and other war materials. They were useful members of society and could not be treated with patronage and contempt."

200 B.C.–1200 A.D.

During this period female education received a great setback due to the deterioration of the religious status of women and the lowering of the marriage age. The girls gradually lost the privilege of Upanayana, the Vedic initiation, and were not considered fit to recite Vedic mantras or perform Vedic sacrifices. In the Vedic period the girls were married at about the age of 16 or 17, but during this period the marriageable age lowered down to 12. Girls in rich, aristocratic and royal families, however, continued to receive a fairly good literary education. Besides the study of Sanskrit and Prakrit works, they were given a good grounding in domestic arts, culminary arts and fine arts like music, dancing, painting, household decoration and garland-making. Educated ladies in cultural families had been known to have contributed to literature.

1200–1800 A.D.

Percentage of literacy among women went down very rapidly during the Muslim rule. Society as a whole became prejudiced against female education. The pardah system stood in the way of girls beyond a certain age being sent to schools, though very young girls had some schooling where possible. Sultana Raziah who ascended the throne of Delhi was an educated princess. Mughal Emperors provided liberal education to the princesses. Gul-Badan Begum, the daughter of Babar and author of the *Humayun-Namah*, Nur Jahan, the celebrated wife of Jahangir, Mumtaz Mahal, the wife of Shah Jahan, Jahanara Begum, the eldest daughter of Shah Jahan. Zibunnisa Begum, the eldest daughter of Aurangzeb were learned ladies of the royal household. Akbar set apart certain chambers in Fatehpur Sikri for a girls' school. Daughters of Rajput chiefs and some Bengali Zamindars were usually able to read and write. During this period some prejudices against education of women through schools prevailed among the people. However, David Hare established a school for girls in Calcutta in 1820. Professor Patton of Elphinstone College, and J.E.D. Bethune also did considerable work in this direction.

1800–1854 A.D.

Touched by the work done by missionaries and philanthropic Englishmen, several great Indians lent their support to the opening of girls' schools and breaking down the traditional popular resistances against women education. Among them, Raja Ram Mohan Roy and Pandit Ishwarchandra Vidyasagar played an important role. By 1850, the stage was set for a change in the State policy. The lead was taken by Lord Dalhousie, the Governor-General of India who declared that no single change in the habits of the people is likely to lead more important and beneficial consequences than the introduction of education for their female children and Government should give its frank and cordial support to the cause. These orders were later on confirmed by the *Educational Despatch of 1854*.

1854–1882 A.D.

With the *Educational Despatch of 1854*, the State promised financial assistance and even direct action. Unfortunately the disturbances of 1857 followed by the declaration of the policy of social and religious neutrality slowed down the official effort. The establishment of municipalities and the levy of the local fund aiding the primary education helped the establishment of special primary schools for girls between 1870 and 1882. The four visits of Miss Mary Carpenter, the English social reformer, to India were of significance. She felt that the establishment of training colleges for women teachers was a must. Her direct access to the highest officers in the country made it possible to give immediate effect to her proposal, and the first training colleges for women primary teachers were established by 1870. By 1882, there were 2,600 primary schools, 81 secondary schools, 15 training institutions and one college for the education of women and girls. First women to get the degrees of an Indian University were two students of Bethune's School, now a college, who graduated themselves from the Calcutta University in 1883.

1882–1902 A.D.

The recommendations of the Indian Education Commission (1882-83) on women education included the support of girls' schools from Public Funds, the payment of liberal grants-in-aid, the offer of freeships, the scholarships, the raising up a class of women for teaching girls through various plans, etc. Unfortunately, the government could not assign adequate grants for the purpose due to a period of financial stringency that followed the report of the Commission, and, therefore, the progress of women education mostly depended on private enterprise. By 1901-02, private effort accounted for 11 out of 12 women colleges, 356 out of 422 secondary schools, 3,982 out of 5,305 primary schools and 32 out of 45 training institutions for women. One significant development during the period was the opening of a career in medicine for women. In 1901-02, there were 76 women in medical colleges and 166 in medical schools. The Lady Dufferin Fund was created for developing medical education for women.

1902–1921 A.D.

The period between the appointment of the Indian Universities Commission in 1902 and the transfer of education to Indian control in 1921 showed better progress in the education of women mainly due to the great public awakening and the first world war. By 1921-22, there were 19 colleges for women, 675 secondary schools and 21,956 primary schools for girls. The burden still lay heavy on private effort, though direct government effort had considerably increased. A very significant development of this period was the considerable rise in the age of marriage. This naturally increased the educational opportunities for girls and their continuance in schools and colleges. The demand of the educated men themselves to have educated wives gave further encouragement to women education. Another significant event of the period was the establishment of S.N.D.T. Women's University in Bombay by Maharshi D.K.Karve in 1916. In 1921-22, there were 197 women in medical colleges, and 334 in medical schools, 67 in colleges for teaching and 3,903 in schools for teaching. A large number of women took up commercial and technical careers.

1921–47 A.D.

The favourable factors for the promotion of women education of this period were : a further rise in the age of marriage, the teachings of Mahatma Gandhi, the phenomenal awakening of Indian womanhood, and the introduction of Provincial Autonomy in 1937. Nonetheless it was also a period of financial stringency and political struggle. In spite of difficulties, women education made considerable progress. In 1946-47, there were 59 arts and science colleges for women, 2,370 secondary schools for girls, 21,479 primary schools for girls and 4,288 institutions for professional, technical and special education for women. Owing to greater initiative shown by the State Governments and local bodies the burden on private effort was considerably reduced and now it accounted for 16,979 women institutions out of a total of 28,196 women institutions. The period also showed an increase in the trend towards co-education. By 1947, a little more than half of the number of girls under instruction were studying in mixed schools.

After 1947

The University Education Commission (1948-49) made certain recommendations regarding women education. But the most important development in the field of women education was the setting up of a National Committee on Women's Education 1958, under the chairmanship of Smt. Durgabai Deshmukh, which examined the problem of women education very comprehensively. As a result of the recommendations of the Committee, a National Council for Education was set up in 1959 under the chairmanship of Smt. Durgabai Deshmukh. State Councils have been set up in the States and Union Territories. Smt. Hansa Mehta Committee was appointed in 1961 by the National Council for Women's Education to examine the problem of curricula for girls at all stages of education. Another Committee was appointed by the Council in May 1965 with Shri M.Bhaktavatsalam, the then Chief Minister of Madras as its Chairman to look into the causes for lack of public support particularly in rural areas for girls' education. The Education Commission 1964-66 also made valuable recommendations regarding women education in India. The Resolution on the National Policy on Education 1968 also laid emphasis on women education.

The National Committee on status of women in India (1974) studied various aspects of the status of women and their education and made useful recommendations. The National Policy on Education (1986) has made important recommendations regarding women's education.

3

WOMEN IN THE CONSTITUTION OF INDIA

PREAMBLE

WE, THE PEOPLE OF INDIA, having solemnly resolved to constitute India into a [SOVEREIGN SOCIALIST SECULAR DEMOCRATIC REPUBLIC][1] and to secure to all its citizens :

JUSTICE, social, economic and political;
LIBERTY of thought, expression, belief, faith and worship;
EQUALITY of status and of opportunity, and to promote among them all
FRATERNITY assuring the dignity of the individual and the [unity and integrity of the Nation][2] unity of the Nation;
IN OUR CONSTITUENT ASSEMBLY this twentysixth day of November, 1949, do HEREBY ADOPT, ENACT AND GIVE TO OURSELVES THIS CONSTITUTION.

PART III : FUNDAMENTAL RIGHTS

Right to Equality

Article 14: *Equality before Law*

The State shall not deny to any person equality before the law or the equal protection of the laws within the territory of India.

Article 15: *Prohibition of discrimination on grounds of religion, race, caste, sex or place of birth*

(1) The State shall not discriminate against any citizen on grounds only of religion, race, caste, sex, place of birth or any of them.
(2) No citizen shall, on grounds only of religion, race, caste, sex,

place of birth or any of them, be subject to any disability, liability, restriction or condition with regard to —

> (a) Access to shops, public restaurants, hotels and places of public entertainment; or
>
> (b) The use of wells, tanks, bathing ghats, roads and places of public resort maintained wholly or partly out of State funds or dedicated to the use of the general public.

(3) Nothing in this article shall prevent the State from making any special provision for women and children.

[(4) Nothing in this article or clause (2) of article 29[3] shall prevent in the State from making any special provision for the advancement of any socially and educationally backward classes or citizens for the Scheduled Castes and the Scheduled Tribes][4].

Article 16: *Equality of opportunity in matters of public employment*

(1) There shall be equality of opportunity for all citizens in matters relating to employment or appointment to any office under the State.

(2) No citizen shall, on grounds only of religion, race, caste, sex, descent, place of birth, residence or any of them, be ineligible for, or discriminated against in respect of, any employment or office under the State.

(3) Nothing in this article shall prevent Parliament from making any law prescribing, in regard to a class or classes of employment or appointment to an office [under the Government of, or any local or other authority within, a State or Union Territory, any requirement as to residence within that State or Union Territory][5] prior to such employment or appointment.

(4) Nothing in this article shall prevent the State from making any provision for the reservation of appointments or posts in favour of any backward class of citizens which, in the opinion of the State, is not adequately represented in the services under the State.

Right against Exploitation

Article 23: *Prohibition of traffic in human beings and forced labour*

(1) Traffic in human beings and *begar* and other similar forms of forced labour are prohibited and any contravention of this provision

shall be an **offence punishable** in accordance with law.

(2) **Nothing** in this article shall prevent the State from imposing compulsory service for public purpose, and in imposing such service the State shall not make any discrimination on grounds only of religion, race, caste or class or any of them.

PART IV — DIRECTIVE PRINCIPLES OF STATE POLICY

Article 39: *Certain principles of policy to be followed by the State*

The State shall, in particular, direct its policy towards securing :

(a) That the citizens, men and women equally, have the right to an adequate means of livelihood;

(b) That the ownership and control of the material resources of the community are so distributed as best to subserve the common good;

(c) That the operation of the economic system does not result in the concentration of wealth and means of production to the common detriment;

(d) That there is equal pay for equal work for both men and women;

(e) That health and strength of workers, men and women, and the tender age of children are not abused and that citizens are not forced by economic necessity to enter avocations unsuited to their age or strength;

[(f) That children are given opportunities and facilities to develop in a healthy manner and in conditions of freedom and dignity and that childhood and youth are protected against exploitation and against moral and material abandonment][6].

Article 39 A: *Equal justice and free legal aid*

The state shall secure that the operation of the legal system promotes justice, on a basis of equal opportunity, and shall, in particular, provide free legal aid, by suitable legislation or schemes or in any other way, to ensure that opportunities for securing justice are not denied to any citizen by reason of economic or other disability.[7]

Article 42: *Provision for just and humane conditions of work and maternity relief*

The State shall make provision for securing just and humane conditions for work and maternity relief.

Article 44: *Uniform civil code for citizens*

The State shall endeavour to secure for all citizens a uniform civil code throughout the territory of India.

PART XV — ELECTIONS

Article 325: *No person to be ineligible for inclusion in, or to claim to be included in a special, electoral roll on grounds of religion, race, caste or sex.*

There shall be one general electoral roll for every territorial constituency for election to either House of Parliament or to the either House of the Legislature of State and no person shall be ineligible for inclusion in any such roll or claim to be included in any special electoral roll for any such constituency on grounds only of religion, race, caste, sex or any of them.

Article 326: *Elections to the House of the People and to the Legislative Assemblies of States to be on the basis of adult suffrage*

The elections to the House of the People and to the Legislative Assembly of every State shall be on the basis of adult suffrage; that is to say, every person who is a citizen of India and who is not less than twenty one years (eighteen years)[8] of age on such date as may be fixed in that behalf by or under any law made by the appropriate Legislature and in not otherwise disqualified under this Constitution or any law made by the appropriate Legislature on the ground of non-residence, unsoundness of mind, crime or corrupt or illegal practice, shall be entitled to be registered as a voter at any such election.

NOTES

1. Substituted by the Constitution (Forty-Second Amendment) Act, 1976, s. 2, for "SOVEREIGN DEMOCRATIC REPUBLIC", with effect from 3.1.1977.

2. Substituted by s. 2 *Ibid.*, for "unity of the nation" with effect from 3.1.1977.

3. Article 29 clause (2). No citizen shall be denied admission into any educational institution maintained by the State or receiving aid out of State funds on grounds only of religion, race, caste, language or any of them.

4. Added by the Constitution (First Amendment) Act, 1951, s. 2.

5. Substituted by the Constitution (Seventh Amendment) Act, 1956, s. 29 and schedule for "under any state specified in the first schedule or any local or other authority with its territory, any requirement as to residence within that state."

6. Substituted by the Constitution (Forty Second Amendment) Act, 1976, s. 7, for clause(f) with effect from 3.1.1977.

7. Inserted by s. 8, *Ibid.*, with effect from 3.1.1977.

8. Substituted by the Constitution (Sixty First Amendment) Act 1988, s. 2, 'twenty-one years'.

4

COMMITTEES, COMMISSIONS IN INDIA: OBSERVATIONS ON WOMEN'S EDUCATION

4.1 UNIVERSITY EDUCATION COMMISSION, (1948-49)*

The University Education Commission noted the importance of women's education and stated that "There cannot be an educated people without educated women. If general education had to be limited to men or to women, that opportunity should be given to women, for then it would most surely be passed on to the next generation."

Fields for Women's Education

The Commission observed : "The greatest profession of women is, and probably will continue to be, that of home maker. Yet her world should not be limited to that one relationship. There are varied conditions which may properly lead a woman to seek fulfilment of her life in other fields. Among the great contributions to human welfare have been some men who determined to forgo home and family in order to commit themselves wholly to the chosen work of their lives. Women should have the same opportunity. The place of wife and mother offers opportunity for exercise of the highest qualities and skills, yet for a woman to decide that she can best fulfil her aims by living a single life should not put her under a social disability. Sometimes also, there is a period before marriage during which a young woman can do useful work, such as teaching or nursing. Sometimes, the loss of a husband makes her the bread winner for the family. When children are grown there often remain ten to twenty-five years of vigorous life in which a woman may wish to have a useful career. Sometimes husband and wife

---

* Published by the Ministry of Education, Government of India, New Delhi, 1950.

wish to share a common occupation through the years. Sometimes with woman, as with men, the needs of home and family·leave time for useful and interesting occupations. For all such circumstances educational opportunities should be available.

One of the desirable developments of Indian life and education for both men and women is a great increase in the kinds of work open to them. If only a few callings are recognised there is excessive competition for the available places; many kinds of ability find no opportunity for expression, and many kinds of needs remain unsupplied. A wholesome and interesting society will have many and varied occupations and professions. The educational system at all levels should prepare men and women for such varied callings."

Co-educational Institutions and their state of affairs. The Commission noted the following :

"There are few truly co-educational colleges in our country. Rather, there are men's colleges to which women have been admitted as students, which is a very different matter. Quite frequently in 'co-educational' colleges nearly all the amenities are for men, and women are little more than tolerated. Often sanitary facilities for women are totally inadequate, and sometimes wholly lacking. Recreation space and facilities for women similarly are inadequate or lacking. One of the most frequent suggestions made to us was that where women and men attend colleges, that a physical directress for women be provided."

"In many co-educational colleges women have little or no share in college life. Women's hostels usually accommodate but few women, and sometimes none at all. According to the comments received, in one city where there are few or no hostels some women students must leave home at 5 a.m. in order to attend classes; and no provisions for refreshments are provided, although the students do not finish their work until mid-afternoon. The Commission received comments to the effect that the attitudes of men students left much to be desired.

"Other weaknesses of 'co-educational' colleges reported to our Commission are that there are too few women teachers, and that examinations are a severe nervous strain to women."

Appraisal of Women's Education. The University Education Commission came across such comments from eminent educationists:

The principal of a college wrote : "Women's present education is entirely irrelevant to the life they have to lead. It is not only a waste but often a definite disability." Another wrote, "The present system of women's education, based as it is upon man's needs, does not in any way make them fit for coping with the practical problems of daily life. Their education should give them a practical bias, especially from the point of view of families, for making them good mothers, teachers and doctors and nurses."

. One experienced woman educator wrote to the Commission : "The modern educated Indian woman is neither happy nor contented nor socially useful. She is a misfit in life. She is highly suppressed, and needs opportunities for self expression, the new education must provide this opportunity."

The Commission felt that to some extent this maladjustment is the price of pioneering. The educated woman is ahead of her time. She is lonely and 'out of place' while creating a new social atmosphere in which her daughters or grand daughters can be natural and at home. But to some extent her discontent is due to her effort, not only to be equal to men, but to be like them in all her interests and activities.

One educator wrote : "It is too late in the day to suggest that women should not have the same courses as men." The remaining question is : "What additional opportunities shall be provided ?"

The Commission was of the view that it was the duty of those in charge of women's education to face these problems and to design adequate lives.

Another educator wrote : "There has been no planning of women's education. It has just happened."

Recommendations

(1) Ordinary amenities and decencies of life should be provided for women in colleges originally planned for men, but to which women are being admitted in increasing numbers;
(2) there should be no curtailment in educational opportunities for women, but rather a great increase;
(3) there should be intelligent educational guidance, by qualified

men and women, to help women to get a clearer view of their real educational interest, to the end that they shall not try to imitate men, but shall desire as good education as men get. Women's and men's education should have many elements in common, but should not in general be identical in all respects, as is usually the case today;

(4) women students in general should be helped to see their normal places in a normal society, both as citizens and as women and to prepare for it, and college programmes should be so designed that it will be possible for them to do so;

(5) through educational counsel and by example the prevailing prejudices against study of home economics and home management should be overcome;

(6) standards of courtesy and social responsibility should be emphasised on the part of men in mixed colleges;

(7) where new colleges are established to serve both men and women students, they should be truly co-educational institutions, with as much thought and consideration given to the life needs of women as to those of men. Except as such colleges come into existence there are no valid criteria for comparing segregated education with co-education; and

(8) women teachers should be paid the same salaries as men teachers for equal work.

Separate Schools between the Age of 13 and 18: The University Education Commission was of the view that there seems to be a definite preponderance of opinion that from the thirteenth or fourteenth year of age until about the eighteenth, separate schools for boys and girls are desirable. The Commission felt that it was not wholly clear whether this opinion was chiefly based on custom or upon experience. The Commission cited the following :

One of India's prominent educators states : "The modern trend is for equality of opportunity for women in all spheres, and it cannot be arrested. There should be no distinctions of any kind of women from men, after the matriculation stage."

On the other hand many, probably a majority of those who commented, favour separate colleges for women when that is feasible, though not to the extent of denying women educational opportunity by excluding them from existing colleges organised primarily for men.

Some of the arguments given are that a woman cannot develop her personality in a men's college; that there is no need for women to undergo the nervous strain of examinations; that women's education should be more in keeping with the temperament and needs of women as wives and mothers; and that overcrowding is more serious for women than for men. 'A pleasing feature of colleges for women has been the intimate relations of students and teachers.' Some of these arguments have greater weight in the absence of truly co-educational colleges where the needs of men and women would be given equal weight in designing the programme.

Co-education at the College Level: As the age of entry to degree colleges would, on our recommendation, be approximately eighteen, college education may be co-educational as it is at present in many medical colleges. Separate institutions at this level would demand unjustified increase in expense. To maintain separate institutions for men and women side by side, duplicating equipment, even when it is very inadequate, would be an undue tax upon limited financial resources. Separate women's colleges commonly have poorer buildings, poorer equipment, and less able teachers. So far as possible, co-educational institutions should be encouraged at the degree level.

4.2 SECONDARY EDUCATION COMMISSION (1952-53)*

Extracts from Chapter IV on Women Education : Some special problems of women's education are reproduced below:

It will be noticed in this Report that no particular chapter has been devoted to the education of women. The Commission feels that, at the present stage of our social evolution there is no special justification to deal with women's education separately. Every type of education open to men should also be open to women. During the course of our visits to various institutions and universities we have noted that women have found admission to practically all the faculties which a generation ago would have been considered as unsuitable for them or beyond their easy reach. It is a matter of gratification that many women have joined the Faculties of Engineering, Agriculture, Medicine, Veterinary Science, Commerce, Law and Teaching as well as the Arts and Science and have taken to research and some have made their mark in it.

---

* Published by the Ministry of Education and Scientific Research, Government of India, New Delhi, 1953.

Our attention has been drawn to the provision in the Constitution that while special arrangements may be made for women and children, there shall not be any discrimination against any citizen on the ground only of religion, race caste, sex or place of birth. It is also laid down under Section 16(a) that there shall be equality of opportunity to all citizens in matters relating to employment or appointment to any office under the State and no citizen shall on grounds only of religion race, caste, sex, descent place of birth, residence be ineligible for or discriminated against in respect of any employment or office under the State. Under the circumstances it will be sufficient if we draw attention to a few points of special consideration in connection with the facilities provided for girls within the general educational framework.

Several delegations on behalf of women's organisations discussed with us various aspects of women's education. It was stated by them that there are two divergent views with regard to women's education. One view is that the only proper place for a women is the home and that the education of girls will, therefore have to be considerably different from that of boys. Such persons may admit with reluctance that in these hard times, some women have to earn their living, but in their heart of hearts, they deplore this fact and consider that training for any profession should be regarded as of minor importance in comparison to the training for home making. The other view is that education should seriously concern itself with the place that women occupy in public life. They point out that India greatly needs the services of women outside the four walls of their homes and that its backwardness in the last century was due in no small degree to the low place in society accorded to women. They insist that women must be given exactly the same education as men, so that they may compete with them on equal terms at school and college as well as in the various professions and services.

There was general agreement, however, that for girls — as well as for boys — education needs to be more closely connected with the home and the community. It should be less bookish in the narrow sense of the word and more practical and should explore the possibility of training the mind through the hands. It should do much more to prepare them for the part they will have to play later as parents and as citizens, i.e., the claims of family life should be considered as important as those of public life. For this reason, it was urged that the teaching of Home Science in Girls' School, (and wherever possible, for girls attending boy's schools) should be radically improved not necessarily with the idea that women's place is restricted to the home, but because it is essential that she should be educated to fulfil her two-fold duty to family and society. If greater attention is given to Home Science, with special emphasis on practical work of every day needs and problems, it will help to bridge the gulf between the school and the life of the home and the community, and be a better preparation for a girl's life after school, in which home making will necessarily play an important part. An educated girl who cannot run her home smoothly and efficiently, within her resources can make no worthwhile contribution to the happiness and the well-being of her family or to raising the social standards in her country.

Co-education

Another issue that was raised in our discussion was that of co-education, which implies the education of boys and girls on a footing of equality in the same institution. So far as the Primary and the University stages are concerned, co-education was generally favoured, but in regard to education at the Secondary stage there was considerable divergence of opinion. Many maintained that, during the period of adolescence, it is desirable that the education of boys and girls should be carried on in separate institutions. On the other hand, it was stated that, in view of the financial considerations and other difficulties in regard to proper personnel etc., this would mean that many girls will not be able to attend schools at all. With the comparatively limited finances that are available for education and with so many other commitments in regard to the expansion and improvement of education, there was some apprehension that, if separate schools were insisted upon, the Secondary education of girls in many parts of the country would be handicapped. Under the present circumstances, there are considerable variations in regard to the social-intercourse of the sexes in different parts of the country. Naturally, in orthodox regions co-education cannot be popular or successful as the atmosphere in the school will be very different from that in the family and the community.

It seems to us, therefore, that there can be no hard and fast policy with regard to co-education and that in this respect the pattern of education in our schools cannot be very much in advance of the social pattern of the community where the school is located. We are, of opinion that where it is possible separate schools for girls should be established as they are likely to offer better opportunities than in mixed schools to develop their physical, social and mental aptitudes and all States should open such schools in adequate numbers. But it should be open to girls whose parents have no objection in this matters, to avail themselves of co-educational facilities in boys' schools.

We have noticed with regret that, because of the larger expenditure which has to be incurred on buildings, equipment and staff in the case of girls' schools. States have generally responded more readily to the demand for boys' education than to the demand for the education of girls. To promote the pattern of society that we envisage for the future the expansion of girls' education must take place *pari passu* with boys' education. In a democratic society where all citizens men and women – have to discharge their civic and social obligations, we cannot envisage differences which may lead to various in the standard of intellectual development achieved by boys and girls.

Conditions for Mixed Schools

This brings us to a consideration of the special facilities that should be provided for girls in mixed schools. We feel that in all such institutions definite rules should be laid down in order to provide for the special needs of girls. In the first place, the staff must be composed of both men and women. Secondly, provision should be made for the teaching of subjects like Home Craft, Music, Drawing, Printing, etc., which specially appeal to girls. Thirdly, necessary amenities should be provided for girls by way of separate sanitary conveniences, retiring rooms, playing fields etc. Even in those institutions where a comparatively small number of girls is admitted — and this will particularly by the case in rural areas for a long time — there should be at least one woman teacher on the staff to attend to their needs and to advice them on all social and personal matters. We need hardly stress the fact that women teachers themselves should have necessary special facilities in the way of retiring room and sanitary conveniences.

In co-educational as well as mixed schools there should be provision for special co-curricular activities suited to girls, in addition to those activities in which they participate side by side with the boys – e.g. Girl Guiding, Home Nursing, Needle Work, etc.

It is also desirable that on the management of such schools there should be women representatives who will be able to see that the necessary facilities for girls are actually provided by the management.

4.3 NATIONAL COMMITTEE ON WOMEN'S EDUCATION (1958-59)*

Background

The problems of education of girls and women acquired a new significance after the attainment of independence. Education panels of the Planning Commission at its meeting held in July 1957, recommended that "a suitable Committee should be appointed to go into the various aspects of the question relating to the nature of education for girls at the elementary, secondary and adult stages and to examine whether the present system was helping them to lead a happier and more useful life." This recommendation was placed before the Conference of the State Education Ministers (held in September, 1957) who also agreed that a special Committee should be appointed to examine the whole question of women's education. The National Committee on Women's Education was accordingly set up by the Government of India in the Ministry of Education.

Chairman: Smt. Durgabai Deshmukh, Chairman, Central Social Welfare Board.

Members: Kumari S. Panadikar; Shri P.N. Mathur; Smt. Kulsum Sayani; Shri J.P. Naik; Smt. Sahra Ahmed; Smt. O.C. Srinivasan; Kumari Sarojini Rajan; Dr. Phulrenu Guha.

Terms of Reference

(a) to suggest special measures to make up the leeway in women's education at the primary and secondary levels.

(b) to examine the problem of wastage in girls' education at these levels.

(c) to examine the problem of adult women who have relapsed into illiteracy or have received inadequate education and who need continuation of education so as to enable them to earn a living and participate in projects of national reconstruction.

(d) to survey the nature and extent of material and other facilities offered by voluntary welfare organisations for the education of such women and to recommend steps necessary to enable them

---

* Published by the Ministry of Education, Govrnment of India, New Delhi, 1959.

to offer larger educational facilities to them.

(e) to examine the possibility and methods of encouraging a larger number of women to go into vocational trades by providing suitable vocational training as a part of formal education or through special courses designed for adult women.

A. Special Recommendations Needing Top Priority

1. The education of women should be regarded as a major and a special problem in education for a good many years to come and a bold and determined effort should be made to face its difficulties and magnitude and to close the existing gap between the education of men and women in as short a time as possible. The funds required for the purpose should be considered to be the first charge on the sums set aside for the development of education.

2. Steps should be taken to constitute as early as possible a National Council for the Education of Girls and Women.

3. The problem of the education of women is so vital and of such great national significance that it is absolutely necessary for the Centre to assume more responsibility for its rapid development.

4. The State Governments should establish State Councils for the education of girls and women.

5. Every State should be required to prepare comprehensive development plans for the education of girls and women in its area.

6. It is also necessary to enlist the co-operation of all semi-official organisations, local bodies, voluntary organisations, teachers' organisations and members of the public to assist in the promotion of the education of girls and women.

7. The Planning Commission should set up a permanent machinery to estimate, as accurately as possible, the woman-power requirements of the Plans from time to time and make the results of its studies available to Government and the public.

B. Other Special Recommendations

1. Primary Education (Age group 6-11):

(1) Concessions in kind (not in cash) should be given to all girls,

whether from rural or urban areas, of parents below a certain income level.

(2) The Government should formulate a scheme for awarding prizes to the village which shows the largest proportional enrolment and average attendance of girls.

2. Middle and Secondary Education (Age group 11 to 17)

(1) At the middle school stage, more and more co-educational institutions should be started.

(2) But for the secondary stage, separate schools for girls should be established specially in rural areas, at the same time giving parents full freedom to admit their girls to boy's schools if they so desire.

(3) All girls (and all boys also) of parents below a prescribed income level should be given free education upto the middle stage.

(4) As far as possible, free or subsidised transport should be made available to girls in order to bring middle and secondary schools, within easy reach.

3. Curriculum and Syllabi

(1) There should be identical curriculum for boys and girls at the primary stage with the proviso that, even at this stage, subjects like music, painting, sewing needle work, simple hand-work, and cooking should be introduced to make the courses more suitable for girls.

(2) At the middle school stage, and more especially at the secondary stage, there is need for differentiation of curricula for boys and girls.

4. Training and Employment

(1) Immediately steps should be taken to set up additional training institutions for women teachers in all such areas of the country where a shortage exists at present.

(2) With a view to inducing women from urban areas to accept posts of teachers in rural schools, women teachers serving in rural areas may be provided with quarters and a village

allowance may be given to such teachers.

(3) The maximum age limit for entry into service may be relaxed, and age of retirement may be extended to 60 provided the teacher is physically and otherwise fit.

5. Professional and Vocational Education

(1) The employment of women on a part-time basis, wherever feasible, should be accepted as policy.

(2) Girls should be encouraged to take up courses in Commerce, Engineering, Agriculture, Medicine, etc., at the university stage by offering them scholarships and other concessions.

(3) It is important to organise campaigns to mobilise public opinion for creating proper conditions in offices and establishments in which women can work freely.

6. Facilities for Adult Women

(1) Educational facilities in the form of condensed courses (a) that prepare women for the Middle School Examination and (b) those that prepare them for the High School or Higher Secondary Examination should be provided more extensively in all States.

(2) Provision should also be made of condensed courses, which train women for suitable vocation after completion of necessary continuation education.

7. Voluntary Organisations

The services of the voluntary organisations should be extensively used in the field of middle, secondary, higher, social and vocational education of women. The existing grant-in-aid codes of the States need a thorough revision. There should be a substantial and significant differenc in the rates of grants-in-aid as between girls' institutions and boys' institutions at all levels. The conditions of aid for girls' institutions should be made easier.

C. General Recommendations

1. Wherever primary education is not free immediate steps should be

taken to make it free. Whenever new shools are started, the rural regions should be given priority consideration.

2. Wastage and Stagnation

(1) As a scientific study of the problem of wastage on an all India basis is needed, the Ministry of education should carry out special studies of this problem in all parts of the country.

(2) The following steps should be taken to reduce the extent of stagnation in class I : (i) all fresh admissions to class I should be made in the beginning of the school year and not later than 60 days after the beginning of the first session; (ii) it should be a specific responsibility of teachers to see that proper attendance is maintained in the school; (iii) the age of admission should be raised to six plus, (iv) standards of teaching should be improved.

(3) The stagnation in classes II to V can be reduced if (i) attendance of children is increased; (ii) standards of teaching are improved; (iii) internal examinations are introduced; (iv) books and educational equipment needed by poor children are supplied in good time.

(4) About 65 per cent of the cases of wastage at the primary level are due to economic causes. This wastage can be eliminated only if provision for part-time instruction is made for those children who cannot attend on a whole-time basis.

(5) About 25 to 30 per cent of the cases of wastage at the primary level are due to the indifference of parents. This cause can be eliminated partly by educative propaganda and partly by a rigorous enforcement of the compulsory education law.

3. Employment of Teachers

(1) The present scales of pay of teachers should be suitably revised.

(2) There should be no distinction between the scales of pay and allowances paid to teachers in Government and Local Board or Municipal institutions and those that are paid to teachers working under private managements.

(3) The triple-benefit scheme called the Pension-cum-Provident Fund-cum Insurance Scheme should be made applicable to every teacher who is employed permanently in an institution.

4.4 COMMITTEE ON DIFFERENTIATION OF CURRICULA FOR BOYS AND GIRLS (1961)*

Background

In its meeting held on May 10, 1961 the National Council for Women's Education authorised the Chairman to set up a Committee to examine comprehensively the problem of curricula for girls at all stages of education. In consultation with the Ministry of Education, the Chairman, Smt. Raksha Saran, set up a Committee on November 1, 1961.

Chairman: Smt. Hansa Mehta.

Members: Kumari S. Panadikar; Kumari S. Sen; Kumari S.Pankajam; Kumari K. Sabarwal; Smt. S.Ray; Smt Chitra Naik; Smt. B.Tarabai; Shri P.N. Mathur; Shri T.C. Sankara Menon; Smt.V.Mulay.

Terms of Reference

(a) To examine the present curricula of school education and to determine the extent to which they take care of the individual and social needs of women in the prevailing circumstances of the country.

(b) To suggest necessary reforms without, at the same time, causing an upheaval in the general pattern of education.

(c) In view of the need of trained women personnel for development projects under social services, to consider the need for providing additional diversified courses of a pre-vocational nature, apart from Fine Arts and Home Science, at the secondary stage.

(d) To review the content of courses under the group "Fine Arts' and 'Home Scinece' and to suggest such modifications as are necessary to enable women to take up some gainful employment.

(e) To examine the types of suitable occupations for which training should be given in the polytechnics and junior teachnical schools that are being set up for girls.

---

* Published by the Ministry of Education, Government of India, 1964.

Sex Difference

According to the traditional view the mere biological difference of sex created different physical, intellectual and psychological characteristics between men and women and these basic sex differences necessitated the provision of differentiated curricula for them. Modern research into sex differences, however, has shown that such a belief has no scientific foundation.

With regard to the intellectual differences between the sexes, it has now been established that women are in no way inferior to men and that the differences in their academic and professional achievements are due mainly to lack of adequate opportunities or to influence of traditional cultural patterns. Similarly, it has been established that there is no scientific justification for the popularly held view that certain subjects are 'masculine'and others 'feminine'.

With regard to psychological differences between the sexes the recent findings are that there are no psychological characteristics related to sex as such and that the different psychological traits which men and women exhibit are the result of social conditioning.

It has also been established that the physical differences between the two sexes are of minor significance. Most of the research relating to the determination of differences and their causes has been carried out in Western countries and it is a matter for regret that no such studies have yet been undertaken in India. The need of such investigations in Indian conditions is imperative.

Equality of Women

"If society is to be organised on this new basis, women will have to be given real and effective equality with men."

In order to enable them to attain *de facto* equality with men and usher in the new social order, the Committee recommended the adoption of the following measures:

(a) The existing gap between the education of boys and girls should be rapidly bridged.

(b) Intensive efforts should be made to educate the public regarding the scientific findings about sex differences and to develop proper attitudes in each sex towards the other. In particular, the public mind will have to be disabused of all traditional concepts of the physical and intellectual inferiority of women. The public in general and the teachers in particular will have to be made to realise that it is unscientific to divide tasks and subjects on the basis of sex and to regard some of them as 'masculine' and others as 'feminine'. Similarly, the fact that the so-called psychological differences between the two sexes arise, not out of sex but out of social conditions will have to be widely publicised and people will have to be made to realise that stereo-types 'masculine' and 'feminine' personalities do more harm than good.

Co-education

(1) Co-education should be adopted as the general pattern at the elementary stage.

(2) At the secondary and collegiate stages, there should be full freedom to the managements and parents either to evoke common institutions or to establish separate ones for girls.

(3) Steps should be taken to appoint women teachers in all educational institutions at the secondary and university stages, which are ordinarily meants for boys. Similarly, some men teachers should also be appointed in separate secondary schools and colleges for girls.

The Role of Women in Society

The Committee felt that in the progressive society like ours the women are expected to share the social and economic responsibilities of men. The Committee noted :

"We do realise that child-rearing and home making will have prior claims on women. We, however, feel that owing to the development of sciences and technology, both these functions will occupy less and less of their time. It would now be possible for women to take up a career of their own and it will be a great social tragedy to allow them to do so. We, therefore, recommend that the education of women should be so planned as to enable them to follow a career of their choice without, in any way, neglecting their responsibilities for child-rearing and home making."

Proposal for Differentiation of Curricula and other allied Problems

"In the ultimate democratic and socialistic pattern of society which we visualise, education will be related to individual capacities, aptitudes and interests which, as stated above, are not related to sex. There, would, therefore be no need in such a society to differentiate curricula on the basis of sex.

But it will be some years before this new social order is created. In the transitional phase in which we are at present, certain psychological differences between men and women as well as certain divisions of social functions based on them will have to be accepted as matters of fact and as a practical basis for building up the curricula for boys and girls. While doing so, however, care should be taken to see that values and attitudes which are essential in the long run are increasingly built up in men and women and that no step is taken which all tend to perpetuate or intensify the existing differences. It is on these fundamental assumptions that the proposals for a differentiation of curricula between boys and girls made in this Report are based."

A. Primary Stage

1. No differentiation should be made in the curricula for boys and girls at the primary stage.
2. The traditional attitude with regard to certain tasks, as 'manly' and others as 'womanly' is generally built up in early childhood through social atmosphere. Simple needle-craft, cooking, music and dancing, introduced in primary schools for boys and girls alike will incidentally counter-act these influences and build up new and healthy attitudes.
3. The proportion of women working as primary teachers should be substantially increased and women should be appointed on the staff of all primary schools. For this purpose the scheme recommended by the National Council for Women's Education for increasing the number of women teachers at the primary stage should be immediately and vigorously implemented.

B. Middle Stage

1. The ultimate objective before the country is to provide free and compulsory education to all children until they reach the age of

14. The curriculum to be provided for this minimum course of general education should be common to boys and girls and no differentiation should be made therein on the basis of sex. This common course should also include a core curriculum of home science.

2. In our opinion, 11 or 12 is too early an age to make the choice of an elective course and no tangible benefit can be derived by introducing electives at this early stage. We, therefore, recommend that special intensive courses of vocational preparation should be organised after the middle school stage.

3. All midle schools provide for the teaching of a craft which is suited to local conditions and, wherever possible for the teaching of more than one craft. Where only one craft has been introduced, it should be obligatory for all boys as well as girls. Where more than one craft has been introduced, each child should have the freedom to choose any craft for which he or she has an aptitude.

4. In all middle schools it is desirable to have mixed staff; but where girls do attend a middle school ordinarily meant for boys, appointment of women teachers on staff should be obligatory.

5. Steps should be taken to expand the provision of facilities for middle school education for girls as largely as possible. This may be done by appointing women teachers on the staff of co-educational schools, or by establishing separate girls' schools. When both these methods are not possible, adequate stipends should be provided to enable deserving and needy girls to stay in hostels and pursue their studies in middle/secondary schools. Wherever necessary and possible, transport facilities should be provided to girls to enable them to attend middle schools which may not be easily accessible from their places of residence.

C. Secondary Stage

In the opinion of the Committee, the best form to organise secondary education would be as follows:

(a) The general courses of secondary education should not attempt to give vocational competence; but craft or handwork or productive labour of some type should form an integral part of such courses.

(b) The Committee recommended the provision of intensive vocational courses which will begin after the middle school stage and be spread over one to three years. These should be run as parallel alternatives to the general courses of secondary education with a view to preparing boys and girls of different vocations in life. They should also be sufficiently diversified to meet the requirements of girls. As a special case, and in view of the comparatively inadequate development of middle school education for girls, especially in rural areas, it may be desirable to admit, to such courses, even those girls who may not have technically completed the elementary school but who may otherwise be in a position to benefit from them. Continuous research and investigations are necessary to ascertain the changing social conditions and employment potential in different parts of the country and to adjust the provision made for these courses accordingly.

(c) At the end of the secondary course, there should be a second bifurcation. Some students would go in for courses in humanities or sciences to prepare themselves intensively for admission to universities. The others would be diverted into various walks of life through intensive training in specialised courses that would aim at giving vocational competence. These courses should have large variety and should be based on the manpower requirements and social needs of different areas as ascertained through continuous programmes of research and investigation.

Textbooks

(1) In textbooks dealing with languages and social studies adequate attention should be paid to the needs, experience and problems of girls by including such topics as special festivals of women, games popular with girls, lives of great women, etc.

(2) One of the important values to be built up through textbooks is to enable each sex to develop a proper respect towards the other.

Vocational Education

(1) Immediate attempts should be directed to expand the provision

of vocational courses at the secondary and higher stages of education, and to relate these courses with man and woman — power requirements of society.

(2) The possibility of employing women on a larger scale on a part-time basis in as many vocations as possible has to be explored.

Measures to Improve Diversified Courses

The following measures are needed to improve the existing diversified courses at the secondary stage to meet the special needs of the girls:

(a) to add further subjects to the existing diversified courses;

(b) to prepare teachers for the teaching of these diversified courses; and

(c) to give financial assistance to the girls' schools to enable them to introduce the teaching of new elective subjects and also to raise the standard of teaching in subjects which have already been introduced.

Home Economics

The Committee recommends that steps should be taken to improve the introduction of home economics.

Music and Fine Arts

This is another group of subjects which is popular with girls. It is, therefore, recommended that steps should be taken to prepare the necessary teachers and to revise the scale of pay, where necessary. Liberal financial assistance should also be made available to girls' schools for the introduction of these courses.

Sex Education

Sex education is essential at the middle and secondary stages. It should not, however, form part of the curriculum and be given by mature, competent and well trained teachers. If satisfactory conditions and competent teachers are not available, it should not be attempted at all.

Provision of other Facilities

To meet the needs of deserving and needy girls, who have no access to separate secondary schools, hostels should be attached to central secondary schools for girls and adequate stipends, to cover maintenance costs, should be provided, on the basis of merit-cum-need. Wherever necessary and possible, transport facilities should also be provided to enable girls to attend separate secondary schools which are not easily accessible from their homes.

4.5 COMMITTEE TO LOOK INTO THE CAUSES FOR LACK OF PUBLIC SUPPORT PARTICULARLY IN RURAL AREAS FOR GIRLS' EDUCATION AND TO ENLIST PUBLIC CO-OPERATION(1963)*

Background

The National Council for Women's Education at its meeting held in April 1963 endorsed the suggestion made by the Union Education Minister in his inaugural address that a small committee be appointed to look into the causes for lack of public support, particularly in rural areas, for girls education and enlist public co-operation. This suggestion was made in view of the serious short-falls in the enrolment of girls. The Committee was to suggest, therefore, ways and means of achieving substantial progress in this field.

The Chairman of the National Council for Women's Education accordingly appointed in May 1963 a Committee with Shri M. Bhaktavatsalam, Chief Minister, Madras, as Chairman.

"The Committee is convinced that it is only through a willing, educated and informed public that any progress can be made at all. Not only is the need urgent, but the ground is also ready for a comprehensive programme for mobilising public co-operation to promote girls' education and giving it constructive channels of expression. It is essential that official action and the programme based on initiative must move forward in close harmony. There has to be a sense of partnership and shared responsibility between official and voluntary agencies. There is also the need for a systematic and sustained programme with an adequate organisation for mobilising community effort.

---

* Published by the Ministry of Education, Government of India, New Delhi, 1965.

Fields for the Co-operation of Public

Direct co-operation of the public should be encouraged in the following fields:

(i) Establishing private schools;

(ii) Putting up of school buildings;

(iii) Contributing voluntary labour for construction of school buildings;

(iv) Helping in the maintenance of school buildings;

(v) Helping in providing suitable accommodation for teachers and students, particularly in the rural areas;

(vi) Popularising co-education at the primary stage;

(vii) Creating public opinion in favour of the teaching profession and to give greater respect to the teacher in the community;

(viii) Undertaking necessary propaganda to make the profession of teaching for women popular;

(ix) Encouraging married women to take up part-time teaching in village schools and to work as school mothers;

(x) Initiating action and participating in educative propaganda to break down traditional prejudices against girls' education.

(xi) Setting up and organising school betterment committees, improvement conferences;

(xii) Supplying mid-day meals;

(xiii) Supplying uniforms to poor and needy children; and

(xiv) Supplying free text-books and writing materials to needy children.

The State Councils for Women's Education are the most suitable agencies for providing the organisation and leadership for mobilising community effort. They should function as a part of the network of which the District Councils at the district level, and the *Mahila Mandals* and similar voluntary bodies at the town and village levels would be strong and active links. These agencies should look upon mobilising of community effort and educating public opinion to promote girls' education as their main and primary responsibility. They should aim at building up in villages and towns teams of voluntary workers, men and women, who are willing to devote themselves to this cause and work actively for its promotion.

State's Responsibility

The State should create public opinion in favour of girls' education through:

   (i) School improvement conferences;

   (ii) Seminars;

   (iii) Radio talks, audio-visual aids and distribution of informative pamphlets and brochures;

   (iv) Enrolment drives, generally in June and special additional drives for girls' education during Dussehra; and

   (v) Assisting voluntary, welfare and other organisations, private individuals and associations engaged in the field of education of girls and women.

Popularisation of Girls' Education

1. *School Improvement Conferences*: School Improvement Conferences should be arranged widely throughout the States and particularly in the less-advanced States in order to encourage people to contribute to educational awakening and advancement.

2. *Schools in All Areas*: The State should continue to help in an abundant measure in providing necessary schooling facilities in all the areas and in all habitations, however small, so that the local population can make use to them. It should be the endeavaour of the state to provide a primary school in each habitation with a population of 300. However, in scattered, hilly or isolated areas, primary schools should be provided where the population is even less than 300, so as to provide every habitation with school within a mile. A middle school in each habitation with population of 1,500 and above, within a radius of 3 miles should be provided. The establishment of secondary schools should be planned in such a way as to cater to the needs of the these primary and middle school leavers. Generally there should be a secondary school within a radius of 5 miles.

3. *Pre-primary Schools*: It is necessary that in rural areas particularly, Pre-Primary schools should be attached to Primary schools so that children get accustomed to schooling even at the tender age.

4. *Sound Buildings*: The existing functional deficiencies of schools should be remedied by replacing buildings which are totally inadequate to modern educational needs. There should be periodical inspection of school buildings and hostels so as to ensure their structural soundness and suitable sanitary facilities.

5. *More Attractive School Work*: School work should be made more attractive and should present education in terms more acceptable to pupils.

6. *Appointment of Women Teachers*: The question of shortage of teachers is bound to remain for a long time and, therefore, concerted efforts have to be made to recruit as many women teachers as possible. Women are by general consent the best teachers for the Primary classes in all schools. It should be the aim of all states to appoint women teachers in primary schools and a greater number of women teachers in mixed schools. A school staffed by women will inspire greater confidence in the parents and make them willing to send their children to mixed institutions.

7. *Special Incentives for Women Teachers*: The basis of recruitment of women teachers should be widened and their conditions of work should be made more attrative. Financial incentives like special allowances for hilly, isolated or any other specific backward rural areas should be given to teachers. Each State may specify areas where such allowances should be available.

8. *Part-time Employment*: Attempts should be made to bring back to the teaching profession married women who have left it in recent years and bring in women from other occupations to supplement the teaching staff.

9. *Condensed Courses for Adult Women*: Condensed courses should be organised on a larger scale for adult women, particularly from rural areas so that they could take up teaching jobs in the villages.

10. *Relaxation in Age Limit of Women Teachers*: In order to attract more women teachers the age limit for the unmarried and married women teachers should be relaxed in the case of those working in village schools. The service conditions of such married women who do part-time teaching work should be made more attractive.

11. *Women Teachers to be Posted Nearer*: Women teachers, as far

as possible, should be posted in or near their own villages.

12. *Improved Salary Scales for Teachers*: The salary scales of all teachers should be improved and the teachers should be paid an economic wage, so that they may be retained in the profession. There should be improvement in the service conditions of teachers. Provision should also be made for retirement benefits.

13. *Special Incentives for Teachers in the Rural Areas*: Special drives should be organised to attract people in rural areas to the teaching profession as the best form of social service needed for the upliftment of the villages.

14. *Training Schools with Hostels*: Training schools with hostels need to be located in the rural centres and near 'difficult' areas where girls from the villages are trained and sent back to work in their own or neighbouring villages. This will help to bring forward teachers with local ties in these areas. The policy of locating the larged majority of training schools in the towns should be reconsidered.

15. *Preference to Women from Rural Areas in Admission*: During selection of trainees for training schools and colleges, special preference should be given to women from rural areas seeking admission.

16. *Increased Training Facilities*: The training facilities available in each State should be of such a magnitude that the annual output of trained teachers would be equal to the demand for additional teachers.

17. *Improvement in Inspection*: The inspecting staff should be adequate and strong if improvement is to be secured and waste reduced. Such a staff can keep close touch with the local conditions and offer sound advice for economical and well directed improvement and development. A separate women inspectorate will help to bring in more girls to school.

18. *Quarters for Women Teachers*: It is only by providing women teachers with quarters near the schools that we can attract many educated women to the teaching profession. As far as possible, the quarters should be built near the school premises, which would help the women teachers to live with social workers, the Gram Sevikas and others and have company and social life. The recommendations made by the Fourth Plan Working Group of the National Council for Women's Education regarding the requirements of teachers' quarters in the Fourth Plan both for

Elementary and Secondary teachers (50,000 quarters for elementary teachers and 10,000 quarters for Secondary teachers) should be seriously considered for implementation, and appropriate advance action initiated as early as possible.

19. *Adequate Hostel Facilities*: The absence of hostel facilities as also the slow progress in the construction of those that have been undertaken, have affected the enrolment of girls, particularly in rural areas. The construction of hostels, therefore, should be included as one of the priority objectives in the Plans of the States and necessary financial assistance for the construction of hostels and maintenance stipend be made available more liberally to local authorities and voluntary organisations working in the field of education of girls and women.

20. *More Responsibility on Local Bodies*: Local bodies should be made responsible for the provision of school buildings, equipment, playing fields and the like and observance of the educational code in the State.

21. *Adult Education*: In the field of social education, a determined effort should be made to increase the number of literacy classes for women in rural areas and to carry out intensive campaigns for the spread of literacy amongst women. Activities in this field should be administered by the Education Departments of the State Governments.

22. *Central Assistance*: A study of conditions prevailing in the less advanced States and the conditions prevailing in some of the advanced States has convinced that the problem of enlisting public co-operation and increasing the enrolment of girls in schools, particularly in the rural areas, is one which needs to be tackled in a co-ordinated manner and from several angles. In the following paragraphs some general recommendations are made as applicable to most of the less advanced States followed by some specific recommendations regarding the individual States.

Such Central Assistance should be :

(a) At the elementary stage for :

    (i) Preparation and employment of women teachers;
    (ii) Grant of free books, writing materials and clothing to girls; and

(iii) Twin quarters for women teachers.

(b) At the secondary stage for:

    (i) Provision of separate schools for girls;
    (ii) Hostels;
    (iii) Grant of free books, writing materials and clothing to girls; and
    (iv) Preparation and appointment of women teachers in increasing numbers.

23. *School Buildings*: The provision of suitable school buildings is one of considerable urgency. For this, either hundred per cent Central assistance or long-term Central loans should be provided.

24. *Free Education for Girls and Central Assistance*: While hundred per cent Central assistance would be necessary for the above schemes and projects, it is of paramount importance that all States should find ways and means of providing funds in order to make education free for all girls up to the secondary stage. Unless this incentive is given, it will be very difficult for the parents in their present economic circumstances to afford girls education.

25. *Special Fund by States for Girls' Education*: It is seen that the States who have not made reasonable provision of girls' education in their plan have also been the States, generally speaking, where progress of girls' education has not been appreciable. The State Government should make all reasonable provision for the advancement of girls' education and earmark such funds.

26. *Community Support for Girls' Education*: If resources that are available are limited and do not meet the full requirements, the concentration of activities should be in rural areas. The State Governments may explore possibilities of raising of local resources for the purpose of meeting the full requirement of the advancement of girls' education.

27. *State Councils for Women's Education*: The States should also use the good offices of the State Councils for Women's Education and strengthen these Councils by providing for them a proper secretariat and suitable financial assistance to meet the

expenses of T.A. and D.A. of the members so that the latter can be in constant touch with the workers in the field and provide them with necessary advice, guidance and encouragement.

28. *Compulsory Education Acts*: Compulsory Education Act should be introduced in states where it does not exist. In addition, State Governments should provide sufficient incentives and carry on propaganda to attract all children to school.

29. *Curriculum*: While the curriculum can be the same for both boys and girls at the primary and middle stages, provision should be made for offering of electives comprising subjects which would be of special interest to girls and which would help them later in their fields of activity. The recommendations made by the Committee of the National Council for Womens' Education in the report "Differentiation of Curricula for boys and Girls" should be carefully studied and action taken by the States to implement them as far as possible.

30. *Double Shifts*: In schools that lack accommodation but have a rush to admission, the double-shift system may be tried as a temporary measure.

31. *Flexibility of School Hours*: Changing of school hours and school holidays to seasonal requirements has been found in some places to be a helpful concession to parents who would otherwise not be in a position to spare the children for attending classes. We are here reminded of the Hartog Committee's observations of the permanent adjustment of school hours to hour of labour especially where it affects children below nine or ten years of age. Such an adjustment of school hours can only be regarded as a temporary measure, and this form of remedy should not be allowed to obscure fundamental principle that the proper place for young children during the day is the school house. In any case, children should attend school before, and not after, they have been engaged in work. While these arguments are relevant, we feel that suitable change of hours of schooling will have to be considered in the backward and hilly areas where due to climate, economic and other conditions parents will not be in a position to send children to school while in fact, they could be employed on the farms during the harvesting season for instance, or some manual work in order to bring in some return to the family. We agree that the adjustment of school hours and school holidays to seasonal requirements

cannot be a uniform feature of a permanent palliative, but till things improve and till the parents and guardians are educated so as to understand the need for proper schooling for their girls and boys, the adjustment of school hours would act as an healthy inducement.

32. *Extra Labour by Less Advanced States*: The less advanced States of Bihar, Jammu and Kashmir, Madhya Pradesh, Orissa, Rajasthan and Uttar Pradesh have their peculiar problems and not all solutions, could be generally applied to solve their difficulties. This much, however, can be said that these States will have to make extra efforts and aims at additional enrolments in classes I-V and VI-VIII. At the secondary stage, the enrolment should be nearly double the present rate. This is necessary for ensuring that there is an adequate supply of women teachers.

4.6 EDUCATION COMMISSION (1964-66)*

The Education Commission fully endorsed the recommendations of the three committees which have examined the problem of womens' education in recent years: (a) The National Committee on the Education of Women under the chairmanship of Shrimati Durgabai Deshmukh; (b) The Committee on Differentiation of Curricula between Boys and Girls under the chairmanship of Shrimati Hansa Mehta; and (c) The Committee under the chairmanship of Shri M. Bhaktavatsalam which studied the problem in the six States where the education of girls is less developed.

The commission observed:

"In the modern world, the role of the women goes much beyond the home and the bringing up of children. She is now adapting a career of her own and sharing equally with man, the responsibility for hte development of society in all its aspects. This is the direction in which we shall have to move. In the struggle for freedom, Indian women fought side by side with men. This equal partnership will have to

---

* Report of the Education Commission (1964-66): *Education and National Development*, Published by Ministry of Education, Government of India, New Delhi, 1966.

continue in the fight against hunger, poverty, ignorance and ill — healthy."

The Commission invited special attention to the following recommendations of the National Committee on Women's Education:-

(1) The education of women should be regarded as a major programme in education for some years to come and a bold and determined effort should be made to face the difficulties involved and to close the existing gap between the education of men and women in as short a time as possible.
(2) Special schemes should be prepared for this purpose and the funds requirement for them should be provided on a priority basis.
(3) Both at the Centre and in the States, there should be a special machinery to look after the education of girls and women. It should bring together officials and non-officials in the planning and implementation of programmes for women's education.

In addition, it will also be necessary to give adequate attention to the education of girls at all stages and in all sectors.

The role of women outside the home has become an important feature of the social and economic life of the country and, in the years to come, this will become still more significant. From this point of view, greater attention will have to be paid to the problems of training and development of women. Opportunities for part-time employment which would enable women to look after their homes and to have a career outside will have to be largely expanded. As the age of marriage continues to rise, full-time employment will have to be provided for almost all young and married women. As the programme of family planning develops, elder women whose children have grown up, will also need employment opportunities. Teaching, nursing and social service are well-recognised areas where women can have a useful role to play. In addition, several new avenues will have to be opened out to them.

Education of Girls — Primary Stage

The education of girls requires special attention in fulfilling the Constitutional directive and should be accelerated on the lines of the measures recommended by the National Committee on Women's Education.

Education of Girls — Secondary Stage

(1) Efforts should be made to accelarate the expansion of girls' education so that the proportion of girls to boys reaches 1:2 at the lower secondary stage and 1:3 at the higher secondary stage in 20 years.

(2) Emphasis should be placed on establishing separate schools for girls, provision of hostels and scholarships, and part-time and vocational courses.

Differentiation of Curricula for Boys and Girls

The recommendation of the Hansa Mehta Committee that there should be no differentiation of curricula on the basis of sex is endorsed. Home science should be provided as an optional subject but not made compulsory for girls. Larger provision should be made for music and fine arts, and the study of mathematics and science should be encouraged.

Education of Women University Stage

(1) At present, the proportion of women students to men students in higher education is 1:4 This should be increased to about 1:3 to meet the requirements for educated women in different fields. For this purpose, a programme of scholarships and provision of suitable but economical hostel accommodation should be developed.

(2) At the undergraduate stage, separate colleges for women may be established if there is a local demand. At the postgraduate level, however, there is no justification for separate institutions.

(3) Women students should have free access to courses in arts, humanities, sciences and technology. Courses in home science, nursing, education and social work need to be developed as these have attraction for a large proportion of girls. Facilities for advanced training in business administration and management should also be provided.

(4) Research units should be set up in one or two universities to deal specifically with women's education.

Women Teachers

(1) The employment of women teachers should be encouraged at all stages and in all sectors of education. Opportunities for part-time employment should be provided for them on a large scale.
(2) Adequate provision should be made for residential accommodation particularly in rural areas.
(3) The condensed courses for adult women operated by the Central Social Welfare Board should be expanded.
(4) Increasing facilities should be provided for education through correspondence courses.
(5) Wherever necessary special allowances should be given to women teachers working in rural areas.

The Resolution on the National Policy on Education (1968) on Girls' Education.

The educational of girls should receive emphasis, not only on grounds of social justice, but also because it accelerates social transformation.

4.7 COMMITTEE ON THE STATUS OF WOMEN (1971-74)*

Background

The Committee on the Status of Women in India was appointed by a resolution of the Ministry of Education and Social Welfare dated 2nd September 1971. The Committee submitted its report entitled *Towards Equality* in December 1974.

Terms of Reference

(1) To examine the Constitutional, legal and administrative provisions that have a bearing on the social status of women, their education and employment.
(2) To assess the impact of these provisions during the two decades on the status of women in the country, particularly in the rural

---

* Published by the Department of Social Welfare, Ministry of Education and Social Welfare, Government of India, New Delhi, 1974.

sector and to suggest more effective programmes.

(3) To consider the development of education among women to determine the factors responsible for the slow progress in some areas and suggest remedial measures.

(4) To survey the problems of the working women including discrimination in employment and remuneration.

(5) To examine the status of women as house-wives and mothers in the changing social pattern and their problems in the sphere of further education and employment.

(6) To undertake surveys or case studies on the implication of the population policies and family planning programmes on the status of women.

(7) To suggest any other measures which would enable women to play their full and prroper role in building up nation.

Composition (when constituted on 2 September 2, 1971)

(1)	Smt. Phulrenu Guha	Chairman
(2)	Smt. Savitri Shyam, M.P.	Member
(3)	Smt. Neera Dogra	Member
(4)	Shri Vikram Chand Mahajan, M.P.	Member
(5)	Smt. Sakina A Hasan	Member
(6)	Smt. Maniben Kara	Member
(7)	Smt. K. Lakshmi Raghuramaiah	Member
(8)	Smt. Lotika Sarkar	Member
(9)	Smt. Shakuntala Masani	Member-Secretary

Composition (Subsequently, vide Resolution dated September 21, 1973).

1.	Dr. (Smt.) Phulrenu Guha	Chairman
2.	Smt. Neera Dogra	Member
3.	Dr. (Smt.) Leela Dube	Member
4.	Smt. Urmila Haksar	Member
5.	Smt. Sakina A. Hasan	Member
6.	Smt. Maniben Kara	Member
7.	Shri Vikram Chand Mahajan, M.P.	Member
8.	Smt. K.Lakshmi Raghuramaiah	Member
9.	Smt. Lotika Sarkar	Member

10. Smt. Savitri Shyam, M.P.   Member
11. Dr. (Smt.) Vina Mazumdar   Member-Secretary

Tenure of the Committee

The Committee constituted in September 1971 was to submit its report within a period of two years. But in view of the magnitude and complexity of task assigned to it, its term was extended from 22.9.73 to 31.3.74 to enable it to complete its report according to terms laid down.

Task Forces and Study Groups

Recognising the wide scope of its enquiry as well as the complex nature of the study, much of which required technical expertise and knowledge in different fields, the Committee appointed Six Task Forces and Two Study Groups to advise it.

Six Task Forces

1. Task Force on Education
2. Task Force on Economic Aspect
3. Task Force on Legal Aspect
4. Task Force on Political Aspect
5. Task Force on Social Aspect
6. Task Force on Employment Aspect

Two Study Groups

1. Study Group on Health
2. Study Group on Dowry

Members of the Task Force on Education

1. Dr. (Miss) Bina Roy, President, University Women's Federation.
2. Shri J.P. Naik
3. Dr. (Miss) C. Nain
4. Mrs. Irene Sinha
5. Smt. Tara Bai

Contents of the Report

The report consists of the following nine chapters besides four appendices.

1. Approach to the Study of Status of Women in India.
2. Demographic Perspective.
3. Socio-Cultural Setting of Women's Status.
4. Women and the Law.
5. Roles, Rights and Opportunities for Economic Participation.
6. Educational Development.
7. Political Status.
8. Policies and Programmes for Women's Welfare and Development.
9. The Role and Influence of the Mass Media on the Status of Women.

Tables in the Report on Educational Development

I   Enrolment Targets and Achievements in the Fourth Plan.

II   Enrolment in the Primary education as percentage of the population in the corresponding age groups: Primary Stage.

III Secondary Stage.

IV Education of Girls and Women in the Pre-Independence period.

V   Education of Grils and Women in the Post-Independence period.

VI Total Enrolment in the Educational Systems — All levels.

VII Percentage Distribution of Boys and Girls in different Stages of the Educational System.

VIII Percentage Distribution of Enrolment of Boys and Girls in Secondary Sections.

IX Enrolment of Women in University Education (All levels included) facultywise — U.P. Board included.

X   Enrolments for University Education (All faculties inclusive stagewise — U.P. Board included).

XI Quinquennial Growth in Enrolment by stage of Education 1960-61 to 1970-71.

XII Out-turn of students at different stages of the educational system.

XIII   Estimated total stock of Educated Persons by sex and levels.

XIV   Degree Holders and Technical Personnel in each subject field, 1971.

XV   Growth of Educational Institutions.

XVI   Percentage of trained Women Teachers in Primary, Middle and Secondary Schools.

XVII   Number of Women Teachers in Colleges and Universities Faculty-wise.

XVIII   Educational level of women by age group.

XIX   Progress of Literacy — 1970-71, Number of Literacy females per mile.

XX   Number of Illiterates by Sex 1951-71.

XXI   Enrolment Ratios (Percentage of Girls in Relevant Age Group) by stages of Education for Girls. Comparison between 1956-57 and 1968-69.

XXII   Enrolment Ratio (Perçentages) by Stages of Education for Girls. Comparison between 1956-57 and 1968-69.

XXIII   Ranking of States for each level of Education, according to Ranges of Enrolment Ratio of Girls — comparison between 1956-57 and 1968-69.

XXIV   Ranking of States for each level of Education, according to Ranges of Enrolment Ratio of Girls — comparison between 1956-57 and 1968-69.

XXV   Percentage of Distribution of literates and illiterates among Members of Scheduled Castes and Scheduled Tribes, India, 1961.

XXVI   Distribution of 1,000 Scheduled Caste and Scheduled Tribe males and females by educational levels, India 1961.

XXVII   Educational imbalance at the district level, literates at per cent of total population.

XXVIII   Views of officials regarding co-education at different levels.

Educational Development

Chapter VI of the Report is devoted to the following aspects of educational development in India:

(i) General

(ii) Education and Women's Status, the 19th Century View.

(iii) Post Independence Era—New Roles and Rights.

(iv) Traces of Ambivalence between the Old and New Views.

Section I: *Progress of Women's Education in India*

A. The Formal Educational System:

(i) Constitutional Provisions and Achievements.
(ii) Development in the Pre-Independence Period.
(iii) Development in the Post-Independence Period.
(iv) Enrolment as an Index of Educational Advance. Problems of Retention, Wastage and Stagnation.
(v) Out-turn.
(vi) Growth of Institutions.
(vii) Women Teachers.
(viii) Inspection.
(ix) Attitude to the Education of Girls and Women.

B. Literacy.
C. Imbalance in Education.

Section II: *Recommendations*

(a) Co-education.
(b) Curricula.
(c) Pre-Primary Schools.
(d) Universalisation of Education for the Age-Group of 6 to 14.
(e) Sex Education.
(f) Secondary Education.
(g) General Recommendations Regarding the Formal System.
(h) Non-Formal Education.
(i) Equality of Sexes as a Major Value to be inculcated through the Educational Process.

Necessity of Education

The Committee observed —

"Emphasis on different arguments justifying the value and necessity of education from the point of view of the individual as well as society has varied according to the historical needs of any society in different stages of its evolution. The first argument regards education as a value in itself, since it develops the personality and the rationality of individuals. The assumption here is that society, recognising the innate value of rationality and learning, accords a high status to the educated. The second argument emphasises the usefulness of educated persons to society at large. Their knowledge, by serving a social purpose, raises their status in society. From the point of view of the individuals, education provides the necessary qualification to fulfil certain economic, political and cultural functions and consequently improves his socio-economic status."

Education and Social Change

The Committee felt —

"With the recognition of the need to direct the process of social change and development towards certain desired goals, education has come to be increasingly regarded as major instrument of social change. The Committee quotes the Education Commission 1964-66 —

"The realisation of the country's aspiration involves changes in the knowledge, skills, interests and values of the people as a whole. This is basic to every programme of social and economic betterment of which India stands in need. . . . If this 'change on a grand scale' is to be achieved without violent revolution (and even for that it would be necessary) there is one instrument and, one instrument only that can be used: Education."

Universal Declaration of Human Rights and Education

The Committee stated —

"One of the expectations from this directed use of education is that it will bring about reduction of inequalities in society, on the assumption that education leads to equalisation of status between individuals coming from hitherto unequal socio-economic strata of society. It was on this argument that the Universal Declaration of Human Rights included education as one of the basic rights of every human being. The Constitution of the UNESCO directs its efforts to achieve 'the ideal of equality of educational opportunity without regard to race, sex or any distinctions, economic or social."

Education and Women's Status (19th Century View)

The Committee recorded:

"The history of the movement for improving women's status all over the world shows emphasis from the beginning on education as the most significant instrument for changing women's subjugated position in society. Increase of educational facilities and opportunities, and the removal of traditional bars on entry of women to particular branches and levels of education, came to be supported by all champions of women's emancipation from the 19th century onwards. Social reformers in India, whether they were modernising liberals or revivalists, also emphasised the importance of education of women to improve their status in society. However, when we look into their justification for this departure from the tradition then prevalent in the country, we notice certain significant omissions. According to the reformers, the main purpose for educating women was not to make them more efficient and active units in the processes of socio-economic or political development, but to make them more capable of fulfilling their traditional roles in society as wives and mothers. The opposition of the orthodox conservatives was countered by the argument that women's education would strengthen the bonds of tradition and the family as the chief unit of social organisation. In their view, the denial of education and early marriage prevented the development of the personality and rationality of women. Stunted and crippled personalities affected the harmony of the family atmosphere, weakening the bonds of the family. Education for women was regarded as a means to improve their status within the family, and not to equip them to play any role in the wider social context. The absence of any economic compulsion was, in fact, the main reason for the slow progress of women's education in this country."

The Committee felt, "Because of their reluctance to interfere in social matters, the colonial authorities generally supported this purely humanitarian and limited view of women's education. The problem of reaching education and health services to the women of this country led to a realisation of the need for women teachers and doctors. Since this was not possible without training women in these professions the importance of the these two vocations outside the familiar roles had to be incorporated in the programmes for women's education."

Post Independence Era — New Roles and Rights

In the discussions on women's education in the post-independence era, a new dimension appeared due to the acceptance of equality of women and their need to play multiple roles in society.

"The general purpose and objective of women's education cannot, of course be different from the purpose and objective of men's education. . . . At the secondary and even at the university stage women's education should have a vocational or occupation bias." *(Five Year Plan*, Government of India, 1951, Chapter XXXIII)

"In a democratic society where all citizens have to discharge their civic and social obligations, differences which may lead to variation in the standard of intellectual development achieved by boys and girls cannot be envisaged." *(Report of the Secondary Education Commission, Government of India*, 1953, Chapter IV)

"In the progressive society of tomorrow, life should be a joint venture for men and women. Men should share the responsibility of parenthood and home-making with women and women in their turn should share the social and economic responsibilities of men." *(Report of the Committee on Differentiation of Curricula for Boys and Girls, Government of India*, 1954, Chapter IV)

The Committee felt that, "The emphasis on education equipping women to carry out their multiple roles as citizen, house-wives, mothers, contributors to the family income and builders of the new society is consistent with the trend of discussions in international agencies on women's education as a basic ingredient for improvement of their status."

Traces of Ambivalence between Old and New Views

The Committee made the following observation—

"In spite of growing recognition of importance of women's education, traces of earlier view which supported it mainly as an equipment for their roles as wives and mothers without conceding any position of equality with men in other spheres of life, can still be found not only in the opinions of individuals, but even in the statements of official agencies'. The Committee quoted the Report of the University

Education Commission, 1949—

"Women's and men's education should have many elements in common, but should not in general be identical in all respects, as is usually the case today. A woman should learn something of problems that are certain to come up in all marriages, and in the relations of parents and children, and how they may be met. Her education should *make her familiar with problems of home management and skills in meeting them,* so that she may take her place in a home with the same interest and same sense of competence that a well trained man has in working at his calling."

The Committee felt that, "An understanding of this ambivalence between the traditional and the new attitudes on women's education is essential for examining the progress of women's education in this country, because it has an impact on academic planning, allocation of resources and development of values in society for both men and women. It lies at the root of all discussions regarding differentiation of curricula between the two sexes and continues to affect social attitudes regarding women's education, its social use and women's roles in society. This in turn has an impact on the class composition of women who are recipients of education. The achievements or the failures in the use of this instrument for transforming women's status have to be measured by these social indicators as well as quantitative ones like enrolment out-turn, number of institutions and teachers, literacy rates and total stock of educated women at different levels and in the light of the stated national objectives."

The Committee refers to the National Policy on Education (1968)—

"The educational system must produce young men and women of character and ability committed to national service and development. Only then will education be able to play its vital role in promoting national progress creating a sense of common citizenship and culture and strengthening national integration."

Progress of Women's Education in India : Formal Education System

The Committee refers to the Constitution of the Republic of India which guarantees equality of opportunity to all citizens irrespective of race, sex, caste and communities and directs the State to "Endeavour to provide within a period of ten years from the commencement of this

Constitution for free and compulsory education for all children until they complete the age of 14 years." The Indian Education Commission in its *Report* (1966) regretted the failure to achieve this target. It emphasised the crucial importance of fulfilling this directive in the coming decades. In view of the immense resources needed for this purpose, the Commission recommended phasing of this programme in the following manner:—

— "by providing five years of effective education to all children by 1975-76 and seven years of such education by 1985-86.
— by making part-time education for about one year compulsory for all children in the age group 11-14, who have not completed the lower-primary stage and are not attending schools. The aim will be to make these children functionally literate and stop all further additions to the ranks of adult non-literates; and
— by efforts to liquidate adult illiteracy."

Targets

The Committee made the following review—

"The following review will indicate that even the targets recommended by the Education Commission have not been achieved, particularly in the case of women. The enrolment targets set for the Third Plan by the National Committee on Women's Education (1959) were equal numbers with boys in the age group 6-11, at least half that of boys in the age group 11-14 and at least one-third that of boys in the age-group 14-17. The targets for the age groups 6-11 and 11-14 have not been reached even at the end of the Fourth Plan. The expected proportion of one-third in the age group 14-17 set for the Third Plan has however been exceeded slightly by the end of the Fourth Plan. The Fifth Five Year Plan notes that in spite of substantial progress in the expansion of educational facilities, the targets laid down for both elementary and secondary education registered a shortfall in enrolment, while those in higher education were exceeded. "But shortfalls have been particularly large in the case of elementary education more so in the case of girls."

Slow Progress of Education among Girls

The Committee stated, "Educational experts now admit that the delay in the achievement of the Constitutional directive is mainly due to the slow progress of education among girls, scheduled castes and scheduled tribes. The discrepancy in the progress of education between boys and girls may be seen in the marked difference in the percentage of boys and girls of the corresponding age groups enrolled in primary, middle and secondary schools."

Development in the Pre-Independence Period

The Committee analysed the situation as, "The foundations of the formal system of education, sponsored and supported by the State, and divided into three well-defined stages (primary, secondary and university) and two main streams (general and vocational) were laid during the first half of the nineteenth century. It was created essentially for men with the ultimate objective of utilising them as government servants. In the initial years girls had little or no access to it, partly because of the traditional prejudices against their formal education and partly because society at that time could not imagine them as government servants. However, as the formal system of education began to spread, the role of education as a liberating influence came to be recognised and increasingly accepted. Thus began the advocacy of the access of girls and women to the formal system of education spearheaded by national leaders, missionaries and a few enlightened officials. It received little response. . . . The movement began in cities and then spread to the towns and villages. Wealth played an ambivalent role. . . . The mass awakening during the freedom movement and the role that women played in the struggle had a great impact on women's education."

Major Recommendations on Education of Women

Two-fold Categorisation

The recommendations of the Committee (1971-74) may be categorised under two headings:

    I. Recommendations regarding Formal System.

II. Recommendations regarding Non-Formal System.

I. Recommendations Regarding Formal System of Education

The Committee discussed these recommendations under the following heads :

1. Co-education.
2. Curricula.
3. Pre-School Education.
4. Universalisation of Education for the Age group 6-14.
5. Sex Education.
6. Secondary Education.
7. General Education.
8. Higher Education.

Co-education

The considerations of efficiency, economy as well as equal opportunity require the acceptance of co-education as a long term policy. In view of the divergent social attitudes, however, we recommend :

(i) Co-education should be adopted as the general policy at the primary level.

(ii) At the middle and secondary stages separate schools may be provided in areas where there is a great demand for them. But the effort to pursue co-education as a general policy at these stages should continue side-by-side.

(iii) At the university level co-education should be the general policy and opening of new colleges exclusively for girls should be discouraged.

(iv) There should be no ban on admission of girls to boys institutions.

(v) Wherever separate schools/colleges for girls are provided, it has to be ensured that they maintain required standards in regard to the quality of staff, provision of facilities, relevant courses and co-curricular activities.

(vi) Acceptance of the principle of mixed staff should be made a condition of recognition for mixed schools. There is a misgiving, however, that this provision may lead to exclusion of girls from some schools. Therefore, it is suggested that this measure may be reviewed a few years after it is implemented.

(vi) Wherever there are mixed schools, separate toilet facilities and retiring rooms for girls should be provided. (Chapter 6, Para 72)

Curricula

(i) There should be common course of general education for both sexes till the end of class X, all courses being open to boys and girls.

(ii) At the primary stage, simple needle craft, music and dancing should be taught to both sexes.

(iii) From the middle stage, differences may be permitted under work experience.

(iv) In clases XI-XII girls should have full opportunity to choose vocational and technical courses according to local conditions, needs and aptitudes.

(v) At the university stage there is a need to introduce more relevant and useful courses for all students. (Chapter 6, Para 81)

Pre-School Education

(i) The provision of three-year pre-school education for all children by making a special effort to increase the number of *balwadis* in the rural areas and in urban slums.

(ii) In order to enable them to fulfil the social functions discussed above, an effort should be made to locate them as near as possible to the primary and middle schools of the locality. (Chapter 6, Para 85)

Universalisation of Education for the Age-Group 6-14

(i) Provision of primary schools within walking distance from the home of every child within the next 5 years.

(ii) Establishment of ashram or residential schools to serve cluster of villages scattered in difficult terrains. Where this is not immediately possible, preparatory schools may be provided for the time being.

(iii) Provision of mobile schools for children of nomadic tribes, migrant labour and construction workers.

(iv) Sustained propaganda by all types of persons, preferably women — officials, and non-officials, social and political workers, to bring every girl into school in Class I preferably at the age of 6. They should visit local schools and involve parents and community leaders in order to promote the schooling of girls, particularly in backward areas.

(v) Provision of incentives to prevent drop-outs. Since poverty is the major cause of drop outs the most effective incentive, in our opinion is the provision of mid-day meals. The rate of children passing the primary level has definitely gone up in States which have introduced mid-day meals. In Kerala, which has highest literacy rate among women, this provision is one of the major factors for the enrolment and retention of children in schools to-day. In reply to our questionnaire, the majority has given highest priority to this incentive. The other important incentives which require to be provided to needy children are free school uniforms, scholarships or stipends and free supply of books and other study material. For girls particularly, the lack of adequate clothing is a great deterrent to attending schools. For schools which do not prescribe any uniform, some provision of clothing is necessary.

(vi) Special incentives for areas where enrolment of girls is low. This will need to be worked out according to local conditions. We suggest special awards or recognition to the community, teachers, students, etc.

(vii) At least 50 per cent of teachers at this stage should be women.

(viii) Provision of at least two teachers in all schools, and conversion of the existing single teacher ones as early as possible.

(ix) Developing a system of part-time education for girls who cannot attend school on a full time basis. This system should provide education to girls at a time convenient to them.

(x) Adoption of the multiple entry system for girls who could not attend school earlier or had to leave before becoming functionally literate.

(xi) Provision of additional space in schools that girls can bring their younger brothers and sisters to be looked after, either by the girls themselves in turn, or by some local women. (Chapter 6, Para 87)

(xii) Opening of schools and greater flexibility in admission procedure in middle schools (multiple only) to help girls to complete their schooling (Chapter 6, Para 88).

Sex-Education

(i) Introduction of sex-education from middle school.

(ii) Appointment of an exert group by the Ministry of Education to prepare graded teaching material on the subject. The group should include some experts on mass media, to advise on the use of films and other mass media for this purpose.

(iii) This material may be used for both formal and non-formal education. (Chapter 6, Para 89)

Secondary Education

(i) Free education for all girls up to the end of the secondary stage.

(ii) Improving the quality of teaching and provision of facilities for important subjects like science, mathematics and commerce.

(iii) Introduction of job-oriented work-experience, keeping in view the needs, the resources and the employment potential of the region e.g. courses leading to training as ANM, typing and commercial practice, programmes oriented to industry and simple technology, agriculture and animal husbandry. (Chapter 6, Para 92)

General Education

(i) Provision of mixed staff in all mixed schools. This should be made a condition of recognition.

(ii) Adequate provision of common-rooms and separate toilet facilities for girls in all schools.

(iii) Adequate arrangements for co-curricular activities for girls in all schools.

(iv) Provision of more need-cum-merit scholarships and hostel facilities of girls. (Chapter 6, Para 93)

Higher Education

(i) Development of more employment opportunities, particularly of a part-time nature, to enable women to participate more in productive activities.

(ii) Development of employment information and guidance service for women entering higher education. Many of them suffer from lack of information regarding job opportunities and regret their choice of subjects when faced by difficulties in obtaining employment. (Chapter 6, Para 96)

II. Recommendations Regarding Non-formal System of Education

Increasing the Social Effectiveness of Women through a Continuous Process

The greatest problem in women's education today is to provide some basic education to the overwhelming majority who have remained outside the reach of the formal system because of their age and social responsibilities as well as the literacy gap. For the sake of national plans for development, it is imperative to increase the social effectiveness of women in the 15—25 age-group even if we cannot do so for the still older groups. Ad-hoc approaches through the adult literacy, functional literacy and other programmes of the Government have proved inadequate. They also draw a sharp distinction between men and women in the context of the training. These distinctions, in our view, are out-of-date. Changes in family life, food habits, family planning all require joint efforts of men and women and continuing this kind of artificial division between the sexes may defeat the purpose of these programmes. As for vocational and occupational skills, the needs of women are greater than those of men. While we do not deny the value of crafts, women's need for vocational training cannot be limited to them. The skills differ according to the industrial and market potential of regions and it is imperative to relate the training to local needs, resources and employment possibilities instead of adopting an artificial sex-selective approach. Ad-hoc approaches through a multiplicity of programmes by various governmental agencies will lead to overlapping, lack of coordination and wastage of resources. The problem is an integrated one and cannot be solved by short term programmes. What is needed is a continuous process. (Chapter 6, Paras 97-101)

Community Involvement and Non-Formal Education

No attempt to professionalise this system will lead to development of the limiting, selective and a rigid approach with fixed curricula and classroom procedures. The prohibitive cost of such professionalisation would inevitably limit its operation to a few selected centres. The teachers in a non-formal system must have other skills of direct relevance to the problems of the community. Without this kind of community involvement, such programmes will lack stability and continuity. (Chapter 6, Para 104)

Participation in Social Life as the Objective of Non-Formal Education

The object of the system should be to provide access to information and use of information for better participation in social life with literacy as the core of the package. Though primarily meant for adolescents, the system should not exclude the young, particularly those who have been denied any formal education. Some of the latter may use it as a stepping stone to enter the formal system if our recommendation regarding multiple entry is accepted. (Chapter 6, Para 105-6)

Limited Role of the Government

The system will have to be organised through community groups. The Panchayats and the Women's Panchayats recommended in Chapter VII would appear to be the ideal bodies for this purpose. Government's role should be limited to providing technical guidance and advice and enabling Government functionaries at the local level to participate in the programmes apart from supportive assistance in the form of literature and reading material. Development of basic libraries in villages and the slum areas of towns is an imperative necessity for this purpose. We therefore recommend concentration of governmental effort on providing this infrastructure. (Chapter 6, Para 107)

Equality of Sexes as a Major Value to be inculcated through the Educational Process

The deep foundations of the inequality of the sexes are built in the minds of men and women through a socialisation process which continues to be extremely powerful. Right from their earliest years, boys and girls are brought up to know that they are different from each other and this differentiation is strengthened in every way possible—through language forms, modes of behaviour of labour etc. They begin to learn very early what is proper or not proper for boys and girls and all attempts at deviation are noticed discouraged and sometimes punished. The sissy and the tomboy are equal objects of derision. There is nothing wrong in this if it were merely a question of distinction. But it soon gets inextricably tied up with the traditional concepts of the roles of men and women and their mutual relationships which are based on inequality. The process of indoctrination affects the development of individual personalities.

The only institution which can counteract the effect of this process is the educational system. If education is to promote equality for women, it must make a deliberate, planned and sustained effort so that the new value of equality of the sexes, can replace the traditional value system of inequality.

Women Teachers

Problems of Women Teachers

Some of the basic problems identified by women teachers, in almost all the states that the Committee visited, are given below :

Resistance from the Family

(a) Women teachers face a certain degree of resistance from their families to their working in rural areas, partly from the general apprehension against women working away from home, and partly from a fear of personal insecurity in villages. This has been aggravated by the deteriorating law and order situation in some villages. There is also a fear that rural society may be unfriendly and even antagonistic to outsiders. We would, however, like to mention that in some states we were told that rural society had now come to accept and even respect women teachers and doctors.

Most of these attitudes are shared by the teachers themselves. Added to them is another cause of resistance from the women, used to life in urban areas, that life in villages would be dull and unattractive.

Lack of Physical Amenities

(b) Apart from these factors, the lack of physical amenities like modern medical facilities, proper accommodation, toilets, transport and schooling for children are real difficulties that deter women from service in rural areas. Even when houses are provided, they are often outside the village, without any consideration for the problems if distance and insecurity that women have to face. If they are within the school, the teachers cannot bring their families. The problem of acccommodation becomes still more acute with married women, if they have to work away from their husbands and families.

RECOMMENDATIONS

The Committee recommended that these problems need to be solved on a priority basis in order to increase the supply of women teachers in rural schools. If this is not done, then the present imbalance in the development of women's education between urban and rural areas will increase. Added to this will be yet another imbalance, that of increasing unemployment among trained and qualified women teachers, whose reluctance to serve in rural areas prevents their employment. The beginnings of this imbalance are already noticeable in many states.

Inspection

The system of inspection of schools varies from state to state. The general complaint, however, is that schools are not inspected regularly. In Himachal Pradesh a retired school teacher informed us that during her 24 years' service, she had faced only three inspections. In some states like Uttar Pradesh and Bihar village schools to be inspected once a year are only those which are within easy reach. In most states all inspections cease during the rainy season.

There is an over-all inadequacy of women on the inspecting staff. Insufficient numbers and over-large jurisdictions contribute to the general inefficiency of inspections. For women in particular, the problems of distance, and inadequate arrangement for transport and night halts create added difficulties. This leads sometimes to serve on the inspecting staff, and the states where the grade of inspectors is the same as that of headmistress of a high school (i.e. Punjab), women members of the service prefer to remain as headmistresses. In Himachal Pradesh, we found that there was no women on the inspecting staff.

States like Himachal Pradesh and Madhya Pradesh do not have a separate women's cadre of inspectors, and girls' schools are often inspected by male inspectors. In the case of single-teacher schools, this sometimes creates a problem. We received some complaints from teachers of misbehaviour, blackmail or exploitation on the part of inspectors.

Attitudes to the Education of Girls and Women

Social attitudes to the education of girls vary, ranging from acceptance of the need to one of absolute indifference. The Committee's survey reveals some interesting trends. A statement that girls should not be given any education received a categorical rejection by 77.8 per cent of respondents. A small minority (16.8%) did, however, agree with this view. In the case of higher education, however, we find a surprisingly hostile attitude since over 64.50 per cent responded that a girl should not be allowed to go for higher education even if she is very intelligent.

In view of the constitutional directive regarding free and compulsory education up to the age of 14, we tried to elicit public opinion on the question of marking education compulsory. In response to our general questionnaire, 77.8 per cent of the respondents, male and female, supported compulsory education for upto the 8th class. A separate questionnaire issued to educationists and administrators regarding measures necessary to improve girls' enrolment in schools also evoked a substantial support in favour of compulsion.

In urban areas, by and large, the acceptance of the need of education for girls is greater than in rural areas. Among the affluent there are two distinct attitudes. Some families are opposed to it for traditional reasons while other have welcomed it as an accomplishment and a symbol of modernisation. Among the middle classes the acceptance is the highest. The attitude among the lower middle class is more difficult to generalise because today's lower middle-class consists of white collared as well as manual workers. Though economically one, socially they are two distinct classes, their attitudes being determined much more by their social background rather than their economic position. While an increasingly large section, conscious of economic necessity, is prepared to make substantial sacrifices for girls' education, a very large number still finds itself unable to do so for economic and social reasons. For the majority of the peole who live below subsistence level, poverty is the predominant factor governing the attitude to girls' education.

Reasons for Variations on Social Attitudes

Reasons for the variations in social attitudes and the consequent slow progress of women's education are both social and economic.

(a) Large majority of girls, by the time they reach the age of eight, are required at home to do various domestic chores, e.g. collecting fire-wood, coal waste, cow dung, fetching water, sometimes from long distances, washing, cleaning, cooking, taking food and water to parents in their places of work, etc.

(b) Majority of girls of this age group have to look after the siblings, especially when their mothers are engaged in earning a livelihood.

(c) A substantial number of girls are engaged in contributing to the family income by their own labour. The prevalence of child labour has long been admitted as the greatest deterrent to the spread of education among children of the poor. The Committee was appalled by the extent and degree of use of young girls of five to fourteen working for twelve hours a day.

(d) Our survey reveals several difficulties in the way of facilities for girls' education. Nearly 53 per cent of the respondents refer to shortage of schools in general, 57.65 per cent to absence of separate schools for girls in many places, 43.57 per cent to over-crowding in schools and 53.95 per cent to distance from house to school. While 39.41 per cent point to the absence of women teachers, 40.46 per cent do not regard this as a difficulty. Other difficulties brought to our notice are the lack of adequate transport arrangement and toilet facilities, as also the prevalence of single teacher schools.

(e) The irrelevance of education as imparted in schools today has been discussed at length by the Education Commission. While endorsing their views, we would like to add that this has a particularly adverse effect on parental attitude to the education of girls, especially in rural areas. Parents who have not as yet accepted the utility of educating girls find in its irrelevance, justification for their apathy. Mothers of young girls told us that except for reading and writing, which the girls could pick up in two or three years, schools taught very little that was useful. One peasant woman in a Punjab village felt that one way of making school education more meaningful would be to train girls to handle and repair tractors. Some women in the Kulu valley wanted training in methods of fruit preservation, so that they could fully utilise the products of their orchards.

(f) Education in the rural areas often results in alienation of the girls from their habitat. While this criticism was voiced in many places, the most vocal opinion was expressed by women in the village of Himachal Pradesh. Since the development of the state and the standard of living of its people depended on the continued efforts of women in agriculture, education in their opinion was becoming an adversary of progress. Girls who completed their formal education in the village did not want to continue living in villages or take part in agricultural activities. The problem became more acute when, owing to absence of secondary school in the villages, they had to study outside, in urban or semi-urban areas. Many of them found village life with its hardships intolerable afterwards. This was particularly brought to our notice in Nagaland and Himachal Pradesh. Most girls who complete secondary school develop a desire for white-collared job, or urban life in some form.

(g) While early marriage or betrothal was undoubtedly the greatest deterrent to progress or girls' education in the past, it is much less so now. Our survey indicates that only 38 per cent of the respondents find early marriage a genuine difficulty for girls' education while 41.5 per cent do not agree with their view.

Marriage Prospects and Education of Girls

The strongest social support for girls' education continues to come from its increasing demand in the marriage market. According to our survey, 64.25 per cent of the respondents felt that education helped to improve marriage prospects of a girl.

4.8 SEVENTH FIVE YEAR PLAN (1985-90)*

The long-term objective of the development programmes for women is

---

* Published by the Planning Commission, Government of India, New Delhi, 1985.

to raise their economic and social status in order to bring them into main stream of national development. Due recognition has to be accorded to the role and contribution of women in the various socio-economic, political and cultural activities.

Women education in the Seventh Plan

1. Efforts will be made to provide 100 per cent coverage for education of girls upto the age of 14 years. Priority will be given to retain girls in schools. Incentives like uniforms, free text books and attendance scholarships will be continued for the needy girls in all schools. Non-formal education will be expanded to benefit girls in 6-14 age group.
2. It has been proposed to provide free education for girls upto the end of the higher secondary stage.
3. The educational content of the adult education programme is to be modified to incorporate new value systems in the community regarding the role of women in the family and community in addition to increasing the coverage of literacy. The number of non-formal education centres for girls will be increased.

In the rural areas, Integrated Rural Development Programme (IRDP), National Rural Employment Programme (NREP), Training of Rural Youth for Self Employment (TRYSEM) and the other such programmes will have a component of functional literacy for women.

4. Talented girls all over the country will be encouraged to pursue higher education. For this, it is proposed to expand the 'Open Learning Systems' including correspondence courses for women.
5. For the promotion of technical and vocational education for girls, more and more polytechniques for women are to be set up during the plan period. Programme for vocationalisation of education for girls is to be expanded.
6. To boost education among the girls belonging to scheduled castes, scheduled tribes and other weaker sections additional facilities would continue to be provided under the 'Development of Backward Classes' sector.
7. Participation of girls and women in sports and games will be encouraged. Stress will be laid to identify sports talent among

women and provision made for sports scholarships, coaching and nourishment support for promising girls to raise their standards of performance in competitive games.

8. Priority will be given to women in teachers' training programmes to increase the availability of trained women teachers.

Social Welfare Programmes for Women

1. Supplementing the services available to women under other development sectors and establishing close linkages with them.
2. Extending grants-in-aid by the Central Social Welfare Board to voluntary organisations to set up a variety of income generating units under the Socio-Economic Programme' for the benefit of needy women.
3. Seeking help from the Norwegian Agency for International Development (NORAD) for taking up diversified occupations and inculcating new skills required by the job market.
4. Giving grants to voluntary organisations for organising condensed educational and vocational training courses for adult women so as to improve their employment prospects.
5. Accelerating construction/expansion programmes of hostels for working women with low-income groups with a view to provide accommodation with improved standards of service at reasonable cost.
6. Involving voluntary agencies in delivering the "Messages" on preventive and promotive health and social and nutritive care for women and children.
7. Encouraging voluntary agencies to provide 'public conveniences' for women at bus stands, markets and theatres etc.

Health Programmes for Women

1. Directing major thrust towards the reduction of the prevailing high maternal and infant mortality rates.
2. Taking up schemes for providing tetanus toxoid to mothers and providing proper ante-natal care on a sizeable scale.
3. Making available the health and family welfare services to all women in the reproductive age group.

4. Providing nutrition supplements, iron and folic acid tablets to mothers for bridging the calorie-vitamin and mineral deficiency gap as well as for fighting anaemia.
5. Expanding considerably the scheme for training of birth attendants and auxiliary nurse mid-wives.
6. Employing mass media, voluntary agencies, village health committees, women's organisations and *dais* to spread knowledge about simple remedies for common disorders.
7. Informing women about misleading advertisements, regarding the use of tonics, health drinks etc.

Employment Programmes for Women

A. Agriculture

1. Paying special attention to improving existing skills of women and imparting to them new skills under the programmes of farmers' training, fodder production, post-harvesting technology, application of pesticides, budding and grafting, training in horticulture, fisheries, poultry etc.
2. Selecting households headed by women beneficiaries under the Integrated Rural Development Programme.
3. Providing adequate opportunities for employment to women under the National Rural Employment Programme (NREP) and Rural Landless Employment Guarantee Scheme(RLEGS).

B. Land-Reforms

Conferring benefits on a large number of households headed by women under the scheme Assignees of Ceiling Surplus Land (ACSL).

C. Industry

Persuading public sector undertakings to sponsor ancillary industries in collaboration with State Level agencies dealing with development programmes for women to provide increased employment opportunities around them.

D. Village and Small Scale Industries

1. Widening scope for specific training programmes for women

entrepreneurs.
2. Promotion of skilled employment, women's participation in various schemes.
3. Making special provisions in terms of infrastructure facilities like industrial sheds for women entrepreneurs.

E. Age Relaxation

Relaxing age limit for women for entry into government services and public sector undertakings.

Programmes for Women in Science and Technology

1. Strengthening programmes for providing gainful employment to women.
2. Sponsoring special training programmes for women in polytechnics and other institutions of technical education in areas such as repair and maintenance of radio, television and other electronic hardware or consumer durables etc.

4.9 NATIONAL POLICY ON EDUCATION (1986) and PROGRAMME OF ACTION (1986)*

National Policy on Education

Part IV entitled 'Education For Equality' devotes two paragraphs to 'Education for Women's Equality':

Education will be used as an agent of basic change in the status of women. In order to neutralise the accumulated distortions of the past, there will be a well conceived edge in favour of women. The national education system will play a possible, interventionist role in the empowerment of women. It will foster the development of new values through redesigned curricular, textbooks, the training and orientation of teachers, decision-makers and administrators, and the active involvement of educational institutions. This will be an act of faith and social engineering. Women's studies will be promoted as a part of various courses and educational institutions encouraged to- take up

---

* Published by the Ministry of Human Resource Development Department of Education, New Delhi.

active programmes to further women's development.

The removal of women's illiteracy and obstacles inhibiting their access to, and retention in, elementary education will receive overriding priority, through provision of special support services, setting of time targets, and effective monitoring. Major emphasis will be laid on women's participation in vocational, technical and professional education at different levels. The policy of non-discrimination will be pursued vigorously to eliminate sex stereo-typing, in vocational and professional courses and to promote women's participation in non-traditional occupations as well as in existing and emergent technologies.

Programme of Action

The Government of India, Ministry of Human Resource Development (*Formerly* Ministry of Education) Department of Education, New Delhi, prepared a programme of Action in August 1986, for the implementation of the National Policy on Education. The programme regarding education of women has been given in a Chapter entitled 'Education For Women's Equality.

Present Situation

Provision of educational opportunities to women has been an important programme in the education sector since independence. Between 1951 and 1981, the percentage of literacy amongst women improved from 7.93 per cent to 24.82 per cent. However, in absolute numbers, illiterate women have increased during this period from 158.7 million to 241.7 million (excluding Assam). Women comprise 57 per cent of the illiterate population and 70 per cent of the non-enrolled children of school stage are girls. In spite of the efforts made so far, the education system has not been able to make sufficient contribution towards women's equality.

Targets

(a) A phased time-bound programme of elementary education for girls, particularly upto the primary stage by 1990, and upto the elementary stage by 1995.

(b) A phased time-bound programme of adult education for women in the age group 15-35 (whose number is estimated to be 6.8 crores) by 1995.

(c) Increased women's access to vocational, technical, professional education and to existing and emergent technologies.

(d) Review and reorganisation of the educational activities to ensure that it makes a substantial contribution towards women's equality, and creation of appropriate cells/units therefor.

Policy Parameters and Strategies

The National Policy on Education (NPE) envisages that education would be used as a strategy for achieving a basic change in the status of women. The National education system would : (i) play a positive interventionist role in the empowerment of women, (ii) contribute towards development of new values through redesigned curricula and text-books, and (iii) women's studies will be promoted as part of various courses. The main features of the targets and implementation strategy will consist of the following :

(i) to gear the entire education system to plan a positive interventionist role in the empowerment of women;

(ii) to promote women's studies as a part of various courses and encouragement to educational institutions to take up active programme to further women's development;

(iii) to widen the access of women in programmes of vocational, technical and professional education;

(iv) to create dynamic managerial structure to cope with the targets envisaged.

Strategy Enunciation and Programme of Action — Empowerment of Women

Women become empowered through collective reflection and decision-making. The parameters of empowerment are :

— building a positive self-image and self-confidence;

— developing ability to think critically;

— building up group cohesion and fostering decision-making and action;

— ensuring equal participation in the process of bringing about social change;

— encouraging group action in order to bring about change in the society;

— providing the wherewithal for economic independence.

Measures to be taken for achievement of Goals

The following measures will be taken for the achievement of the above parameters :

(a) Every educational institution should, by 1995, take up active programmes of women's development built around a study and awareness of the women's predicament and for promotion of communication and organisation among women.

(b) All teachers and Non-Formal Education/Adult Education (NFE/AE) instructors should be trained as agents of women's empowerment. Special training programmes will be developed by NCERT, NIEPA, Directorate of Adult Education (DAE), SCERTs, State Resource Centres (SRCs) and UGC to incorporate in all training programmes of teachers and NFE/AE instructors elements which would motivate them to work for women's empowerment. Voluntary agencies and activist groups for women's development will be involved in these training programmes.

(c) Women teachers and women instructors in adult/non-formal education programmes should receive special orientation to enable them to play an activist role towards women's equality.

(d) Special programmes should be developed by research institutions, voluntary institutions and professional groups of artists to promote general awareness and self-image amongst women through a variety programmes like discussions, street plays, skits, wall papers, puppet shows etc.

(e) An environment should be created in which practically all sections of the society will commit themselves and work for achieving this objective enunciated in the National Policy on Education. Keeping in view the important role played by media in this sphere, clear policy guidelines should be developed by radio and TV in 1986-87 and measures taken to persuade films and other media on these lines.

(f) Preference in recruitment of teachers upto school level should be for women. This will create a greater confidence in the rural areas and motivate the parents to send girls to the school.

(g) The common core curriculum is a powerful instrument for the empowerment of women through the incorporation of values commensurate with the new status of women. The Women's Cell in the NCERT will be revived and given the responsibility for preparing the component of the core curriculum relating to women's equality. The Cell should also accelerate its work of eliminating sexist bias and sex stereo-types from school text-books. The Women's Cell of NCERT should take active help of all persons on playing its assigned role.

(h) Sensitisation of teacher, trainers, planners and administrators to women's issues will be taken up as a major programme by NIEPA and appropriate State level agencies, through initial training, in-service training and refresher courses. NIEPA should also have a strong cell for planning and execution of these programmes.

Women Studies: Four Dimensions

Women's studies programme has 4 dimensions—teaching, research, training and extension.

Teaching : In teaching, the following activities will be taken up :

(i) Incorporation of issues relating to women's status and role in the foundation course proposed to be introduced by University Grants Commission for all undergraduate students;

(ii) Incorporation of the women's dimension into courses in different disciplines;

(iii) Elimination of sexist bias and sex stereo-types from text-books.

Research : Under research, the following steps will be taken :

(i) Encouraging research on identified areas and subjects which are crucial in advancing knowledge in this area and to expand the information base;

(ii) Critical appraisal of existing Tools and techniques which have been responsible for the disadvantages suffered by them and where necessary reformation of research methodology.

Training : The followinng measures will be taken under training :

(i) Dissemination of information and interaction through seminars/workshops on the need for Women's Studies and its role in University education;

(ii) Orientation of teachers and researchers to handle women-related topics and to incorporate women's dimension into general topics;

(iii) Workshops for restructuring the curriculum.

Extension : Under extension, it is proposed to encourage educational institutions to take up Programmes which directly benefit the community and bring about the empowerment of women.

These would include actual implementation of development programmes directly aimed at women's empowerment such as adult education, awareness building, legal literacy, informational and training support for socio-economic programmes of women's development, media, etc.

Universalisation of Elementary Education and Adult Education

Following steps have been envisaged;

(1) The present programme of non-formal centres for girls on 90:10 pattern will be extended to all educationally backward pockets of the country. NFE Centres should be community based. Responsibility of planning, selection of instructors and monitoring should be with the community including parents. Increased assistance to voluntary agencies to run non-formal education centres for girls should be given.

(2) In the rural areas, girls are kept busy at home in sibling and household care, in fetching fuel, fodder and water, or in earning a day's wage. Therefore, special support services referred to in the Policy need to cover all these areas upto 1995. Early childhood education centres are important support service in increasing enrolment and retention of girls in schools. Programmes of social forestry, drinking water supply, mid-day meals, and other nutrition programmes, smokeless chullahs and other devices aimed at eliminating drudgery from women's

lives should be formulated by the Ministry and organisation concerned upto 1990 to converage with the objective of universalisation of education.

(3) Skill development linked to emloyment or work opportunities in the villages or local areas are   required to be given overriding priority so that there is an incentive on the part of the parents to educate the girls.

(4) Mass scale adult education programme for women in the age group 15-35 should be developed to eradicate illiteracy amongst women by 1995. As majority of women in this age group are workers, literacy per se may not have any relevance for them. It is, therefore, necessaary to develop adult education programmes for women linked with upgrading of their skills and income generating activities.

(5) Skill development for girls and women should be continuous process of learning starting from the NFE centres and AE centres. Continuing Education Centres should be set up in a phased manner which should organise vocational training, provide opportunities for retention of literacy skills and application of this learning for improving their living conditions.

(6) The skill development given by the Continuing Education Centres will be supported by other programmes of non-formal, vocational training and skill development to be administered by a variety of organisations and institutions, such as Polytechnics, Community Polytechnics, ITIs, Shramik Vidyapeeths, Central Social Welfare Board, State Social Welfare Advisory Boards, Voluntary agencies, Krishi Vigyan Kendras, Women's Centres in Agricultural and Home Science Colleges as part of their extension activities. Besides, industries which employ women should themselves run non-formal vocational training courses. For effective learning and monitoring Women's Bureau is to be set up in the Department of Education.

Women's Access to Vocational, Technical and Professional Education and to Existing and Emergent Technologies

Following measures will be taken in this direction :

(1) At each stage in school education; or a part of work experience

or vocationalisation, girls should be exposed to a variety of vocational training activities. The method of vocational training should be both through the formal and non-formal courses. The choice of skills to be taught will depend on the natural resources, traditional occupations and new activities being taken up through government and private investment.

(2) There are 104 ITIs functioning exclusively for women and 97 wings in general ITIs reserved for women. It is proposed that these institutions be revamped during the period 1987-90 on the following lines :

(i) Diversification of trades and courses, will be done, keeping the job potential of the area in mind. There will be an efficient placement system which will enable the institutions to have continuous dialogue with employers. The idea behind this diversification is that while girls will continue to receive preferential treatment in trades/occupations, for which they are particularly well suited (e.g. teaching and nursing), this will not beocme a barrier for their participation in technical and professional courses of higher level and equal opportunities will be provided for them in all vocational, technical and professional courses.

(ii) There will be a strong element of vocational counselling in each ITI/RVTI/NVTI, polytechnics, suitable orientation should also be provided in the schools as preparation for motivating the girls to choose non-traditional courses.

(iii) Information about credit, banking, entrepreneurial development etc. will be provided by the ITI/NVTI/RVTI/ Polytechnics and community polytechnics alongwith practical on-the-job training. The implementation of the apprenticeship scheme will be strengthened to increase the coverage of women.

(iv) In order to substantially enlarge the opportunities to women for craftsmen's trainings, shift system will be introduced in existing ITI's — one in the morning and the other in the afternoon.

(v) DCE&T office should have a separate Directorate of Women's Vocational Training.

(vi) The women's access to technical education will be improved qualitatively and quantitatively. The choice of trades/disciplines offered to women at Certificate/Diploma/Degree levels in all types of technical education institutions, will be made keeping in view the objective of bringing about women's equality. Necessary incentives, as spelt out in the section of Technical Education will be provided.

Management Structure at Centre and State Level

It includes the following :

(1) The interventions and programmes referred to above will be planned, coordinated, monitored and evaluated continuously both at the national and state level. Each of the organisations responsible for the programme will have to be strengthened. The Women's Cell in the NCERT will be revived and strengthened. NIEP and Directorate of Adult Education will have strong cells to plan and administer Women's training programmes. The Women's Cell in the UGC will be strengthened in order to monitor the implementation of various programmes at higher education level.

(2) At the State level, Women's Cell should be set up in all the States with adequate supporting staff to be headed by an officer of at least Joint Director's status.

4.10 NATIONAL COMMISSION ON SELF-EMPLOYED WOMEN AND WOMEN IN THE INFORMAL SECTOR (1987-88)*

Introduction

The Commission appointed on January 5, 1987 under the Chairperson of Ela R. Bhatt, submitted its report to the Government of India on June 1988. The Commission covered and studied the entire gamut of unprotected laouring women to include self-employed and wage labour, paid and unpaid labour and contract labour. *Interalia*, the Commission made recommendations on the education of women.

---

* Published by the Ministry of Human Resource Development, Department of Women and Child Development, New Delhi.

Education

Education is both an important instrument for increasing and bettering the chances of women's employability and for empowering women as they learn to think for themselves, become confident and also develop the capability of recognising more acutely the areas of exploitation. This fact has also been recognised and accepted in the National Policy on Education, 1986, by the Government, wherein, it has been mentioned that :

> Education will be used as an agent of basic change in the status of women. In order to neutralise the accumulated distortions of the past, there will be a well-conceived edge in favour of women. The National Education System will play a positive, interventionist role in the empowerment of women, it will foster the development of new values through redesigned curicula, textbook, the training and orientation of teachers, decision-makers and administrators, and the active involvement of education institutions.

However, although in principle the fact of empowering women through education has been recognised in the National Policy on Education and the Programme of Action, the Commission suggests that following steps be taken by which the working women themselves and their children, specially the girl child, may benefit.

1. Since one of the reasons for poor enrolment of a girl child and even poorer retention of their enrolment is their contribution in helping the working mothers in domestic work and looking after younger children and also contributing to the family economy as child labour, it is necessary that *there should be shifts for girls at suitable times* so that they can assist their mothers in work and go to school. It should be possible for all the school going children in a family to attend the same shift, or else, the girl will be required to remain home to mind the younger children.

2. To encourage parents to send their girls to afternoon shifts, it should be desirable that *a woman helper is provided on an honorarium basis for accompanying the children from the house and back to ensure their enrolment and safety.*

3. The same helper as mentioned at (b) above or another *helper's services could be utilised for looking after the siblings below school age of the girls going to the school in the premises of the school itself.*

It may be a room, a verandah or a temporary shed constructed for the purpose.

4. It would be preferable to have *a regular creche attached to the primary school where the younger children could be taken care of so that the older child can attend the school.*

5. *Incentives for sending the girls to school* will have to be given to promote their education. In many states like Haryana, cash per month and free uniform is given to scheduled caste girls. Similar facilities including mid-day meals, free textbooks and exercise books, could be extended to all girls students at least up to the primary school level. If the girls are attracted to education, they are likely to move away eventually from the back breaking traditional occupation of their mothers to better employment.

6. The syllabli need to be made more relevant for the children of rural areas. Practical subjects like animal husbandry, cattle care, soil conservation, agriculture, social forestry may be added and such options offered along with subjects like history, geography, modern science and physics.

7. Under the Government Scheme of Condensed Courses being implemented by the Central Social Welfare Board, the adolescent girls and above, who acquire education in a non-formal manner, have to appear in the same examination for which children from public schools from metropolitan cities also appear. This needs to be changed. In certain situations, a good grounding in languages, mathematics, general knowledge and some subjects relevant to their life situation, should suffice to get them a school certificate for the purpose of getting jobs at certain levels.

8. It has been mentioned in the Programme of Action, issued by the Ministry of Human Resource Development, that women teachers should be preferably recruited at the school level to give greater confidence to the parents to send their girl children to the school. The Commission would like to add that it is possible to have more women teachers only of they are posted in their home villages, or nearby villages, to which they belong or into which they marry. Certain States have a policy not to post anyone within 20 kilometers of their home town. Such a policy should be totally discouraged. Women employees, like teachers or extension workers, need the security of the home and they cannot stay away from their families because of the basic responsibility if looking after the children. And if married, the husband and wife should be posted in the same area or as close geographically possible.

9. The Commision recognises the fact that in the rural areas there are not enough trained women who can be appointed as teachers. Urban based teachers posted in rural areas do not tend to stay in the village to which they are posted, resulting in loss of school hours for the children. The Commission therefore, recommends and innovation in the basic requirements of school teachers. *For primary schools, girls who have completed secondary school or have achieved even middle school level, may be give an intensive training for a period of one year or nine months in certain training colleges of the State Government. Their training, boarding and lodging should be free. After the training, they should be posted in their home villages, or in the vicinity or their villages.* Only in this manner, will it be possible for the schools to have women teachers who will stay there and not absent themselves from schools. We wish to reiterate again, that increasing women teachers would have a direct bearing on the recruitment of girls which would, eventually, improve their chances of employment or self-employment in the non-traditional sector.

10. The primers under the adult education programme do not have sufficient material related to women workers which will be of interest to the labouring workers. There are certain exceptions. For example, the Commission's studies reveal that the primers in Tamil Nadu were of a high quality in this respect.

11. The textbooks both in the formal and informal educational systems perpetuate labouring women's invisibility and stereotyped sex biased concept of women. The revision of *the textbooks and the primers need to be carried out keeping the objective of bringing of women into greater focus.*

12. Greater emphasis has to be given on the vocational aspect of education. More experiments need to be undertaken to combine general and vocational education, specially for the rural areas. For a country as large as ours and to cater to the needs of the vast majority of labouring women in poverty, there cannot be a single model of education. *Various alternatives of education need to be developed.* These alternatives may be developed in a decentralised manner, preferably with an area specific approach.

13. The vocational training, which is being imparted at present is also stereotyped and sex biased. Trades which are more remunerative, and involving modern technology, are by and large beyond the reach of girls thereby restricting their options for employment. This needs serious attention.

14. *For the vocational training of girls, there should be a revolving fund from which they may be given scholarships to bear the cost of training and hostel facilities and they should reimburse the amount after they get suitable jobs.* This amount can be recycled again to help their equally deprived sisters. Experience of a private trust in this regard has been successful. After the girls get vocational training. They must be helped in job placement.

15. *It is necessary to convince the parents of poor girls regarding the relevance of education to the lives of their daughters.* This is possible if education and vocational training have a direct relation to their chances of employability and leading to enhancement in their remuneration. Further if the parents can be convinced that by providing education, the girls would also have the option of alterantive methods of employment, they may send their daughters for education more readily. One of the important reasons for women' submitting to exploitation is that they do not have a viable economic alternative.

16. The Commission does realise that literacy in itself is not a solution to the basic problems of poor women, viz. exploitation and hunger; and therefore, literacy has to be understood in the wider context of the social structure. Therefore, the Commission recommends that any attempt to eradicate poverty should lead the women to deal with the question of equality, social justice and development. Therefore, it is crucial to have teaching materials and teachers who deliver the service with these objectives. Ultimately the poor women should gain self-confidence to deal with her environment.

5

NATIONAL PERSPECTIVE PLAN FOR WOMEN'S EDUCATION
(1988 to 2000 A.D.)*

The programmes for women's education will have to be implemented as a priority so that women attain a comparable level of education by 2000 A.D. The strategy to be adopted for raising literacy levels and education among women has to keep in view the vast cultural, geographical and ecological variations and also the problems relating to poverty and ignorance. The cultural and geographical variations call for decentralization of educational planning. Within the national perspective, planning, implementation and monitoring of educational programmes has to be done at district and block levels, keeping in view the socio-economic and geographic parameters of the area. The vocational and occupational components have to be designed in accordance with the availability of resources and job opportunities in the regions. Voluntary organizations and women's groups active in the area should be involved in the task.

In view of the social and cultural handicaps that have operated against women's education and taking account of the multiple roles that women are required to play, the need for adopting a set of objective specific to women's education is imperative. The objectives to be achieved by 2000 A.D. in regard to women's education are :

(i) Elimination of illiteracy, universalisation of elementary education and minimization of the dropout rate in the age group 6-14 years and stagnation to negligible proportions.

(ii) Ensuring opportunities to all women for access to appropriate

---

* National Perspective Plan for Women 1988-2000 A.D. was prepared by a 14-member group, headed by Mrs. Margaret Alva, the then Minister of State for Women, Youth Affairs and Sport.

level, nature and quality of education and also the wherewithal for success comparable with men.

(iii) Substantial vocationalization and diversification of secondary education so as to provide a wide scope for employment and economic independence of women.

(iv) Making education an effective means for women's equality by (a) Addressing ourselves to the constraints that prevent women from participating in the educational process; (b) Eliminating the existing sexist bias in the system; (c) Making necessary intervention in the content and processes of education to inculcate positive and egalitarian attitudes; and (d) Ensuring that teachers' perceive this as one of their essential roles.

(v) Providing non-formal and part-time courses to women to enable them to acquire knowledge and skills for their social, cultural and economic advancement.

(vi) Impetus to enrol in various professional degree courses so as to increase their number in medicine, teaching, engineering and other fields substantially.

(vii) Creating a new system of accountability, particularly in respect of the basic educational services, to the local community, inter alia, by active involvement of women.

In brief, it is reiterated that the goals and strategies spelt out in the National Policy on Education, POA and the National Literacy Mission will ensure a much larger access for women to education.

High priority has to be accorded to creating awareness, through the various communication media, of the need for women's education and their active participation in economic and political development of the nation.

The curricula for school as well as university education have to be reviewed and revised so as to remove sex bias, inculcate among the masses a recognition of equality between men and women, and make women aware of their own potential as well as provide them necessary opportunities to develop their capabilities in every field. Greater accessibility of educational facilities to girls is to be achieved by reducing the distance of schools from village habitations, and expanding non-formal elementary eduation, adult education, and the open school system. Appointment of lady teachers in schools would help draw more girls to schools and instil confidence among their parents. Towards this end, provision of quarters for lady teachers would be essential. Efforts should be directed at training local women as teachers. Provision of creche facilities and balwadis near the elementary and secondary schools for girls would enable the girls to attend schools and ensure care of younger siblings. Incentives like mid-day meals' better rates of scholarships, freeships, etc. would go a long way in preventing dropout.

Above all, better health facilities, smaller families, and relief from drudgery through improved technology for household chores, are essential pre-requisites for better enrolment of girls at schools and higher educational institutions. Inputs from other sectors are, therefore, important. Greater coordination of health, employment, welfare and education interventions will have an effect on the status of women and girls.

According to Educational Statistics for 1984-85 published by the Ministry of Human Resource Development, the enrolment of girls at primary level, which covers the age group 6-11 years, is 331.9 lakhs. Surveys and field research have pointed out that there is 25 per cent inflation in the enrolment figures, and 22 per cent enrolment is outside the age group. Thus the effective emrolment gets reduced by about 47 per cent. Accordingly, the coverage for 1984-85 for 6-11 age group may be estimated as 176 lakhs. The population projected for the age group is 422.7 lakhs. This means that only 40.7 per cent of the girls in the age group 6-11 are enrolled in schools. On a similar basis, the enrolment of 11-14 years age group gets reduced to 48.1 lakhs (from 90.7 lakhs) which is only 19.2 per cent of the population of 249.9 lakhs estimated for the age group. The population projections for the girls in the age group 6-11 years and 11-14 years for 1989-90 are 462 lakhs and 267 lakhs respectively. In order to have full coverage, the additional enrolment required would be 286 lakhs for 6-11 years age group 219 lakhs for 11-14 years age group, the total being nearly 5 crores. The task appears to be stupendous. Alongwith enrolment, there is the problem of very high dropout rates. Stemming from highly inflated enrolment rates and subsequent dropouts in the 6-11 years age group, enrolment of 11-14 years age group girls, even at primary level, may not be possible even by 1995.

In view of the social and cultural handicaps that have operated against women's education, the need for adopting a set of objectives specific to women's education is imperative. These would need to encompass the elimination of illiteracy and measures for retention of girls in schools, substantial vocationalization and diversification to enhance economic opportunities for women, improvement in the quality of education in terms of the values it promotes and inculcates and finally the provision of access to professional courses for women. Such measures would be necessary as also efforts to remove the inherent prejudices working against women's education.

RECOMMENDATIONS

1. Awareness needs to be generated among the masses regarding the necessity of educating girls so as to prepare them to effectively contribute to the socio-economic development of the country, to strengthen their role in society and to realise their own capacities. The media and various forms of communication have to be geared to this end.

2. A fruitful rapport has to be established between the community at large and the teachers and other education personnel. As per the programme of Action under National Policy on Education 1986, every educational institution should actively participate in bringing about such awareness.

3. Involvement of local leaders, voluntary agencies and women's groups is also necessary. Mahila mandals need to be *revitalized* and reoriented to provide an effective forum for the purpose. One measure to achieve this could be to assign the responsibility to mahila mandals for ensuring that all children in a community attend school. An incentive scheme should be introduced to motivate panchayats to ensure 100 per cent enrolment of girls in their respective villages.

4. Early childhood care and education introduces children into the school system gradually and smoothly. When children get used to attending schools, it ensures in some measure retention of children, including girls, at elementary stages also. Hence there is need to have a comprehensive and effective programme of early childhood care and education linked to an integrated package of learning for women. The most comprehensive example of this is the Integrated Child Development Services Programme which needs to be universalized.

5. For improving enrolment and minimising drop-outs and wastage in case of girl students, it would be helpful if learning is made more attractive by providing adequate teaching materials in schools.

6. The number of teachers should also be increased so that the interaction between the teacher and the taught, which is so essential for good education, also increases. This would help in the retention of girls

in schools and would be more effective if teachers from the area are employed. In single teacher schools, the teacher must be a woman. In the case of two-teacher schools, at least one teacher must be a woman. In Orissa all jobs of primary teachers have been reserved for women.

7. School curricula should be imaginatively developed to stimulate creativity largely through play rather than overburdening children with formal or rote learning. Regional language should normally be the medium of instruction.

8. School timings should be flexible and fixed to suit local conditions and the needs of the working girl and must be available within the walking distance of the child. A substantial increase is required in the number of schools for girls.

9. In addition to incentives like free textbooks, free supply of uniforms, award of attendance scholarships and mid-day meals, facilities such as proper school building, safe drinking water, and toilets, etc. need to be provided to encourage school enrolment and retention of girls especially girls from educationally deprived social groups and from hilly tribal desert and remote rural areas and urban slums.

10. Local talent must be developed in order to meet the need for recruiting women teachers at the primary and elementary levels especially in rural and tribal areas. In this endeavour national agencies like CAPART and CSWB, voluntary agencies, mahila mandals and local self-governmennt agencies can make a significant contribution. They can also play a useful watchdog function to ensure that educational and other programmes are run efficiently and effectively.

11. There should be a reservation of 50 per cent posts for women teachers in elementary schools. Women teachers working in the rural areas should be provided suitable accommodation.

12. Multi-entry system for girls who cannot attend schools continuously should be adopted.

13. Wherever necessary, schools meant exclusively for girls may be set up. The recommended distance of 3 kilometres for locating a middle school is a handicap for many girls. To ensure participation of girls in middle schools, it is necessarry to provide hostel facilities.

14. The Savitribai Phule Foster Parents Scheme of Maharashtra could be adopted in other States/Union Territories to help girls of poorer families to at least complete primary school. Under the scheme, well-to do persons and organisations are persuaded to adopt one or more out of school girls and contribute in cash or kind or both @ Rs.25

per month for her education. The money can be spent on uniforms, stationery or anything else, needed by the girl or also partly used to alleviate the economic distress of the parents. The Zila Parishad, Block Education Officer and Headmaster play a pivotal role in implementing the scheme, which is purely voluntary and if district level officers for coordination of programmes for women are appointed they could also actively take it up.

15. Condensed courses of education at elementary and middle school levels for girls must be started in all the rural areas and for weaker sections of the urban community.

16. Many girls in the 11-14 years age group would first have to be brought into the primary stage through non-formal education. By devising alternative education approaches non-formal schooling and through like intelligent use of technology, the pace of middle school education can be accelerated. If retention upto 75 per cent is achieved upto class V, universal elementary education may be possible in some parts of country by 2000 A.D. Other backward areas would have to be given much more attention in professional as well as financial terms to enable them even to universalize primary education for girls by 1995. The National Literacy Mission will need to address these issues on a priority basis.

17. Special efforts are necessary for bringing tribal children particularly, girls into school system. Tribal dialects, extreme poverty, problems of commuting, rigidity of formal education and its irrelevance to the tribal culture and the tribals distrust of the ways of the mainstream society, must be borne in mind in formulating strategies.

18. The educational forecasts, may look more achievable if the system is opened up for flexible non-formal education which the below average states' should be persuaded to adopt in a large measure. The existing educational infrastructure, particularly, in tribal and rural areas should be made effective and responsible.

19. Non-formal education is an alternative to the formal system which has the potentiality of becoming the major programme of education for girls who cannot attend school during normal school hours due to various reasons. The Central Government is already implementing a centrally sponsored scheme under which grants to the extent of 90 per cent are provided towards maintenance of non-formal education centres exclusively for girls in nine educationally backward states. The programme should be strengthened further and extended to

other states where education of girls is lagging behind. It should at least cover all the pockets of low enrolment of girls and areas of high dropout rate. Besides literacy, it must also provide relevant information on skill development and inculcation of positive self-image among girls.

20. Secondary education for girls should entail :

(i) A ten year course in general education learning and diversified higher secondary education which may be either terminal or lead to further professional preparation; and (ii) Diversified courses after Grade VIII in technical subjects, viz., agricultural technology, health services, food production activities, such as, dairy and poultry and non-traditional areas need to be untroubled. A legal literacy component is also recommended at this stage.

21. Diversified courses leading to occupational preparation should be of parallel duration to the general secondary courses. In addition, there should be a variety of short and long term, whole time, part-time and apprentice courses. The trend of thinking is now to place emphasis on the last. Keeping in view the rapid modernization and advancement in technology for agriculture, there is an urgent need for skilled artisanship for promoting productive activities on the one hand, and a variety of learning programmes for adjustment of the rural society to socio-economic change, on the other. Efforts should be made to ensure that girls have every opportunity to enter into apprenticeship in areas that are non-conventional and incentives be provided for the same. Further, at least 30 per cent seats should be reserved for girls in apprenticeship training courses on a non-transferable basis.

22. General and vocational training courses should be combined so that prospects of career immediately on completion of schooling may attract girls from weaker sections. While designing the vocational courses, available occupational opportunities as well as the need to overcome market stereotypes should be kept in view.

23. Since secondary education has remained almost beyond the reach of weaker sections, liberal incentives and other facilities to release the girls from household chores appear to be essential. It would also help to locate the institutions in the areas of their habitation.

24. Multiple entry system should be introduced in the secondary classes. Part-time education facilities should also be made available.

25. Condensed courses should be organised in cooperation with

local vocational training institutions to cover all rural area and areas inhabited by weaker sections in urban areas. Such courses may be organized for small groups of girls, and combined with job training. Efforts should be made to cover at least 215 lakhs women in the age group 15-30 years under the condensed courses programme; wherever possible the condensed courses of the CSWB should be expanded and strengthened. New programmes that are to be initiated must avoid duplication in the areas where the CSWB's programmes exist.

26. Correspondence courses and self study programme can be especially useful for girls desirous of continuing education but are unable to do so because of circumstances. Apart from imparting elementary education and knowledge about farming techniques, the curriculum for non student girls should include courses of training in occupational skills. Similar programmes should also be designed for girls in the urban areas.

27. The open school system should be expanded extending the facility to all the girls in rural and backward areas.

28. Science education for girls has been neglected so far. Secondary schools for girls must be helped to build good science programmes over the Eighth Five Year Plan. Special scholarships for girls opting for science courses need to be instituted at the secondary and higher education levels.

29. Special scholarships may also be offered to rural women, who opt for teachers' training, especially those who complete the condensed courses at the secondary stage.

30. There is a need to open more colleges and polytechnics for girls, especially in rural areas.

31. Incentives like scholarships, freeship, etc., should be provided to enable girls from rural areas to pursue higher education for girls belonging to weaker sections. In addition to freeships and scholarships, bursaries should also be provided to meet their requirements for food and lodging.

32. Girls should be encouraged to enter professional courses. Reservation of seats for girls in such courses may be considered to level out the existing bias in access to certain professional streams.

33. Vocational counselling and guidance service should be organised exclusively in a more meaningful way to help girls in colleges and universities opt for suitable courses relevant to their talents and interests, and free of traditional bias.

34. Vocational and technical education for women, both formal and

non-formal, should be a major feature of the programmers of rural universities. The women's wings of the universities could undertake large scale extension programmes in order to activate girls and women in the surrounding areas to take advantage of educational and occupational facilities of various types, particularly those leading to meaningful employment, essential for reducing women's marginalization.

35. In order to increase the representation of rural girls in higher education courses, 30 per cent seats, may be reserved for girls to begin with.

36. All agencies involved with preparation of curricula, prescription of textbooks and organization of educational processes will have to evince awareness towards women's issues. University/College Departments of Women's Studies, appropriate voluntary agencies; women's groups, etc., should be involved in giving a new perspective to the various issues of content and process of education. Women's universities and women's centres in colleges need to take an active role in women's development and in influencing the attitudes of future generations.

37. Facilities for part-time self study and correspondence courses should be provided on a large scale to enable girls who are not in a position to join higher education institutions on a regular basis, to continue their studies.

38. In addition to courses leading to degree/diploma, short courses in specific subjects through summer school sessions, and ad hoc programmes like seminars, workshops, etc., should be organized for working women with a view to upgrading their knowledge and skills, not necessarily leading to degrees.

39. Integrated learning programmes for women are recommended which will not only lay emphasis on literacy but on empowering women through awareness building on social issues, bringing about attitudinal change, promoting skill training for employment, providing information on health care, nutrition and hygiene as well as on legal rights. Such programmes are beginning and must continue to be designed and structured so as to be relevant for the vast majority of rural women. The revised scheme linked to ICDS known as the 'Women's Integrated Learning for Life', should be introduced as an integral part of the non-formal education system.

40. Entrepreneurship development programmes should be organized separately for education of women in the age group 18-30

years, with a minimum of matriculation level of education. The objective of such training should be to (i) Make them aware of the various opportunities for self-employment; (ii) Motivate them to take up self-employment; (iii) Impart needed skills and training; (iv) Promote motivation for achievement among them; and (v) Create access to resources such as capital credit, etc.

41. A large number of girls cannot participate in whole-day education programmes. Provision of non-formal and part-time programmes with flexible schools hours and sensitivity to the agricultural cycle are, of particular importance. In addition to the primary and upper primary stage, distance learning opportunities need to be provided at secondary and higher secondary level.

42. Adult education will have to be composed of three-inter-related strands aimed at :

(i) Continuous flow of new information especially to rural and tribal areas, particularly to inculcate positive attitudes towards women;
(ii) Continuous training of the people in the use of modern tools and methods of production, and
(iii) Acquisition of permanent reading and computation skills.

Following from the above, three types of programmes may be offered to the learner :

(i) Information and literacy.
(ii) Information and training in new technology and literacy.
(iii) Information and training in new technology with or without literacy. Continuous information flows relating to human affairs, gender relations and the use of science and technology for betterment of life would be the common factor in all the three programmes.

43. The growing availability of communication media should be directed towards keeping up information flows and portraying positive images of women in non-conventional roles. Audio-visual materials, combined with non-formal training arrangements, could impart to various population groups the kind of instruction they need in the use of new technologies. Involvement of mass media in motivating women to attend literacy classes is most essential.

44. Rapid strides in the development of technologies and tools for the reduction in women's drudgery and easy access to work places, water and fuel supply, child care, health services and population control can contribute significantly to the success of learning programmes for women. Women's literacy programmes would succeed better if they centre around women's concerns and also provide opportunities of recreation and sharing of experiences.

45. District plans should be prepared keeping in view literacy requirements of the learners, identifying agencies which can take up such programmes in district.

46. All women working in industries or employed elsewhere should be made literate by the employers by allotting time from the working hours for their education. Place of teaching, teachers and teaching materials should be arranged by them. Necessary legislation to this effect may be enacted.

47. At least 50 per cent seats in pre-service courses in all teachers training institutions should be reserved for women. Spatial planning to ensure that women from rural areas are selected as teachers is essential.

48. Provision of composite teacher training courses for women who have had insufficient education to improve their educational qualifications along with their training, should be made.

49. The existing Integrated Rural Development Programme, National Rural Employment Programme, Development of Women and Children in Rural Areas Training of Youth in Self-Employment Programme, Integrated Child Development Programme, etc., should have a component of literacy for their women beneficiaries. Training should be provided to the functionaries of various development department by the Directorate of Education in the States.

50. The State Resources Centres should produce suitable learning material for women on a priority basis. Literature for neoliterates should be suitably devised by experts, keeping in view the needs of different groups of learners.

51. Decentralisation is the key to the successful application of the strategies outlined above. In this decentralised approach, the village cluster of the block level is seen as most appropriate for the delivery of programmes. It is, therefore, necessary that the block is allocated a flexible budget so as to make funds available to village clusters/villages for innovative educational activities and for equalisation of educational opportunity.

52. An overall coordination of health, welfare and educational inputs would be, most desirable. This would entail (a) Convergent policies in these sectors; (b) Coordination of delivery mechanisms, and (c) Pooling of allocations.

53. The strategies spelt out in the National Policy of Education, 1986, the Programme of Action for its implementation and the National Literacy Mission and the successful achievement of the goals, imposed in these documents, would be important for improvement in the status of women.

PART II

STATISTICAL INDICATORS

6

STATISTICAL INDICATORS

A. PRE-INDEPENDENCE

TABLE 6.1:   Progress of Enrolment Among Boys and Girls

Year	Percentage of Boys Enrolment to Total Enrolment	Percentage of Girls Enrolment to Total Enrolment
1881-82	94.4	5.6
1886-87	92.2	7.8
1891-92	90.8	9.2
1896-97	90.5	9.5
1901-02	88.2	11.8
1906-07	87.8	12.2
1911-12	85.7	14.3
1916-17	84.0	16.0
1921-22	82.7	17.3
1926-27	83.3	16.7
1931-32	80.4	19.6
1936-37	77.7	22.3
1941-42	76.8	23.2
1946-47	76.6	23.4

TABLE 6.2:   Number of Girls per 100 Boys

Year	Number of Girls Per 100 Boys
1881-82	06
1901-02	11
1921-22	21
1931-32	24
1936-37	30
1946-47	31

TABLE 6.3: Enrolment of Girls in Primary Schools

Year	Total	Girls
1881-82	20,61,541	1,24,491
1886-87	25,37,502	2,04,117
1891-92	28,37,607	2,70,802
1896-97	32,09,825	3,17,561
1901-02	32,04,336	3,45,397
1906-07	39,37,866	5,13,248
1911-12	49,88,142	7,85,508
1916-17	58,18,730	10,36,125
1921-22	63,10,400	11,98,550
1926-27	82,56,760	15,49,281
1931-32	94,54,360	20,77,103
1936-37	105,41,790	26,11,577
1941-42	1,20,18,726	31,23,643
1946-47	1,30,36,248	34,75,165

TABLE 6.4: Enrolment of Girls in Middle Schools

Year	Total	Girls
1881-82	1,58,425	
1886-87	3,16,253	20,140
1891-92	3,41,135	88,668
1896-97	3,42,996	31,449
1901-02	3,59,909	34,386
1906-07	4,15,066	49,352
1911-12	5,16,605	46,527
1916-17	6,14,074	77,031
1921-22	6,44,414	92,466
1926-27	10,59,866	1,30,321
1931-32	13,42,468	1,77,488
1936-37	13,63,346	2,33,214
1941-42	13,40,841	2,42,794
1946-47	17,81,390	3,21,508

TABLE 6.5: Enrolment of Girls in High Schools

Year	Total	Girls
1881-82	52,937	2,054
1886-87	1,02,159	5,574
1891-92	1,32,159	6,574
1896-97	1,92,159	8,574
1901-02	2,62,859	10,309
1906-07	2,98,276	11,885

Contd.

Contd.

Year	Total	Girls
1911-12	4,07,765	16,884
1916-17	5,72,261	24,948
1921-22	5,94,910	36,698
1926-27	7,94,210	54,826
1931-32	9,55,051	92,538
1936-37	11,33,488	1,34,290
1941-42	13,33,948	1,67,539
1946-47	21,93,439	2,80,772

TABLE 6.6:   Enrolment of Girls in Technical and Industrial Schools

Year	Total	Girls
1881-82	520	—
1886-87	2,582	—
1891-92	4,902	—
1896-97	4,494	—
1901-02	6,152	167
1906-07	7,940	266
1911-12	12,990	130
1916-17	13,580	2,677
1921-22	15,359	2,770
1926-27	26,172	4,121
1931-32	28,771	5,050
1936-37	32,286	6,345
1941-42	37,189	8,103
1946-47	36,048	1,004

TABLE 6.7:   Enrolment of Girls in Other Professional and Special Schools

Year	Total	Girls
1881-82	3,980	515
1886-87	10,870	894
1891-92	16,830	1,280
1896-97	20,125	2,292
1901-02	30,228	2,625
1906-07	60,164	4,624
1911-12	1,66,939	26,239
1916-17	1,30,024	14,665
1921-22	1,17,347	8,829
1926-27	3,02,432	10,784
1931-32	2,42,323	14,805
1936-37	2,44,700	17,102
1941-42	4,41,219	32,766
1946-47	4,62,843	15,086

TABLE 6.8:   Enrolment of Girls in Professional Colleges

Year	Total	Girls
1881-82	—	—
1886-87	2,411	27
1891-92	3,292	31
1896-97	4,363	43
1901-02	5,358	87
1906-07	6,250	113
1911-12	6,636	90
1916-17	11,504	180
1921-22	13,662	266
1926-27	17,951	345
1931-32	18,483	579
1936-37	21,226	955
1941-42	27,025	1,625
1946-47	44,437	2,903

TABLE 6.9:   Enrolment of Girls and Boys in Arts and Science Colleges

Year	Total	Boys	Girls
1881-82	7,205	7,199	6
1886-87	8,127	8,119	8
1891-92	12,985	12,940	45
1896-97	14,420	14,333	87
1901-02	17,651	17,544	177
1906-07	18,918	18,758	160
1911-12	29,648	29,369	279
1916-17	47,135	47,293	842
1921-22	45,933	44,670	1,263
1926-27	71,968	70,035	1,933
1931-32	81,010	79,644	2,966
1936-37	97,554	91,513	6,041
1941-42	1,32,129	1,20,451	11,778
1946-47	2,12,306	1,89,002	23,304

TABLE 6.10:   Enrolment of Girls in Normal Teacher Training Schools

Year	Number of Normal Schools		Enrolment in Normal Schools	
	Total	Girls	Total	Girls
1	2	3	4	5
1881-82	108	15	3,973	515
1886-87	135	27	4,949	616
1891-92	153	37	5,206	793
1896-97	186	45	5,725	1,113

Contd.

Contd.

1	2	3	4	5
1901-02	179	46	5,702	1,292
1906-07	377	63	9,180	2,278
1911-12	575	85	12,873	1,508
1916-17	801	111	18,631	2,651
1921-22	1,072	146	26,931	4,157
1926-27	695	166	25,274	4,664
1931-32	634	209	28,768	6,945
1936-37	563	217	27,314	7,379
1941-42	615	239	31,700	9,265
1946-47	649	206	38,873	10,835

TABLE 6.11:	Enrolment of Girls:Stagewise

Year	College Stage	High School Stage	Middle School Stage	Primary School Stage	Professional Collegiate Stage
1881-82	6	2,054	Included under High	1,24,491	—
1886-87	10	5574	4,430	2,47,664	27
1891-92	45	6926	6,106	2,99,013	31
1896-97	87	9,190	7,170	3,44,216	43
1901-02	177	10,677	8,133	3,80,282	37
1906-07	160	2,558	10,553	5,51,764	113
1911-12	270	1,544	15,687	8,20,793	90
1916-17	842	4,021	18,872	11,15,492	120
1921-22	1,263	5,818	24,655	12,97,643	266
1926-27	1,933	6,776	32,961	16,91,697	345
1931-32	2,966	14,581	70,612	22,62,935	575
1936-37	6,041	29,399	1,22,207	28,17,745	956
1941-42	12,600	42,000	2,91,606	32,99,467	1,743
1946-47	20,304	83,270	2,81,606	37,28,793	2,903

Note:	There is variation *vis-a-vas* Table 6.3 to 6.8 perhaps because of the term stage.

TABLE 6.12:	Number of Girls Who Passed Various Examination: Stagewise

Year	Matriculation and Above	Intermediate	B.A./B.Sc. Hons.	M.A./M.Sc.	Research
1921-22	1,001	195	85	6	—
1926-27	1,312	379	191	27	—
1931-32	2,567	713	302	37	—
1936-37	5,592	1,494	834	75	—
1941-42	10,932	3,724	1,829	240	3
1964-77	12,924	4,227	2,319	384	4

TABLE 6.13:   Number of Women and Men Teachers: Stagewise

Year	Women	Men	Total
1926-27			
Primary Schools	26,156	2,85,694	3,11,850
Middle Schools	5,325	41,760	47,085
High Schools	3,350	38,037	41,387
1931-32			
Primary Schools	33,524	3,18,018	3,51,542
Middle Schools	6,153	57,387	6,404
High Schools	5,225	44,390	49,615
1936-37			
Primary Schools	48,243	3,38,072	3,76,315
Middle Schools	7,927	51,688	59,615
High Schools	6,823	51,031	57,854
1941-42			
Primary Schools	45,742	3,46,339	3,92,079
Middle Schools	8,747	54,116	62,863
High Schools	8,185	58,128	66,316
1946-47			
Primary Schools	55,575	3,50,548	4,06,123
Middle Schools	11,619	61,794	72,413
High Schools	11,643	76,219	87,862

B. AFTER INDEPENDENCE

(i) School Education

TABLE 6.14:   Enrolment and Percentage of Girls, 1950-51 to 1986-87: Stagewise

Year	Number of Girls in Primary Classes I-V	Number of Girls in Middle Classes VI-VIII	Number of Girls in Secondary 10+2 Intermediate (IX + above)
1950-51	54,00,000 (28.17%)	5,00,000 (16.1%)	2,00,000 (14.3%)
1960-61	1,14,00,000 (32.6%)	16,03,900 (23.9%)	6,00,000 (18.2%)
1970-71	2,13,00,000 (37.4%)	39,00,000 (29.3%)	19,00,000 (25.0%)
1980-81	2,85,00,000 (38.6%)	88,00,000 (32.97%)	35,00,000 (29.4%)
1986-87	3,61,00,000 (40.1%)	1,02,00,000 (35.4%)	54,00,000 (30.7%)

Note: Figures in Parentheses indicate percentage to total enrolment (Boys and Girls).

TABLE 6.15: Enrolment Ratio of Girls and Boys in Classes I to VIII, 1986-87: Statewise

State/U.T.	Classes I-V — 6-11 Years		Classes VI to VIII	
	Boys (Girls)	Total	Boys (Girls)	Total
1	2	3	4	5
Andhra Pradesh	116.4 (86.7)	101.6	42.2 (24.2)	33.25
Assam	97.2 (82.8)	90.2	69.1 (61.6)	65.5
Bihar	107.0 (52.8)	80.4	47.1 (15.5)	31.6
Gujarat	126 (98.0)	112.3	64.9 (40.9)	53.2
Haryana	98.2 (72.1)	85.5	78.3 (40.5)	60.5
Himachal Pradesh	118.9 (103.2)	111.2	106.7 (72.8)	90.8
Jammu & Kashmir	96.1 (62.0)	79.6	63.3 (35.8)	49.9
Karnataka	104.5 (85.9)	95.3	83.7 (54.1)	69.0
Kerala	108.6 (105.8)	107.2	96.8 (94.3)	95.8
Madhya Pradesh	117.3 (75.8)	97.1	66.5 (24.8)	46.0
Maharashtra	126.2 (108.9)	117.8	79.9 (53.3)	67.0
Manipur	127.8 (105.0)	116.5	82.6 59.9	71.4
Meghalaya	100.7 (97.3)	99.0	62.7 (50.3)	56.4
Nagaland	118.6 (117.7)	118.1	55.43 (48.1)	51.9
Orissa	111.7 (78.0)	95.0	49.2 (27.0)	39.1
Punjab	97.1 (91.3)	94.4	67.1 (54.4)	61.2
Rajasthan	109.6 (46.7)	79.1	61.8 (16.2)	39.8
Sikkim	141.3 (115.2)	128.4	63.3 (50.5)	57.1
Tamil Nadu	138.6 (122.4)	130.6	91.9 (65.4)	78.8

Contd.

Contd.

1	2	3	4	5
Tripura	139.2		57.6	
	(85.8)	113	(41.8)	49.8
Uttar Pradesh	96.5		59.9	
	(53.4)	76.2	(23.2)	42.7
West Bengal	134.9		70.7	
	(96.5)	115.8	(54.6)	62.7
A & N Islands	108.4		95.0	
	(94.7)	100.5	(82.7)	89.2
Arunachal Pradesh	112.8		51	
	(75.9)	94.5	(30.4)	41
Chandigarh	44.8		41.3	
	(45.9)	45.9	(40.9)	41.2
Dadra & Nagar Haveli	102.4		50.9	
	(75.3)	89.4	(32.1)	41.7
Delhi	92.63		87.9	
	(94.9)	93.7	(81.4)	85
Goa, Daman & Diu	135.7		114.2	
	(123.1)	129.4	(97.0)	105.8
Lakshadweep	152.2		119.3	
	(143.6)	148	(81.3)	100.3
Mizoram	137.1	123	65.6	
	(139.5)	123.4	(62.1)	63.9
Pondicherry	133.1		117.4	
	(118.7)	12.6	(81.6)	99.5
India	111.8		66.5	
	(792.0)	96	39	53.1

TABLE 6.16:   Number of Girls and Boys in Vocational Courses at +2 Stage, 1986-87

1. Number of Institutions with Vocational Courses		1706
2. Number of Students in Class XI	Boys	41,318
	Girls	26,862
	Total	68,180
3. Number of Students in Class XII	Boys	39,070
	Girls	19,321
	Total	58,391
4. Total: Classes XI and XII	Boys	80,388
	Girls	46,183
	Grand Total	1,26,571

Notes:

1. Not a single girl opted for vocational courses in Uttar Pradesh. Total number of boys taking up vocational courses was 1700.
2. In Goa, girls outnumbered boys in opting for vocational courses.

(ii) Higher Education

TABLE 6.17:   Enrolment of Women, 1950-51 to 1986-87

Year	Total Women Enrolment in Thousands	Number of Women per Hundred Men
1950-51	40	14
1955-56	84	17
1960-61	150	23
1965-66	271	24
1975-76	595	33
1981-82	817	38
1982-83	880	39
1983-84	940	40
1984-85	992	41
1985-86*	1059	42
1986-87*	1125	44

* Estimated

TABLE 6.18:   Number of Women's Colleges, 1970-77 to 1988-89

Year	Total Number of Colleges	Number of Women's Colleges
1970-77	4,317	543
1980-81	4,722	609
1984-85	5,590	712
1985-86	5,813	741
1986-87	6,040 *	771 *
1987-88	6,190 *	800 *
1988-89	6,300 *	830 *

* Estimated

TABLE 6.19:   Enrolment of Women: Statewise 1986-87: Statewise

Sl. No.	State/ Union Territory	Total Enrolment	Women Enrolment	Percentage of Women Enrolled
1	2	3	4	5
1.	Andhra Pradesh	2,79,822	73,005	26.1
2.	Assam	81,001	23,342	26.8
3.	Bihar	2,65,095	40,040	15.1
4.	Gujarat	2,13,549	73,219	34.3
5.	Haryana	73,637	29,971	40.7
6.	Himachal Pradesh	20,250	5,174	25.6

Contd.

Contd.

1	2	3	4	5
7.	Jammu & Kashmir	29,455	10,577	35.9
8.	Karnataka	2,54,049	69,437	27.3
9.	Kerala	1,43,593	72,359	50.4
10.	Madhya Pradesh	2,72,458	84,461	31.0
11.	Maharashtra	4,78,643	1,65,925	34.7
12.	Manipur	11,046	3,593	32.5
13.	Meghalaya/Nagaland	9,205	3,554	38.6
14.	Orissa	73,637	16,876	22.9
15.	Punjab	1,36,229	62,015	45.5
16.	Rajasthan	1,80,412	40,619	22.5
17.	Tamil Nadu	2,61,413	95,431	36.5
18.	Uttar Pradesh	5,08,098	1,08,853	21.4
19.	West Bengal/Tripura/ Sikkim	2,87,186	1,01,962	35.5
20.	Delhi	1,03,092	44,891	43.5
	Total	36,81,870	11,25,304	30.6

* Estimated

TABLE 6.20:   Percentage of Enrolment of Women, 1975-76 to 1986-87

Year	Total Enrolment	Women Enrolment	Percentage of Women Enrolled
1975-76	24,26,109	5,95,162	24.5
1976-77	24,31,563	6,27,346	25.8
1979-80	26,48,579	7,89,042	26.0
1980-81	27,52,437	7,48,525	27.2
1981-82	29,52,066	8,16,704	27.7
1982-83	31,33,093	8,80,156	28.1
1983-84	33,07,649	9,40,253	28.4
1984-85	34,04,096	9,92,139	29.1
1985-86*	35,70,897	10,58,612	29.6
1986-87*	36,81,870	11,25,304	30.6

* Estimated

TABLE 6.21: Distribution of Enrolment, 1975-76 to 1986-87: Sexwise and Statewise

Year	Graduate			Postgraduate			Research		
	T	W	%	T	W	%	T	W	%
1975-76	21,46,919	5,26,260	24.5	2,19,826	54,824	24.9	18,381	4,477	24.4
1976-77	21,41,542	NA	NA	2,18,128	NA	NA	21,910	NA	NA
1979-80	23,07,924	5,95,493	26.0	2,65,251	71,963	27.1	29,570	7,331	24.8
1980-81	24,01,485	6,52,808	27.2	2,73,337	77,001	28.2	32,171	8,780	27.3
1981-82	25,88,759	7,16,249	27.7	2,85,892	81,645	28.6	34,588	9,581	27.7
1982-83	27,57,893	7,73,342	28.0	2,96,103	86,380	29.2	36,731	10,673	29.1
1983-84	29,12,487	8,25,409	28.3	3,13,110	93,728	29.9	36,249	10,615	29.3
1984-85	29,99,621	8,71,571	29.1	3,22,541	98,415	30.5	38,160	11,332	29.7
1985-86*	31,42,389	9,99,461	29.6	3,39,235	1,04,803	30.9	39,280	12,703	32.3
1986-87*	32,40,046	9,88,017	30.5	3,49,778	1,11,405	31.5	40,500	13,504	33.3

* Estimated

TABLE 6.22:　Distribution of Enrolment, 1975-76 to 1986-87: Sexwise and Facultywise

(i)

Year	Arts			Science			Commerce		
	T	W	%	T	W	%	T	W	%
1975-76	10,79,990	3,92,737	36.4	4,63,841	1,11,714	24.1	4,14,946	27,551	6.6
1976-77	10,78,967	NA	NA	4,43,013	NA	NA	4,30,387	NA	NA
1979-80	10,76,076	3,97,914	37.0	5,08,763	1,40,098	27.5	5,16,170	68,051	13.2
1980-81	11,14,417	4,20,276	37.7	5,33,859	1,53,868	28.8	5,54,253	88,067	15.9
1981-82	11,90,177	4,54,990	38.2	5,78,766	1,65,666	28.6	6,28,031	1,04,964	16.7
1982-83	12,59,587	4,87,620	38.7	6,23,545	1,79,650	28.8	6,69,813	1,16,837	17.4
1983-84	13,38,106	5,17,017	38.6	6,53,092	1,89,685	29.0	7,03,638	1,31,379	18.7
1984-85	13,72,277	5,40,686	39.4	6,69,563	2,00,632	30.0	7,38,506	1,42,222	19.3
1985-86*	14,39,071	5,81,813	40.4	7,03,467	2,14,581	30.5	7,67,743	1,46,724	19.1
1986-87*	14,83,794	6,18,467	41.6	7,25,328	2,28,099	31.4	7,91,602	1,55,967	19.7

* Estimated

(ii)

Year	Education			Engg/Tech			Medicine		
	T	W	%	T	W	%	T	W	%
1975-76	76,641	30,110	39.3	96,067	2,061	2.1	1,05,140	19,208	18.3
1976-77	75,512	NA	NA	1,00,040	NA	NA	1,13,151	NA	NA
1979-80	72,981	34,497	47.3	1,18,607	4,428	3.7	1,12,194	24,426	21.8
1980-81	71,204	33,708	47.3	1,28,937	4,949	3.8	1,10,020	26,797	24.4
1981-82	71,168	34,383	48.3	1,30,189	5,866	4.5	1,13,794	29,792	26.2
1982-83	74,167	34,893	47.0	1,42,440	7,173	5.0	1,13,902	31,648	27.8
1983-84	74,679	35,337	47.3	1,53,131	8,469	5.5	1,18,989	33,676	28.3
1984-85	76,522	36,555	47.8	1,59,046	10,052	6.3	1,18,890	35,190	29.6
1985-86*	82,131	40,227	49.0	1,64,261	9,634	5.9	1,28,552	37,898	29.5
1986-87*	84,683	42,762	50.5	1,69,366	10,240	6.0	1,32,547	40,286	30.4

* Estimated

(iii)

Year	Agriculture			Vet./Science			Law		
	T	W	%	T	W	%	T	W	%
1975-76	30,160	432	1.4	6,377	91	1.4	1,41,298	7,053	5.0
1976-77	31,860	NA	NA	6,700	NA	NA	1,40,680	NA	NA
1979-80	39,962	1,101	2.8	7,435	202	2.7	1,77,448		
1980-81	39,231	1,311	3.3	7,648	249	3.3	1,74,374	11,948	6.9
1981-82	39,318	1,390	3.5	8,173	352	4.3	1,74,445	12,309	7.1
1982-83	39,425 **	1,595	4.0	8,797	424	4.8	1,83,153	13,576	7.4
1983-84	41,588	1,719	4.1	9,268	470	5.1	1,94,555	15,156	7.8
1984-85	41,741	2,045	4.9	9,413	506	5.4	1,95,708	15,745	8.0
1985-86*	46,422	2,011	4.3	10,713	529	4.9	2,07,112	16,726	8.1
1986-87*	47,864	2,138	4.5	11,046	563	5.1	2,13,549	17,780	8.3

* Estimated
** Revised

(iii) All Types

TABLE 6.23: Enrolment, 1985-86 to 1986-87: Sexwise and Classes/Stagewise

Category	1985-86		1986-87	
	Boys *(Girls)*	*Total*	*Boys* *(Girls)*	*Total*
Ph.D./D.Sc./D.Phil.	19,696 (8,905)	28,601	21,068 (10,465)	31,533
M.A.	1,12,508 (69,569)	1,82,077	1,19,309 (71,777)	1,91,086
M.Sc.	53,090 (26,234)	79,324	52,816 (26,315)	79,131
M.Com.	54,332 (11,714)	66,036	52,882 (9,100)	61,982
B.A./B.A.Hons.	7,98,686 (4,87,778)	12,86,464	8,57,399 (5,47,997)	14,05,396
B.Sc./B.Sc.Hons.	4,52,077 (1,91,681)	6,43,758	4,64,038 (2,07,851)	6,71,889
B.Com./B.Com. Hons.	5,98,456 (1,58,071)	7,56,527	6,00,973 (1,69,269)	7,70,242
B.E./B.Sc.(Engg.)/ B.Arch.	1,34,870 (8,550)	1,43,420	1,59,629 (22,792)	1,82,421
B.Ed./B.T.	47,822 (37,396)	85,218	50,408 (38,744)	89,152
M.B.B.S.	56,462 (23,628)	80,090	53,440 (25,327)	78,767
Intermediate/ Junior Colleges	1,10,927 (3,01,230)	14,10,509	12,80,706 (3,97,662)	16,78,368
Pre-Degree/ Pre-University (Two Year Course)	2,21,011 (1,53,165)	3,74,176	1,74,546 (1,37,112)	3,11,658
Pre-University (One-Year Course)	52,029 (27,612)	79,641	50,841 (26,630)	77,471
Higher Secondary (10+2) Pattern (XI-XII Classes)	12,33,290 (6,36,465)	18,69,755	19,26,885 (9,40,500)	28,67,385
Higher Secondary Old Pattern	11,64,791 (4,54,126)	16,18,917	1,28,174 (32,708)	1,60,882
Higher/Post Basic (IX-X Classes)	80,29,339 (35,87,923)	1,16,17,262	86,21,512 (38,51,420)	1,24,72,962
Middle/Senior Basic(VI-VII)	1,81,32,301 (99,92,455)	2,81,24,756	1,85,43,453 (1,02,36,646)	2,87,80,099
Primary/Junior Basic(I-IV)	5,17,26,426 (3,47,32,763)	8,64,65,189	5,38,50,028 (3,61,43,018)	8,99,93,046
Pre-Primary/ Pre-Basic	6,75,600 (5,60,150)	12,35,750	6,96,183 (5,75,401)	12,71,584
Teacher Training School	46,688 (50,871)	97,559	46,984 (45,901)	92,885
Polytechnic Institutions	1,12,165 (12,360)	1,24,525	1,64,454 (34,088)	1,98,542
Technical Industrial Arts and Crafts School	12,16,773 (65,837)	2,82,610	2,33,640 (74,639)	3,08,279

Source: Selected Educational Statistics 1985-86 and 1986-87.

TABLE 6.24: Literacy Rate, 1981: Percentage Literacy Rates According to Ranking: (Sexwise and Statewise)

State/Union Territories	Rank	Males	Females	Persons (Total)
Kerala	1	75.26	65.73	70.74
Chandigarh	2	69.00	59.31	64.79
Delhi	3	68.40	53.07	61.54
Mizoram	4	64.46	54.91	59.88
Goa, Daman and Diu	5	65.59	49.56	56.66
Pondicherry	6	65.84	45.71	55.85
Lakshadweep	7	65.24	44.65	55.07
A & N Islands	8	58.72	42.14	51.56
Maharashtra	9	58.79	34.79	47.18
Tamil Nadu	10	58.26	34.99	46.76
Gujarat	11	54.44	32.30	43.70
Nagaland	12	50.06	33.89	42.57
Himachal Pradesh	13	53.19	31.46	42.48
Tripura	14	51.70	32.00	42.12
Manipur	15	53.29	29.06	41.35
West Bengal	16	50.67	30.25	40.94
Punjab	17	47.16	33.69	40.86
Karnataka	18	48.81	27.71	38.46
Haryana	19	48.20	22.37	36.14
Orissa	20	47.10	21.12	34.23
Meghalaya	21	37.89	30.08	34.08
Sikkim	22	43.95	22.20	34.05
Andhra Pradesh	23	39.26	20.39	29.94
Madhya Pradesh	24	39.49	15.53	27.87
Uttar Pradesh	25	38.76	14.04	27.16
Jammu & Kashmir	26	36.29	15.88	26.69
Dadra & Nagar Haveli	27	36.32	16.78	26.67
Bihar	28	38.11	13.62	26.20
Rajasthan	29	36.30	11.42	24.38
Arunachal Pradesh	30	28.94	11.32	20.79
INDIA	—	46.89	24.82	36.23

TABLE 6.25: Women Teachers, 1950-51 and 1986-87

Sl. No.	Category	1950-51	1986-87
1	2	3	4
1.	Primary Schools	5,35,000	15,22,000
2.	Secondary/High Schools	85,000	9,79,000
3.	Senior Secondary/Higher Secondary	1,27,000	11,99,000
	Total	7,47,000	37,00,000

Contd.

Contd.

1	2	3	4
	4. Percentage of Female Teachers		
	(a) Primary Schools	15.3	30.56
	(b) Upper Primary Schools	15.2	32.18
	(c) Secondary Schools	15.7	28.12
	(d) Higher Secondary Schools	—	29.33
	5. Percentage of Trained Teachers		
	(a) Primary Schools	58.5	86.66
	(b) Upper Primary Schools	53.3	87.33
	(c) Secondary Schools	55.5	90.23
	(d) Higher Secondary Schools	—	88.55

TABLE 6.26: Some Profiles of Women

1.	Women illiterate	over 75%
2.	Rural illiterate Women	83%
3.	Women Working in unorganised sectors	over 90%
4.	Of 3 above, unskilled labour in agriculture and construction	83%
5.	Women having full time employment in organised sectors	14%
6.	Maternity benefits and childcare available in organised sectors	3.5%
7.	Registered unemployed school graduates	51 lakh
8.	Pragmatic women who are anaemic	65%
9.	Sex Ratio	993 females to 1000 males
10.	Expectation of life at birth	51.6 as against 52.9 for males
11.	On an average working hours per day for rural women worker	18 hours
12.	Property owned by women	less than 1%

In India, women constitute about 30 per cent of the graduates, 31 per cent of the post-graduates, 33 per cent of research workers, 42 per cent of Arts enrolment, 31 per cent of Science, 19.7 per cent of Commerce, 50 per cent of Education, 10 per cent of Engineering/Technology, 30 per cent of Medicine, 4 per cent of Agriculture, 8.3 per cent of Law and 41 per cent of other subjects. The overall per cent is 31 per cent (Estimated figures for 1986-87)

PART III

INDEX TO SCHOLARLY WRITINGS IN INDIAN EDUCATIONAL JOURNALS AND NEWSPAPERS SINCE INDEPENDENCE

7

INDEX TO SCHOLARLY WRITINGS IN INDIAN EDUCATIONAL JOURNALS AND NEWSPAPERS SINCE INDEPENDENCE*

7.1 BASIC INDEX

Abildgaard, Jorgine, 1958, Physical education for girls, *Shiksha* 11 (1) July, p. 62-65.

Access of women to education, 1960, *Indian Journal of Adult Education* 21(11) November , p. 18.

Achanta, Laxmi Devi, 1983, Measurement of values of rural women, *Indian Journal of Extension Education* 19 (3-4) September-December, p. 83-89, refs, tabs.

Acharlu, K.S., 1966, Teacher's wife in rural education, *Educational India* 33(2) August, p. 72, letter to editor.

————, 1977 Two-hour rural school for small villages, *Educational India* 43 (10) April, p. 223-26.

Activities of Kasturba Trust : Gujarat Branch, 1964, *Indian Journal of Adult Education* 25(4) April, p. 5.

Adarsh Bala, 1976, Milton's misogyny, *Journal of Indian Education*, 1(5) January, p. 45-50.

Adhila Haque *see* Haque, Adhila.

Adult education of women in the changing pattern of society: Seminar working paper, 1968, *Indian Journal of Adult Education* 29 (10) October, p. 6-9.

Advancement of women through access to education, 1970, *Education Quarterly* 22 (3) October, p. 49-55.

Agarwal, Bina, 1976, Exploitation utilization of educated women power, *Journal of Higher Education* 2(2) August, p. 185-95, refs, tabs.

---

* Includes significant articles in newspapers and other Journals

Agrawal, Mamta, 1981, A study of the impact of education on social and cultural modernisation of Hindu and Muslim women, *Indian Educational Review* 16(1) January, p. 72-77.

Agarwal, S.M., 1965, Impact of education on employment of women as career girls, *Education and Psychology Review* 5 (1) January, p. 34-37.

Ahmad, Karuna, 1979, Equity and women's higher education, *Journal of Higher Education* 5 (1) Monsoon, p. 33-49.

————, 1984, From secondary to higher education: Focus on women, *Journal of Higher Education* 9 (3) Spring, p. 349-62, refs. The social context of women's education in India, 1921-81: Tentative formulations, *New Frontiers in Education* 15(3), p. 1-36.

Aiyar, Shahnaz Auklesaria *see* Aklesaria Aiyar, Shahnaz.

Alagappa University, Centre for Woman's Studies and Rural Technology, 1989, Seminar on women and development, *University News* 27 (2), p. 31.

All India Council for Women's Education, 1958, *Education* 37 (6) June, p. 1-3, editorial.

Amiruddin, Mir, 1949, Women's role in adult education, *Educational India* 16 (5) November, p. 138-39.

Amrik Singh, 1988, Empowerment of women, *Tribune* July 13, 1988.

————, 1988, New deal for women, *Hindustan Times* June 27.

————, 1988, What happens to briliant girls? *Tribune* 27 August.

Amrit Kaur *see* Kaur, Amrit.

Anand, Kulwant, 1965, Attitudes of Punjab University women students towards marriage and the family, *Indian Journal of Social Work* 26, p. 87-90.

Aneja, Nirmala, 1966, Use of higher education by women, *Social Welfare* 13, p. 1-3.

Anklesaria Aiyar, Shahnaz, 1988, Need to improve girls' education, *Indian Express* 13 August.

Anusuya, Gyanchand *see* Gyanchand, Anusuya.

Atienza, Maria Fe G., 1966, The Philippine Women's University and extramural education for women, *Indian Journal of Adult Education* 27 (7) July, p. 11-16.

Avadhesh Dayal, 1965, women's education, *Education* 44 (7) July, p. 31-34.

Azmat, Rehana, 1970, A thought on girls education, *Education* 49 (3) March, p. 12-15.

Bagree, Asha, 1980, Appropriate education for women, *Hindu* 9 July, p. 5.

Bala, Adarsh *see* Adarsh Bala.

Ban on male teachers for girls schools held void, 1979, *Times of India* September 1, p. 3.

Banerjee, Nirmala, 1989, Trends in women's employment, 1971-81: Some macro-level observation, *Economic and Political Weekly* 24 (17), p. 10-22 WS

Barnabas, Manorama, 1978, Designing education for tomorrow's woman: Curricular aspects, *New Frontiers in Education* 8 (1) January-March, p. 27-41, refs, tabs.

Basnet, Neelam, 1989, Status of women's education in Nepal, *New Frontiers in Education* 19 (1), January-March, p. 106-9.

Basu, Soma, 1989, Can education liberate eve? *Patriot* June 18.

Beg, Shahnaz Hashmi, 1975, Educational problems of the Muslim women, *Journal Indian Education* 1 (4) November of, p. 8-13.

Behl, R.K., 1988, Whither women's education? *Tribune* February 28.

Benjamin, Margaret, 1965, Progressive school : Alexander Girls English Institute, Bombay, *Indian Education* 4(8-9) July-August, p. 36-37.

Bhagat, Bankim Bihari, 1983, Making the other half literate, *Indian Express* 26 February, p. 6.

Bhagat, P., 1981, Evaluation of condensed courses of education for adult women, *Indian Journal of Adult Education* 42 (10) October, p. 17-20. refs.

Bhandari, R.K. 1982, Educational development of women, *Education Quarterly* 34(3) July, p. 12-14.

————, 1982, Development of women's education, *New Frontiers in Education* 12(4) October-December, p. 32-37.

Bhansali, Kamalini H., 1969, Education of women in modern India: Some achievements and problems, *Education Quarterly* 21(1) April, p. 36-43.

————, 1975, Women and the continuing education, *Journal of Indian Education* 1 (4) November, p. 18-23.

Bhatnagar, Bimla, 1960, Social education for women, *Education Quarterly* 12 (47) Autumn, p. 240-41.

Bhatnagar, Suman Rani, author *see* Saxena, Daya and Bhatnagar, Suman Rani.

Bhave, Asha, M., jt author *see* Ravi, Jhani and Bhave, Asha M.

Bhushan, L.I., 1981, Development of women's social freedom scale: A report, *Asian Journal of Psychology and Education* 7 (2) July, p. 34-38.

Big educational schemes for women proposed, 1987, *Patriot* December 9, p. 5.

Bodet, Jaimes Torre, 1950, Excerpts from the address to the Conference of the International Federation of University Women at Zurich on 12 August 1950, *Education* 29 (15) 25 August, p. 27-29.

Bose, A., 1975, Census figures reveal discrimination against women, *Organiser* 24 (39) p. 5.

Britain's schools undertake new experiment: Further extension of co-education, 1948, *Education* 27 (20) 30 November, p. 22-23.

Brockway, K.N., 1953, Changes in girls education, 1927-52, *Teaching* 25 (4) June, p. 143-44.

————, 1953, Secondary education for Indian girls, *Journal of Education and Psychology* 10 (4) January p. 201-04.

Buch, M.B., 1968, Issues and problems in women's education in India, *Education Quarterly* 20 (1) April p. 34-37.

Buch, M.B., jt author *see* Santhanam, M.R. and Buch, M.B.

Call to promote women's education, 1986, *National Herald* January, 14, p. 6.

Castello, Kathleen, 1962, Women's education in Japan, *Educational Review* 68 (4) April, p. 94.

Central grants for women's upliftment, 1986, *Statesman* December 20, p. 8.

Chainani, R.S., 1982, Woman and her Education, *Progress of Education* 57 (4) November, p. 77-80.

Chakrabarti, Ashok Kumar, 1977, Causes of women's unemployment in India, *Economic Affairs* 22 (5), p. 177-84.

Challenge of women's education, 1979, *Hindu* October 29, p. 6, November 2, p. 9.

Chanana, Karuna, *see* Ahmad, Karuna.

Chandler, E.M, 1980, *Education of adolescent girls*, Allen and Unwin, London, 217 p.; Book Review, 1981, *Education Quarterly* 33(3) July, p. 44-45.

Chandra Govind, 1965, Adult education programme for women, *Naya Shikshak* 8(2) October, p. 71-75.

Chandra Reddy, T., jt author *see*, Venkata Rami Reddy, A., and Chandra Reddy, T.

Chandrasekaran, Rajkumari, 1977, Role of voluntary organisations in meeting the needs of women in the fields of adult education and female literacy, *Indian Journal of Adult Education* 38(5) May, p. 16-24, refs.

————, 1980, Designing curriculum and technology for women's adult education programmes, *Indian Journal of Adult Education* 41(4) April, p. 19-27.

————, 1983, Women power must be exploited too! *Hindu* 25 October, p. 19.

Chandy, Anna, 1962, Problems of women's education, *Educational Review* 68(5) May, p. 101-03.

Chattopadhyay, Kamladevi, 1969, Role of women in modern India, *Education Quarterly* 21 (1) April, p. 12-14.

————, 1983, *Indian women's battle for freedom*, Abhinav Pub, New Delhi, 184 p.; Book Review, 1983, *New Frontier in Education* 13 (1) January-March, p. 72-73.

Chhabra, Rai, 1980, Establishing linkages between women's literacy programmes status issues and access to family planning, *Indian Journal of Adult Education* 41(4) April, p. 6-9.

Chinnappa, Padmavati, 1949, The education of women adults, *Education* 28 (19) 30 November, p. 12-14.

Chiplunkar, VV, 1987, Education and development of women: Project Maher, *Journal of Educational Planning and Administration* 1(2), p. 173-90.

Chitnis, S., 1975, International Women's Year: Its significance for women in India, *Social Action* 25(3), p. 203-220.

Choksi, M., 1956, Co-education in India, *Education Quarterly* 8(32) December, p. 377-79.

Chopra, Kamala, 1970, Reading interests of adolescent boys and girls, *Educational India* 37 (1) July, p. 16-19+; *Progress of Education* 44(12) July, p. 412-18, refs, tabs.

Chowdhury, Neerja, 1986, Education for equality, *Statesman* May 26, p. 5.

Christian, J.A., 1980, A correlational study of students performance, *Journal of Institute of Educational Research* 4(1) January, p. 16-19, refs.

Co-education in India, 1956, *Education Quarterly* December, p. 377-83 Contents: M. Choksi, p. 377-79; 2. Vijay Mulay, p. 379-81; 3. N. K. Sundaram, p. 381-82; 4. K.C.Khanna, p. 382-83;

Co-education in the United States, 1960, *Education* 39(8) August p. 13-15.

Concern over higher drop-out among girls, 1985, *National Herald*, 14 April, p. 12.

Council recast for women's education, 1978, *Palnot*, July 3, p. 5.

D' Souza *see* filing as (De Souza).

Dayal, Avadesh *see* Avadesh Dayal.

De, S.K., 1959, Progress of women's education in India, *Education* 38(7) July, p. 5-11.

Decusker, Mahesh, 1977, A study into the corrleation between the scholistic achievements and the achievement in co-curriculum activities of girl students of higher secondary schools of Sagar town, *Progress of Education*, 51(12) July, p. 221-25, refs, tabs.

Delhi, grand old lady (Hindu Girls Higher Secondary School, Delhi), 1979, *Femina* December 23, p. 33.

Demonstration home, 1961, *Journal of Indian Adult Education* 22(9) September, p. 16-18.

Desai, Haribhai, G., jt author *see* Uchat, D.A. and Desai, Haribhai G.

Desai, Neera, 1977, Pattern of higher education of women and role of a woman's university, *Journal of Higher Education* 3(1), p. 5-19.

Deshmukh, Durgabai, 1960, womens education: A major problem, *Educational India* 27(3) September, p. 78-82.

———, 1960, Expansion of women's education under the Third Plan, *Education Quarterly* 12 (48) Winter, p. 289-93.

———, 1960, Women's education: A major problem, *Educational India*, 27(3), Septemper, p. 8-82.

De Souza, Austin, A., 1961, Education of women in the U.K. and the U.S.A., *Education Quarterly* 13(50) Summer, p. 182-80.

Deulkar, Durga, 1960, Place of home science in secondary education for girls, *Teacher Education* 4(2), February, p. 29-32.

Devadas, Rajammal P., 1956, Rural women's uplift: Role of the Gram- sevika, *Indian Journal of Adult Education* 17 (1) March, p. 37-43.

———, 1969, Vocational education for women, *Education Quarterly* 21 (1) April, p. 15-21.

Dewani, Lakshman, 1989, Nehru and emancipation of Indian women, *Patriot*, December 16.

Dey, Chhaya, 1981, Reform entails a pre-definition process, *Progress of Education*, 56(4), November, p 85-88.

Dharam Vir, 1972, Women education: An effort in Central India, *Indian Journal of Adult Education*, 33(8), August, p. 9.

Dighe, Anita, 1985, Non-formal education for women, *Social Change* 15 (3), p. 40-45.

Divan, Sharada, 1961, S.N.D.T. Women's University: Dr Karve's experiment, *Educational India* 27(11-12) May-June, p. 389-91.

Diwakar Shastri see Shastri, Diwakar.

D' Souza *see* (filing as) De Souza.

Dubey, V.K., *et. el*, 1978, Training rural women for change, *Indian Journal of Adult Education* 39(7) July, p. 35-38.

Duncan, Margaret, 1971, Continuing education of women, *Indian Journal of Adult Education* 32 (4) April, p. 9-12.

du Sautey, Peter, 1960, Educating grandmothers, *Indian Journal of Adult Education* 21 (11) November, p. 12-14.

Dutt, Sumitt Sunitee, 1959, National planning and vocations for women, *Educational Forum*, 4(1) January, p 8-11.

Dutt, V.C., 1956, Women's Education, *Shiksha* 9 (2) October, p. 89-94

Dutta, S.C., 1962, Condensed course for adult women : A new experiment in adult education, *Indian Journal of Adult Education* 23 (8) August, p. 3-4.

————, 1980, Women's education for civic and social responsibilities, *Indian Journal of Adult Education* 28 (12) December, p. 3-4.

————, 1985, Development of non-formal structure to educate women, *Indian Journal of Adult Education* 46 (4) April, p. 11-13.

[Editorial], 1975, *Journal of Indian Education* 1 (4) November, p. 1-2.

Educating the daughters, 1988, *Tribune*, December 30, editorial.

Educating women 'crucial', 1984, *Patriot*, February 12, p. 3.

Education for women, 1959, *Educational India* 25 (11-12) May-June, p. 424-25, editorial.

Education for women, 1959, *Educational India* 26(5) November p. 154-56, editorial.
Smt. Durgabai Deshmukhs's address at National Council for Women's Education.

Education of girls, 1964, *Educational India* 30(8) February, p. 276-77, editorial.

Education of girls best investment : Reserve Bank of India study, 1980, *Economic Times*, October 18, p. 7.

Education of women, 1953, *Educational India* 20(3) September, p. 91-93, editorial.

Education of women, 1964, *Educational India* 30 (9) March, p. 307-08, editorial .

Education plan for girls benefits 8,000, 1984, *Times of India* (Bombay), April 9, p. 4.

Engler, M., 1949, Adult education for women, *Educational India* 16 (5) November p. 139.

Faget, Claire, 1966, African women help in rural education and training, *Educational India* 32 (9) March, p. 329-30.

Female education still far from good, 1983, *Hindustan Times*, June 21, p. 12.

Female literacy growing, 1984, *Patriot*, June 5, p. 5.

Female literacy still deemed unnecessary, 1986, *Indian Express*, October 13, p. 4.

Fernandes, Marjorie, 1984, Development of women's education : Problems and suggestions, *Indian Journal of Adult Education* 45 (9), p. 4-9.

Fernandez, Marilyn, 1985, University education for what : The case of Kerala women, *New Frontiers in Education* 15 (1), p. 82-85.

The Five Year Plan and women's education, 1952, *Educational India*, 19 (2) August, p. 56-59, editorial.

Free education upto 10+2 for girls soon, 1985, *Times of India*, February 6, p. 16.

Fund appeal for women's literacy network, 1986, *Patriot*, April 30, p. 3.

Gandhi, T.K., 1951, Girls' education, *Shiksha* 3(3) January, p. 46-49.

Ganguly, Shailaja, 1975, Can women manage : Management as a career for women, *Education Quarterly* 27 (2) July, p. 4-6.

Geldens, Maria, 1956, The women's welfare scheme in Uttar Pradesh, *Indian Journal of Adult Education* 17 (3), March, p. 5-11; 17(3) September, p. 5-11.

George, Mary, 1954, Women's role in social education under the community projects, *Indian Journal of Adult Education* 15 (1) March, p. 17-22.

Ghosh, Dhirendranath, 1955, Vidyasagar and women's education in Bengal, *Journal of Education* 2 (3-4) Conference Number, p. 157-63.

Gill, Betty, 1948, Indian girls study in Australia, enjoy student life at domestic college, *Education* 27(12) 31 July, p. 6-7.

Girls and women's education in India today, 1960, *Education Quarterly* 21 (1) April, p. 1-46.

Contents : Education of women in India, Phulrenu Guha, p. 1-4; Article 45 and primary education of girls, Lakshmi N. Menon, p. 5-8; Imbalances in the progress of girls education, Sulabha Panandikar, p. 9-11; Role of women in modern India, Kamaladevi Chattopadhyay, p. 12-14; Vocational education for women, Rajammal P. Devadas, p. 15-21; Co-education at what stages and why, Hansa Mehta, p. 22-25; Adult women and the spread of literacy, Anusuya Gyanchand, p. 26-28; Voluntary organisation and women's education, Raksha Saran, p. 29-32; Towards a new social outlook, Sarojini Mahishi, p. 33-35; Education of women in modern India : Some achievements and problems, Kamalani Bhansali, p. 36-43; Education of tribal women and girls, B.H. Mehta, p. 44-46.

Girls education, 1950, *Education* 29 (21) 25 November, p. 3-4, editorial.

Girls education, 1950, *Shiksha* 3(1) July, p. 26-27; 3(2), October p. 65-67

————, 1951, *Shiksha* 3(3) January, p. 46-49; 3(4) April, p. 24-28; 4(1) July, p. 105-107; 4 (2) October, p. 122-24.

Gopal Krishna, 1958, Women's education in India, *Educational India* 25 (2), August p. 45-48.

Gopalaratnam, D.L., 1947, The educated girl in India, *Educational India* 13 (8) February, p. 265-66.

Gopalaratnam, Ranga, 1962, Life in a women's college, *Education Quarterly*, 14 (56) December, p. 267-69.

Gore, M.S., 1987, Education for women's equality I & II, *University News* 25 (16) p. 2-5; 25 (17) p. 4-7.

Govind, Chandra *see* Chandra Govind.

Greenough, Richard, 1963, Barriers against schooling for girls, *Educational Review* 69 (6) June, p. 130-31.

Group discussion reports, 1984, *Indian Journal of Adult Education*, 45 (12) December, p. 20-27

Guha, Phulrenu, 1968, Content of literacy for women, *Indian Journal of Adult Education* 29 (11) November, p. 15-16.

————, 1969, Education of women in India; A historical perspective, *Education Quarterly* 21(1) April, p. 1-4.

Gupta, Madhu and Gupta, Prabhu, 1979, Family problems of adolescent girls as related to problems in other areas and delinquent tendencies, *Journal of Education and Psychology* 37 (1) April, p. 67-72 refs.

————, 1979, Delinquent tendencies in the adolescent girls at different age levels and their effect on verbal learning, *Asian Journal of Psychology and Education* 4 (3) November, p. 6-8.

Gupta, Prabhu, jt. author *see* Gupta, Madhu and Gupta Prabhu.

Gupta, Radhika, jt author, *see* Saraswathi, T.S. and Gupta, Radhika.

Gupta, S.L., 1983, Factors influencing the growth of girls education at the elementary stage, *Indian Educational Review* 18 (4) October, p. 77-82.

————, 1983, A study of private costs of schooling girls at the elementary state, *EPA Quarterly Bulletin* 6 (2) July, p. 31-40, tabs.

Gyanchand, Anusuya, 1969, Adult women and the spread of literacy, *Education Quarterly* 21(1), April, p. 26-28.

Haksar, N.J., 1976, What Women's Year should mean, *Mainstream* 16(18) p. 29.

Haque, Adhila, 1978, Understanding rural school going girls; An implication for non-formal education, *Indian Journal of Adult Education* 39 (4) April, p. 27-31, tabs.

————, 1978, Needs of rural school going girls : Implication for non-formal education, *Indian Journal of Adult Education* 39 (10) October, p. 9-13, tabs.

Harby, Mohamed Khairy and Mehrez, Zenab Mohmoud, 1961, Education of women in the U.A.R., *Education Quarterly* 13 (50) Summer, p. 178-81.

Hariani, Kamla, 1970, Educational and vocational aspirations and planning by high school girls, *Journal of Education and Psychology* 28(3), October, p. 122-28, refs, tabs.

Hasan, Masuma, 1989, Women's education in Pakistan, *New Frontiers in Education* 19 (1) January-March, p. 80-89.

Hema Kumari, T.A., 1977, Role of the mother and education achievement of the child, *Education Quarterly* 28(3) October, p. 16-21.

Hodgkin, Edward, 1949, Women's college celebrates centenary, *Educational India* 15 (12) June, p. 345-46.

Hooja, G.B.K., 1987, Women's status, family life, education and the media, *University News* 25 (14), p. 4-6.

Hooja, Meenakshi, 1981-82, Women of Rajasthan: A demographic profile, *Prasar* 8 (3-4) October-January, p. 1-17, tabs.

Hookens, William Edward, 1949, On co-education, *Education* 28 (7) 15 April, p. 21-22.

Ida Singh, 1981, Continuing education for women in slums, *Experiments in Education* 9 (6) August, p. 99-102.

Inamdar, Hemant V., 1984, A separate university for women, *Progress of Education* 59 (5) December, p. 90-94.

Indian Universities Association for Continuing Education, 1989, Empowerment of women-multi-disciplinary perspectives, *University News* 27 (4), p. 9-10.

Indian Women's University: S.N.D.T. University, 1980, *Progress of Education* 24(8) March, p. 312, editorial.

Indira, K., 1988, New vista for Indian girl, *Indian Nation*, October 2.

Indrasen, Lila, 1969, Report on progress of girls and women's education in the states : Pondicherry, *Education Quarterly* 21 (1) April, p. 49-50.

Irudaya Rajan, S. *see* Rajan, S. Irudaya.

Israney, S.M., 1989, Status of women in the academic world : Indian context, *University News* 27 (23), p. 11-14.

Jacob, A., 1982, Education for women and girls today in cities in India, *Education Quarterly* 34 (4) October, p. 11-13.

Jacob, Ayesha, 1975, The place of women's education in the ten plus two scheme, *Education Quarterly* 27(2) July, p. 16-17.

Jacob, Plamthodathil, S., 1985, Women students programme in co-educational context : A case study, *New Frontiers in Education* 15(1) January-March, p. 77-81.

Jagan Nath, 1988, India hopes to attract more girls to schools, *Indian Nation*, September 8.

Jain, Devaki, 1975, Content of education : Its relevance to the status of women, *Education Quarterly* 27 (2) July, p. 7-9.

Jain, M.K., 1959, Women's education in India, *Educational Review* 65 (5) May, p. 97-98.

Jain, Shobhita, 1984, Women and peoples ecological movement, *Economic and Political Weekly* 20 (27).

Jaishankar, V., 1979, Role of women's education in India, *Hindu*, October 9, p. 3.

Jayaraman, Kunthala, 1975, Education for women: A five year plan, *Journal of Higher Education* 1(2) Autumn, p 255-56.

Jayaweera, S., 1979, Programmes of non-formal education for women, *Indian Journal of Adult Education* 40(12) December, p. 33-45.

Jha, J., and Saxena, Bimla, 1983, A study of disadvantages associated with different socio-economic groups of girls studying in secondary schools, *Journal of Education and Psychology*, 41(1-2), April-July, p 12-16.

Jhansi Rani *see* Rani, Jhansi.

Job oriented course for women needed, 1984, *National Herald*, September 23, p. 3.

Jobless women, 1967, *Educational India* 33 (1) April, p. 345-46. editorial.

John, Pushpita, 1982, New approaches to higher education for women, *Education Quarterly* 34(4) October, p. 28-30.

Joshi Vibha and Menon Geeta, 1986, Research on women's education in India : A review, *Perspectives in Education* 2(2) April, p. 77-79.

Kalia, Narendranath, 1984, Changing images of males and females: How of feminist sex role liberation in Indian school text books, *Indian Education* 13(10-11) January-February, p. 10-16.

Kamla Kumar *see* Kumar, Kamla.

Kapoor, M., 1978, Women's education for national development, *Indian Journal of Adult Education* 39(7) July, p. 32-34.

Kapoor, Ranga, 1975, Career opportunities for women, *Education Quarterly* 27(2) July, p. 10-12.

Kapur, H. L., 1983, Progress in girls education, *National Herald*, October 23, p. 2.

Kapur, R. K., 1969, Vatsalyadham Post-basic for Girls, *Educational India* 35(7) January, p. 241-42.

Karlekar, Kalyani, 1960, Special curriculum for girls in secondary education, *Teacher Education* 4 (2) February, p. 33-36.

Karve, B. D., 1953, The future of girls' secondary education, *Journal of Education and Psychology* 10(4) January, p. 236-40.

Kashyap, S. S., 1976, Impact of women's education, *Education Quarterly* 28(2) July, p. 21-22.

Katiyar, S. N., 1982, Modernization and the rural women, *Teacher Today* 24 (3) January-March, p. 20-26, refs.

Kaur, A., 1979, Adult Education programmes for illiterate women in the age group 15-35, *Indian Journal of Adult Education* 40(12) December, p. 19-32.

Kaur, Amrit, 1979, Women education in India today, *Naya Shikshak* 21(4) April-June, p 9-24, tabs.

Kaur, Harjit, jt. author *see* Satvir Singh and Kaur, Harjit

Kerala gets Ist prize for girls education, 1984, *Hindustan Times*, May 25, p. 4.

Khanna, K. C., 1956, Co-education in India, *Education Quarterly* 8(32) December, p. 382-83.

Khanna, Kailash, 1977, Effectivity of follow-up material for girl dropouts in a slum of Delhi, *Indian Journal of Adult Education* 38(12) December, p. 10-16, tabs.

Khitha, Sadhana, jt. author, *see* Kumar, Kamla and Khitha, Sadhana.

Kidwai, Mohsina, 1984, Develop unconventional measures of education, *Indian Journal of Adult Education* 45(12) December, p. 9-11.

Kim, Okgill, 1978, The place of women's colleges: The Korean experience: EWHA University, *New Frontiers in Education* 8(1) January-March, p. 47-56, appen.

Koshy, T. A., 1975, Non-formal education for rural women: An experimental project for the development of the young child, *Indian Journal of Adult Education* 36(1-2) January-February, p. 17-19.

Krishna, Gopal *see* Gopal Krishna.

Krishnaraj, Maithrey, 1977, Employment pattern of university educated women and its implications, *Journal of Higher Education* 2(3) Spring, p. 317-27, appen, refs.

Kulwinder Singh, 1985-1986, Academic motivation among high school students in relation to academic achievement and sex, *Journal of Education and Psychology* 43(3-4) October January, p. 164-68.

Kumar, Kamla and Khitha, Sadhana, 1982, Women in science and technology, *Education Quarterly* 34(4) October, p 8-10, refs.

Kumar, Rajni, 1982, Secondary education for girls: The what and the how, *Education Quarterly* 34 (4) October, p. 31-33.

Kumar, Usha A., 1975, Job oriented education for girls: Some practical and theoretical considerations, *Education Quarterly* 27(3) October, p 14-15.

Kurien, Mathew, 1989, Women education and global survival, *Deccan Herald*, July 8.

Labha Singh, 1965, Co-education in India, *Educational Review* 71(11) November, p. 246.

Lakshminarayana, M., 1985, Non-formal education for women, *EPA Quarterly Bulletin* 8(1-2) April-July, p. 40-44.

Lal, Mohan *see* Mohan Lal.

Lal, Prem Chand, 1951, Education of women and girls in India today, *Education* 30(14) August 31, p. 7-11.

Leadership development, among rural women, 1983, *New Frontiers in Education* 13(2) April-June, p. 73-104.

Lebra, Joyce, *et al*, 1986, *Women and work in India: Continuity and change* Promila, New Delhi, 310 p. Book Review, *New Frontier in Education* 16(2) April-June, p. 106-08.

Leela, R. H. , 1968, Stray thoughts on the education of Indian girls, *Educational Review* 74(5) May, p. 97-98.

Mahishi, Sarojini, 1969, Towards a new social outlook, *Education Quarterly* 21(1) April, p. 33-35.

Maithreyi Krishnaraj *see* Krishnaraj, Maithreyi.

Maitra, S. N., 1972, Women's primary and supplementary books, *Indian Journal of Adult Education* 33(6) June, p. 14-15.

Majumdar, Vina *see* Mazumdar, Vina

Mane, M. G. , 1984, Educate women to reduce inequalities, *Indian Journal of Adult Education* 45 (12) December, p. 7-8.

Mangal, Shavinder K. and Roy, Sunita, 1983, Participation and interest of rural school going girls in household and farm activities, *Indian Journal of Extension Education* 19(1-2) January-June, p. 69-73.

Manohar Rao, G., 1969, Reports on the progrss of girl's and women's education in the states, Andhra Pradesh, *Education Quarterly* 21(1) April, p. 47-48.

Maria Fe G. Atienza *see* Atienza, Maria Fe G.

Masuma Hasan *see* Hasan, Masuma.

Mathias, T. A., 1988, Women's education and development: The key to brighter future in Asia, *New Frontiers in Education* 18(3) July-September, p. 42-57.

Mathur, B. S., 1948, Current thoughts, on education, *Education* 27(18) October 31, p. 31-32.

Mathur, V. S., 1955, Should boys and girls study together, *Educator* 4(3) July. p 135-37.

————, 1979, Indian women's right to education, *Education Quarterly* 31(1) April, p. 18-20.

Mazumdar, Vina, 1975, Educational development and changes in women's status, *Journal of Indian Education* 1(4) November, p. 3-7.

————, 1975, Higher education of women in India, *Journal of Higher Education* 1(2) Autumn, p. 156-65, tabs.

————, 1981, Women's studies: Challenge to educational system, *Economic and Political Weekly*, May 16, p. 890-92.

Measures to boost women's education, 1983, *Indian Express*, June 14, p. 4.

Mehrez, Zenab Mohmoud, jt author *see* Harby, Mohamed Khairy and Mehrez, Zenab Mohmoud.

Mehta, B. H., 1969, Education of tribal women and girls, *Education Quarterly* 21(1) April, p. 44-46.

Mehta, H. P., jt. author *see* Mehta, Perin H. and Mehta, H. P.

Mehta, Hansa, 1969, Co-education: At what stages and why? *Education Quarterly* 21(1) April, p. 22-25.

Mehta, Perin H., 1968, The felt needs of female students and their implications for education, *NIE Journal* 3(1) September, p. 13-18, refs.

————, H. and Mehta, H. P., 1974, Vocational preparations and the employ ability of women, *Education Quarterly* 26(2) July, p. 1-4, refs.

Mehta, Sushila, 1961, Where shall we look for leaders? *Indian Journal of Adult Education* 22(2) February, p. 9-10.

————, 1964, Literacy among women, *Indian Journal of Adult Education* 25(11) November, p. 11-12.

Menon, Geeta, jt. auther *see* Joshi, Vibha and Menon, Geeta.

Menon, Lakshmi N., 1969, Article 45 and primary education of girls, *Education Quarterly* 21(1) April, p. 5-8.

Menon, Laxmi, 1989, Emancipation of women, *University News* 27(23) p. 6-10.

Mir Aniruddin see Amiruddin, Mir

Mishra, Lakshmi, 1961, Democratic India and women education, *Education Quarterly* 13(50) Summer, p. 119-22.

————, 1962, The importance of the social attitude in the development of women's education in India, *Shiksha* 14(4) April, p. 148-51.

————, 1980, Adult education programme and women, *Educational Review* 86(3) March, p. 41-43.

Misra, Prabha, 1969, Report on the progress of girls and women's education in the states: Rajasthan, *Educational Quarterly* 21(1) April, p. 50-51.

Mitra, Ashok, 1978, Employment of women, *Manpower* 14(1) 1978, p. 1-29.

Mohan Lal, 1961, Problems of girls education in rural areas, *Education Quarterly* 13(50) Summer, p. 167-69.

Mojumdar, Modhumita, 1988, Education for equality, *Statesman*, June 15.

More funds urged for women's education, 1985, *Indian Express*, October 1, p. 7

Mother Teresa Women's Universty, 1987, Methodology for women's studies, *University News* 25(50), p. 81.

————, 1988, Implementation of NEP with special reference to education for women's equality: Report, *University News* 26(24), p. 17.

————, 1989, Seminar on women's studies as an academic discipline, *University News* 27 (17), p. 16.

Motwani, Clara, 1961, Education of women in Ceylon, *Education* 13(50) Summer, p. 175-77.

Mukherjee, H. B. , 1961, Tagore on women's education, *Education Quarterly* 13(50) Summer, p. 123-27.

Mukherjee, L., 1956-1957, Education of women in India: Past and present, *Education* 35 (12) December, p. 5-9; 36 (1) January, p. 5-10.

Mukerji, Latika, 1954, Women and adult education, *Indian Journal Adult Education* 15(3) March, p. 13-16.

Mukerji, S., 1985, Benefits, we derived from present education, *Yojana* 29(22), p. 28-30.

Mulay, Sumati, 1976, Uttar Pradesh literacy and family planning behaviour of rural women, *Indian Journal of Adult Education* 37(1) January, p. 9-10, tabs.

Mulay, Vijay, 1956, Co-education in India, *Education Quarterly* 8(32) December, p. 379-81.

Munshi, K. M., 1948, Educational sparks, *Education* 27(19), November 15, p. 35-37.

Murray, A. R., 1956, Women's education at Oxford and Cambridge, *Educational Review* 62(9) September, p. 169-70.

Murugkar, Lata, 1983, Developmental goals and women's higher education, *Journal of Higher Education* 8(3), Spring, p. 321-26, refs.

Nagappa, T. R., 1980, Adult Education for women, *Indian Journal of Adult Education* 41(8) August, p. 23-25, refs.

Naik, Chitra, 1970, Social transformation and equal educational opportunity for girls and women, *Naya Shikshak* 13(1) July-September, p. 59-66.

Nair, G. Ravindran *see* Ravindran Nair, G.

Nair, K. R. Ramachandran *see* Ramchandran Nair, K. R.

Nanda, Anant, 1951, The school and the adolescent girls, *Educational Forum* 2(3) July, p. 27-30.

Nath, Jagan *see* Jagan Nath

Nayar, Usha, 1975, Women, education and work: A review, *Journal of Higher Education* 1(2) Autumn, p. 283-92, refs.

————, 1986, Women's education in South Asia, *Patriot*, January 16, p. 4.

Need for women's equality stressed, 1986, *Indian Express*, December 21, p. 3.

New thrust to primary education for girls, 1985, *Hindustan Times*, July 9, p. 10.

New vocational training programme for women, 1984, *Statesman*, February 28, p. 4.

Nigam, Raghuvir Sahay, 1970, Universities and female education, *Educational India* 36(7) January, p. 233-34.

————, 1980, Adult education for women, *Educational Review* 86(3), March p. 49.

Nimbkar, Krishnabai, 1955, Rural women's uplift: The role of the Bharatiya Grameen Mahila Sangh, *Indian Journal of Adult Education* 16(4) December, p. 25-29.

————, 1961, Voluntary organisations and womens education, *Indian Journal of Adult Education* 22 (3), March, p. 5-7.

Ninan, Sevante, 1982, Women reluctant to educate daughters, *Indian Express*, November 11, p. 3.

Non-formal adult education for women, 1984, *Indian Journal of Adult Education* 45 (12), p. 13-19.

Norris, Louis William, 1955, How to educate a woman, *Educational Review* 61(9) September, p. 169-71, repr.

Nuita, Yoko, 1969, Trends in continuing education of women in Japan, *Indian Journal of Adult Education* 30(10) October, p. 5-7.

Oak, A. W., 1984, Life-styles of home science graduates, *Research Bulletin* 19(3-4) September-December, p. 10-32. tabs.

Padma, K., 1983, Attitude of literate women of Hyderabad Slums, *Experiments in Education* 11(8) October, p. 138-40.

Padmanabhan, N. S., 1962, Wither women's education? *Educational Review* 68(4) April, p. 90-92.

Padmavati, S., 1975, Higher medical education for women, *Journal of Higher Education* 1(2) Autumn, p. 256-58, refs.

Panandikar, Sulabha, 1969, Imbalances in the progress of girls education: Extent and remedy, *Education Quarterly* 21(1) April, p. 9-11.

Panda, K. C., 1962, A comparative study of attitudes of students reading in co-educational and single sex institutions towards co-educational practices in India, *Journal of Education and Psychology* 19(4) January, p. 190-98, refs, tabs.

Panda, S. N., 1969, Women's education in India, *Indian Educational Review* 4(2) July, p. 151-53.

(Review Article of the book *Education of women in India* (1921-66) by Lakshmi Misra, Macmillan, 1966.)

Pande, Mrinal, 1988, Where do the women toppers go? *Hindustan Times*, August 19.

Pandey, Balaji, 1985, Eradicating illiteracy among women, *Statesman*, September 11, p. 6.

Pandeya, Ram Prasad, 1975, Education; Social attitutes and women's progress, *Educational Review*, 81(10) October, p. 193-96.

Pandit, Pratibha, 1964, Arya Kanya Mahavidyalaya, Baroda, *Indian Education* 3(12) November, p. 15-18.

Paranjape, S. D., 1974, Problems of graduate employed women: A socio-psychological study and attitude survey, *Indian Dissertation Abstracts* 2(2), p. 101-103.

Passi, B.K., 1970, Patterns of vocational aspirations of higher secondary school adolescents in relation to sex and residential background, *Journal of Education and Psychology* 28(3) October, p. 57-63 +, tabs.

Patnaik, Narasinga, 1949, Education for women, *Educational Review* (55(2) February, p. 28-29.

Pillai, J. K., 1976, Educating women for national development, *Education Quartely* 27(4) January, p. 31-33.

————, 1977, A suggested programme for checking the problems of dropouts with special reference to girls, *New Frontiers in Education* 7(4) October-December, p. 48-55.

————, 1982, The dual role of women, *New Frontiers in Education* 12(4) October-December, p. 39-42.

————, 1989, Strategies for empowerment of women, *University News* 27 (23), p. 1-2.

Prem Chand Lal *see* Lal, Prem Chand

Priority for women's education, 1959, *Educational India* 25(8), February, p. 314-16, editorial.

Problems of women's education, 1958, *Educational India* 25(2) p. 53-56, Editorial, August.

Programmes for the promotion of girls education in the new Fourth Plan, 1968, *Education Quarterly* 20(1) April, p. 32-33.

Proper education solution to women's problems, 1983, *Hindu*, February 6, p. 13.

Pushpamma, P., 1980, Special curriculum for girls, *Hindu*, October 7, p. 3.

Rabindranathan, M. R., 1975, Development of women's education at the University stage, *Journal of Higher Education* 1(2) Antumn, p. 258-62, refs, tabs.

Rai, Kamala, 1984, Problems of girls in co-educational institutions, *National Journal of Education* 7 (1) September, p. 29-38, refs, tabs.

————, 1985, Adjustment of secondary school girls studing in co-education and segregated institutions in relation to their socio-economic status, *National Journal of Education* 7(2) May, p. 46-55.

Rai, S., 1975, Education of our rural women folk, *Education Quarterly* 27 (2) July, p. 18-19.

————, 1985, Morie female teachers must in rural schools, *Hindustan Times*, February 6, p. 20.

Rajan, S. Irudaya, 1988, Progress of female literacy in India, *Yojana* 32(21), p. 10-12.

Rajani Kumar *see* Kumar, Rajani.

Raksha Saran *see* Saran, Raksha.

Rallia Ram, Mayawanti, 1975, Muslium educated women in North India, *Journal of Higher Education* 1(2) August, p. 250.

Ram, Sita *see* Sita Ram.

Ram, Mayawanti Rallia *see* Rallia Ram, Mayawanti.

Ramachandran, Padma, 1975, The World Conference on Women, *Journal of Indian Education* 1(4) November, p. 24-27.

Ramachandran Nair, K. R., 1981, Women's education and women's colleges, *University News* 19(6) March 15, p. 59-60.

Raman, Usha, 1988, Why few women take to Science? *Deccan Chronicle*, November 27.

Rami Reddy, A. Venkata *see* Venkata Rami Reddy, A.

Rana, Kamala, 1980, NAEP and the involvement of educational women, *Prasar* 7(1-2) April-July, p. 39-47.

Rana, R. P. S., 1982, Economic aspect of women education, *University News* 20(23), p. 719-724.

Rani, Jhansi and Bhave, Asha M., 1982, Actual and desired type of participation by rural women in selected areas of decision-making, *Indian Journal of Extension Education* 18(1-2) January, p. 83-89, tabs.

Ranjit Singh and Saini, R.K., 1984, Socio-personal correlates and gain in the knowledge of correspondence course trainees, *Indian Journal of Adult Education* 45(4) April, p. 30-33, tabs.

Rao, B. S. Vasudeva *see* Vasudeva Rao, B. S.

Rao, G. Manohar *see* Manohar Rao, G.

Rao, Lakshmi Venkata *see* Venkata Lakshmi Rao.

Rao, Waman, 1952, Co-education and present Indian opinion, *Educational Review* 58(12) December, p. 230-34.

Ravi Kant Singh, 1985, Women's education crucial for child welfare: Children of India, *Patriot*, January 3, p. 6; 4 January, p. 5.

Ravindran Nair, G., 1983, Education : Why do more girls drop out? *Kurukshetra* 31(15), p. 14-16.

Rawat, B., jt. author *see* Srivastava, R.K. and Rawat, B.

Razdan, Prithvi Nath, 1953, Educating the destitute, *Educational India* 19(7) January, p. 203-07.

————, 1955, The Kashmir government's educational policy, *Educational India* 22(1) July, p. 8-12.

Recommendations, 1984, *Indian Journal of Adult Education* 45 (12) December, p. 29-31.

Reddy, A. Venkata Rami *see* Venkata Rami Reddy, A.

Reddy, T. Chandra, jt. author *see* Venkate Rami Reddy, A. and Chandra Reddy T.

Reports on the progress of girls and women's education in the states, 1969, *Education Quaterly* 21(1) April, p. 47-53,

Contents: Andhra Pradesh, G. Manohar Rao, p. 47-48; Madhya Pradesh, Vimla Sharma, p. 48-49; Pandicherry, Lila Indrasen, p. 49-50; Rajasthan, Prabha Misra, p. 50-51; Tamil Nadu, Sarojini Vardeppan, p. 51-53.

Re-thinking on women's education, 1980, *Educational Review* 70(9) September, p. 218, editorial.

Roberts, Funice Carmichael, 1954, Curricula for women, *Educational Review* 60(10) October, p. 196-98.

Roy, Sunita, jt. author *see* Mangat, Shavinder K. and Roy, Sunita.

Roy, Sushila, 1959, Women education in villages, *Naya Shikshak* 2(3) July, p. 76-79.

Rural women and community development, 1958, *Indian Journal of Adult Education* 19(2) June, p. iv-v.

S.N.D.T. Women's University and Institute of Marketing and Management, Association of Women Entrepreneurs and Executives, 1989, Seminar on 'Working Women — challenges ahead, *University News* 27 (23), p. 31-32.

Sabha, V. R., 1953, Educating the destitute, *Education* 32(1) January, p. 13-19.

Safaya, Raghunath, 1964, Part-time employment of women teachers, *Educational Review* 70 (4) April, p. 86-87.

Saini, R.K., jt. author *see* Ranjit Singh and Saini, R.K.

Saksena, Gopala Krishna, 1952, Co-education: The need of the hour, *Educational India* 18(10) April, p. 283-86.

Sandhu, D. K. and Shukla, A. N. , 1981, Content analysis of Tiranjan programme of AIR Jallunder, *Indian Journal of Extension Education* 17(3-4) July-December, p. 7-16, refs.

The Sangrahalaya: A nucleus for work among women in rural areas, 1960, *Indian Adult Education* 21(1) January, p. 13-16.

Sautey, Peter du *see* du Santey, Peter.

Santhanam, M. R. and Buch, M. B., 1971, Sex of the teacher as a factor of teacher classroom behaviour, *Indian Educational Review*, 6(2) July, p. 47-68, refs, tabs.

Santoso, Maria Ulfah, 1948, Brief survey of the Indonesian women's movement, *Education* 27(5) March 15, p. 24-27.

Sapra, Ramlal, 1950, Girls education in schools, *Education* 29 (15) August 25, p. 24-26.

Saradmoni, K., 1975, Waiting for hopeful tomorrow: International Women's Year, *Mainstream* 13(43), p. 11-12, 24.

Saran, Raksha, 1960, Education of women, *Educational India* 26(8) February 5, p. 263-64.

(Address of Mrs. Raksha Saran at the 29th session of the All India Women's Conference, Madras, 1959).

————, 1962, Expanding women's education in the third Plan, *Shiksha* 15(2) October, p. 50-55.

Saran, Raksha, 1965, International understanding and co-operation through education-teachers role: A symposium: Women education, *Education Quarterly* 17(67) September-December, p. 142-44.

————, 1965, Teachers role in the eradication of the social taboos in girls education, *Education* 17(67) September-December, p. 175-77.

————, 1969, Voluntary organisation and women's education, *Education Quarterly* 21(1) April, p. 29-32.

Saraswat, Renuka, 1974, Sex education: How a college girl looks at it, *Education Quarterly* 26(1) April, p. 21-22.

Saraswathi, T. S. and Gupta, Radhika, 1985, Educate a woman and you educate a family, *Perspectives in Education* 1(1) January, p. 49-54, refs, tabs.

Satvir Singh, 1975, Women's education in India: A statistical presentation, *Journal of Indian Education* 1(4) November, p. 34-38.

————, and Kaur, Harjit, 1976, The relationship of motives, aspiration and anxiety among women teachers at different professional levels, *Asian Journal of Psychology and Education* 1(2) July p. 1-11, refs, tabs.

Saunders, Fay, E., 1980, Discrimination and inequalities between the sexes and school, *Journal of Indian Education* 5(5) January, p. 35-42.

Saxena, Bimla, jt. author *see* Jha, J. and Saxena, Bimla.

Saxena, Daya and Bhatnagar, Suman Rani, 1985, A comparative study of time utilization pattern of tribal and non-tribal women in Rajasthan, *Indian Journal of Extension Education* 21(1-2) January-June, p. 83-85, tabs.

Saxena, Usha, 1985, Women in India: Education and employment status, *Economic Times*, May 17, p. 5.

————, 1985, Women in India: Job opportunities and education, *Economic Times*, May 18, p. 5.

Saxena, Vinodini, 1956, The heroes of adolescent college girls, *Education* 10(4) October, p. 213-31, refs.

Scheme to promote girls education, 1982, *Times of India*, December 25, p. 9.

Seddey, S. C., 1983, Trends in professional education among women, *Journal of Higher Education* 8(3), Spring, p. 327-34.

Seethamma, M. N., 1947, Women and adult education, *Indian Journal of Adult Education* 8 (1) January, p. 7-9; 8(3) March, p. 7-8.

Sehgal, Krishna, 1979, The impact of sex and academic discipline on the level knowledge of current affairs, *Progress of Education* 53(12) July, p. 223-271, tabs.

Sen Gupta, Kamala, 1956, Home and school cooperation as experienced in Lady Irwin School, *Educational Forum* 1(3) July, p. 18-20.

Sengupta M., 1989, Women's status: What is the concept of equality? *Hindu*, February 7.

Seth, M., *et al*, 1983, Group interaction among adult women participating in the functional literacy programmes in Delhi, *Indian Journal of Extension Education* 19(1-2) January-June, p. 62-68, refs, tabs.

————, 1983, Group interaction among women participants of functional literacy programme in Delhi: A study, *Indian Journal of Adult Education* 44(10) October, p. 24-28, refs, tabs.

Seth, Mridula, 1977, Production centre as venues for non-formal education of women, *Indian Journal of Adult Education* 38(7), p. 36-38.

Seth, Padma, 1975, The status of women and their legal rights, *Journal of Indian Education* 1 (4) November, p. 28-33.

Shafi, Rafat S., 1978, Literacy and nutrition education in context of adult education programme for young females, *Indian Journal of Adult Education* 39(2) February, p. 17-27, refs.

Shah, Gunvant B., 1975, Genesis of women's education in India, *NIE Journal* 9 (3) January, p. 1-9, refs, tabs.

————, 1976, Non-formal education for women, *Indian Journal of Adult Education* 37, June, p. 13-15.

Shah, Madhuri R., 1978, The deal is still unfair, *New fronteirs in Education* 8 (1) January-March, p. 57-59.

Shahare, M. L., 1984, Eradicating women's illiteracy : A Challange, *Indian Journal of Adult Education,* 45(12) December, p. 32-38.

Shamsuddin, 1960, Status of women in ancient India, *Progress of Education* 35(1) April, p-10-12.

————, 1976, Development of women's education in Madhya Pradesh, 1956-1974, *Education Quarterly* 27(4) January, p. 34-36.

————, 1977, Development of women's education in new Madhya Pradesh, *Educational India* 43(7) January, p. 155-58.

Sharma, Jan, 1989, Stress on education of girls in Nepal, *Pioneer,* January 13.

Sharma, Kumud, 1985, Women and media: A care for critical correction, *Indian Journal of Adult Education* 46(9) September, p. 27-30.

Sharma, Narayan Prasad, 1988, Women and higher education, *Yojana* 32(21), p. 6-8.

Sharma, Prabhu Datta, 1973, Women's education: A curricular model for India, *Education Quarterly* 25(2) July, p. 12-15.

Sharma, Premlata, 1984, Study habits and underachievement among rural girls, *Journal of Education and Psychology* 42(3) October, p. 115-18, refs.

Sharma, Radha Rani, 1982, Education of women in India: Inequalities and bottlenecks, *Education Quarterly* 34(4) October, p. 20-27, refs, tabs.

Sharma, S. and Singh, T. R., 1984, Rural women's level of knowlege and persuation for the acceptance of solar cooker device, *Indian Journal of Extension Education* 20(1-2) January-June, p. 47-51, refs.

Sharma, S. R., 1989, Delhi tops in women's education, *National Hearald,* April 23.

Sharma, Savitri, 1978, A study of the influence of socio-economic backgrounds in regard to the development of different types of values among female college students, *Asian Journal of Psychology and Education* 3(1) January 1978, p. 21-29, refs, tabs.

————, 1980, Women students in India: Status and personality, Concept Publishing Company, New Delhi, 171 p;
Book Review, *Indian Education* 9(12) March, p. 45-47; *Education Quarterly* 32 (2) July, p 46-47; *Teacher Education* 14(10-11) January-April, p. 76-77; *Teacher Today* 23(1) July-September, p. 103; *Indian Educatonal Review* 15(2) April, p. 128-29; *Yojana,* June 1, p 29.

Sharma, Vimla, 1969, Reports on the progress of girls and women's education in the states, *Education Quarterly* 21(1) April, p. 48-49.

Shastri, Diwakar, 1989, Women's universities or universities for women: Mission of women's institutions in higher education, *University News* 27(23), p. 3-5.

Shervani, Nusrat, 1981, Muslim girls' education, *National Hearald,* February 21, p. 7.

Shrimali, K. L. , 1959, Future of women's education, *Educational India* 25 (7) January, p. 248-50.

Shukla, A. N., jt. author *see* Sandhu, D. K. and Shukla, A. N.

Shukla, M. M., 1949, Sex differences in inducive reasoning during early adolescence, *Journal of Education and Psychology* 6(4) January, p. 172-76.

Shukla, Sureshchandra, 1981, Perspectives on women's education, *National Journal of Education* 3(2) March, p. 7-16.

Singh K. P., 1974, A comparative study of the attitudes of working and non-working women towards women's education and employment, *Interdiscipline* 11(3), p. 89-100.

Singh, R. P., 1969, Wanted a teacheress: A study in newspaper advertisements, *NIE Journal* 4(1) September, p. 50-52.

Singh, T. R., jt. author *see* Sharma, S. and Singh, T. R.

Singh *see also* under full name

Singhal, Sushila, 1984, The development of educated women in India: Reflections of a social psychologist, *Comparative Education* 20(3), p. 355-369.

Sita Ram, 1960, Progress of women's education in Uttar Pradesh, *Shiksha* 12(3) January, p. 39-43.

Some facts and figures about women in Soviet Russia, 1957, *Education* 36 (5) May, p. 26-27.

Souza, Austin A. D' *see* D'Souza, Austin A.

Srinivasan, K., 1962, Women and we, men, *Educational India* 28(11-12) May-June, p. 351-53.

Srivastava, B. K., jt. author *see* Varma, P. C. and Srivastava, B. K.

Srivastava, K. N., 1961, Women's education in rural communities, *Education Quarterly* 13 (50) Summer, p. 170-74.

Srivastava, R.K., and Rawat, B., 1982, Attitudes of Harijan women towards education : A comparative study of a city and surrounding villages, *Indian Journal of Adult Education* 43(7) July, p. 27-31, refs, tabs.

Srivastava, Saroj, 1963, Education of women teachers, *Education Quarterly* 15(57) March, p. 16-19.

Srivastava, Sumita, 1985, College going girls: their occupational choices, goals and problems, *Journal of Indian Education*, 11(2) July, p. 40-44.

Statement and recommendations of the Consultation on "Designing Education for Tomorrow's Women", held at Women's Christian College, Madras, under the auspices of All India Association for Christian Higher Education in December 1977, 1978, *New Frontiers in Education* 8(1) January-March, p. 81-84.

States told to make up lag in girls education, 1983, *Hindustan Times*, June 17, p. 4.

Sudha, B. G. and Goetha, S., 1982, Problems of girls as a function of material employment and anxiety, *Journal of Institute of Educational Research* 6(1) January, p. 28-37, refs, tabs.

————, and Tirath, Lalitha G., 1979, The effect of personality trial variation on the intensity of problems of girls, *Journal of Education and Psychology* 37(2) July, p. 103-14, refs.

Suman Singh, 1988, Need to define women's education, *Pioneer*, July 6.

Sundaram, N. K., 1956, Co-education in India, *Education Quarterly* 8(32) December, p. 381-82.

Surana, M.L., 1985, Girl dropouts in rural Haryana, *Indian Educational Review* 20(2) April, p. 109-116.

————, 1989, Strategies for political empowerment of women, *University News* 27 (23), p. 17-18.

Suryakumari, A., 1988, Women's interests, *University News* 26(45) p. 1-3.

Swaminathan, M. S., 1982, Women and rural development, *New Frontiers in Education*, 12(3) July-September, p. 56-63.

Swaminathan, Mina, 1982, Needed two revaluations in one non-formal education for women and girls, *Education Quarterly* 34(4) October, p. 5-7.

Talesra, Hem Lata, 1986, Higher education among women: An analyses of the situation in a district of India, *Prospectives in Education* 2(2) April, p. 121-24.

————, 1986, Women's higher education: A feudal background, *Journal of Indian Education* 11(6), p. 66-74).

Tawde, Sunanda S., 1958, Progress in education in rural and urban areas, *Teaching* 31(2) December, p. 48-54.

Thakkar, Usha, jt. author *see* Watson, Leonard E. and Thakkar, Usha.

Thanki, Harijiwan, 1968, Gurukul's role in girl's education in Gujarat, *Indian Education* 7 (10-11) September-October, p. 32-34.

Tirath, Lalitha, G., jt. author *see* Sudha B. G. and Tirath, Lalitha G.

Tripathi, Harsh, jt. author *see* Vyias, K. C. and Tripathi, Harsh.

Tripathi, Madhukanta, 1985, Women's struggle for the new roles, *National Journal of Education* 7 (2) May, p56-60, appendix, refs.

Trown, E. A., 1981, Headships for women: Long term effects of the re-entry problem, *Educational Studies* 7 (1), p. 41-45.

Turkia, Rauni, 1962, Adult education for Tunisian women, *Indian Journal of Adult Education* 23(7) July, p. 11-16; 23(9), September 62, p. 4 +

U. P. Universities urged to set up adult education department, 1967, *Indian Journal of Adult Education* 28(5) May, p. 4.

Uchat, D. A. and Desai Haribhai, 1982, Self concept of female students of single sex colleges and co-educational colleges, *Journal of Institute of Educational Research* 6(2) May, p. 32-36. refs.

Ulfah Santosa, Maria *see* Santosa, Maria Ulfah.

Umar, Zafar, *see* Zafar, Umar.

United Nations World Conference of the International Women's Year, 1975, *Journal of Indian Education* 1(4) November, p. 43-45.

Uploankar, U. T., 1983, Occupational aspirations of college students, *Social Change* 13(2), p. 16-26.

Uplift of women through Education, 1986, *National Herald*, March 12, p. 5.

Ury, Glaude M., 1972, Women in U.S. school history textbooks, *Educational Review* 78 (9) September, p. 197-203.

Vaish, J.D., 1962, Help younger and weaker brothers and sisters, *Educational India* 29(4) October, p. 133-35.

Varadan, V., 1964, For women: A different education? *Educational Review* 70(4) April, p. 75-78.

Vardappan, Sarojini, 1969, Reports on the progress of girl's and women's education in the states: Tamil Nadu, *Education Quarterly* 21(1) April, p. 51-53.

Varma, P. C. and Srivastava, B. K., 1983, A study of attitudes of teachers trainees towards women's participation in social activities and professions, *Asian Journal of Psychology and Education* 11(1), p. 21-27.

Vasudeva Rao, B. S., 1986, Adult education programme : A study on womens performance, *Indian Journal of Adult Education* 47 (6) June, p. 8-12, tabs.

Venkatalakshmi, V., 1960, Women and commercial education, *Educational India*, 27(1) July, p. 17-18.

Venkataraman, Leela, 1975, Change of attitute towards education of women, *Education Quarterly* 27(2) July, p. 13-15.

Venkata Rami Reddy, A and Balakrishna Reddy, P., 1984, Creativity of adolescent boys and girls in relation to some variables, *Indian Educational Review* 19 (1) January, p. 60-72.

Venkata Rao, Lakshmi, 1948, Adult education in the city of Mysore with special reference to education among women, *Indian Journal of Adult Education* 9(1) January p. 21-24.

Verma, S., jt. author *see* Verma, T. and Verma. S.

Verma, T., and Verma, S., 1985, Training needs of rural women: An action research, *Indian Journal of Extension Education* 21(3-4), July-December, p. 104-07, tabs.

Verma, Vinod Kumar, 1988, Status of women: Students view, *Tribune*, August 28.

Vir, Dharam *see* Dharam Vir.

Vyas, K. C. and Tripathi, Harsh, 1967, Education for high school girls, *Educational India* 33(10) April, p. 338-40.

Waman Rao *see* Rao, Waman.

Wasi, Muriel, 1978, The case for co-educational colleges vs. women's colleges, *New Frontiers in Education* 8 (1) January-March p. 42-46.

————, 1982, Educating women in India: Ends and means, *Education Quaterly* 34(4) October, p. 1-4.

Watson, Leanard E. and Thakkar, Usha, 1989, The management development of women administrators: Some considerations, *University News* 27 (23) p. 15-16.

Welfare project for U. P. women: Prai's poineering efforts, 1966, *Indian Journal of Adult Education* 27 (4) April, p. 1-2, editor.

Wells, Inez Ray, 1960, Girls in commercial education in commerce schools, *Teacher Education* 4 (2) February, p. 19-23.

Wiser, W. H., 1958, The lamplighter: Review of a guide-book for development work among rural women, *Indian Journal of Adult Education* 19 (2) February, p. 25-28.

Women and education, 1952, *Educational Review* 58 (6) June, p. 108-09, repr.

Women and education, 1952, *Education Quartely* June p. 104-05.

Women and education, 1952, *Educational India* 19 (1) July p. 7-8.

Women and education, 1952, *Progress of Education* 25 (12) July, p. 335-37.

Women and education, 1952, *Shiksha*, July, p. 7-10 repr.

Women and health, 1981-1982, *Prasar* 8(3-4) October-January, p. 18-25.

Women and scientific education, 1966, *Educational India* 33 (3) September, p. 92-93, editorial.

Women's access to education: Geneva Conference examines problem, 1952, *Educational India* 19 (3) September, p. 99.

Women's education, 1948, *Educational India* 14 (8) February, p. 229, Editorial.

Women's education, 1948, *Educational India* 15(3) September, p. 97-98, editorial.

Women's Education in Bangladesh, 1989, *New Frontiers in Education*, 19(1) January-March, p. 96-105.

Yoko Nuita *see* Nuita, Yoko.

Yoon, Young Soon, 1983, Women's studies: is it relevant? *Samya Shakti* 1 (1), p. 5.

Young Soon Yoon *see* Yoon, Young Soon.

Zafar Uman, 1979, Acquisition of general information: Role of sex and general intelligence, *Educational Review* 85 (2) February, p. 25-28, refs, tabs.

7.2 SUBJECT INDEX

ACADEMIC ACHIEVEMENT

Decusker, Mahesh, 1977, A study into the correlation between the scholistic achievements and the achievement in co-curriculam activities of girl students of higher secondary schools of Sagar town, *Progress of Education* 51(12) July, p 221-25, refs, tabs.

Hema Kumari, T.A., 1977, Role of the mother and education achievement of the child, *Education Quarterly* 28(3) October, p 16-21.

Kulwinder Singh, 1985-1986, Academic motivation among high school students in relation to academic achievement and sex, *Journal of Education and Psychology* 43(3-4) October-January, p 164-68.

See also
> Motivation in Education
> Performance: Academic
> Underachievers.

ACCESS TO EDUCATION

Anon, 1952, Women's access to education: Geneva Conference examines problem, 1952, *Education India* 19(3) September, p 99.

————, 1960, Access of women to education, *Indian Journal of Adult Education* 21(11) November, p 18.

————, 1970, Advancement of women through access to education, *Education Quarterly* 22(3) October, p 49-55.

Greenough, Richard, 1963, Barriers against schooling for girls, *Educational Review* 69 (6) June, p 103-131.

See also
> Right to Education.

ADOLESCENT GIRLS

Anon, 1981, (Book review), *Education Quarterly* 33(3) July, p 44-48. Review of the book : Chandler, E.M., 1980, *Education of Adolescent Girls*, Allen and Unwin, London, 217 p.

Chopra, Kamala, 1970, Reading interests of adolescent boys and girls, *Educational India* 37(1) July, p 16-19 + tabs; *Progress of Education* 44(12) July, p 412-18, refs, tabs.

Nanda, Anant, 1951, The school and the adolescent girls, *Educational Forum* 2(3) July, p 27-30.

Passi, B.K. 1970, Patterns of vocational aspirations of higher secondary adolescents in relation to sex and residential background, *Journal of Education and Psychology* 28(3) October, p 57-63 +, tabs.

Saxena, Vinodini, 1956, The heroes of adolescent college girls, *Educator*, 10(4) October, p 213-31, refs.

Shafi, Rafat S., 1978, Literacy and nutrition education in context of adult education programme, for young females, *Indian Journal of Adult Education* 39(2) February, p 17-27.

Shukla, M.M., 1949, Sex differences in inducive reasoning during early adolescence, *Journal of Education and Psychology* 6(4) January, p 172-76.

Venkata Rami Reddy, A., and Balakrishna Reddy, P., 1984, Creativity of adolescent boys and girls in relations to some variables, *Indian Educational Review* 19(1) January, p 60-72.

ADOLESCENT GIRLS : DELINQUENCY

Gupta, Madhu and Gupta, Prabha, 1979, Family problems of adolescent girls as related to problems in other areas and deliquent tendencies, *Journal of Education and Psychology* 37(1) April, p 67-72, refs.

Gupta, Madhu and Gupta Prabha, 1979, Delinquent tendencies in the adolescent girls at different age levels and their effect on verbal learning, *Asian Journal of Psychology and Education* 4(3) November, p 6-8.

ADOLESCENT PSYCHOLOGY

See

Adolescent Girls

ADULT EDUCATION

Anon, 1962, Women's education, *Indian Journal of Adult Education* 23(2) February, p 15-16.

————, 1968, Adult education of women in the changing pattern of society : Seminar working paper, *Indian Journal of Adult Education* 29(10) October, p 6-9.

————, 1968, Extension of project on farmer's education and functional literacy urged, *Indian Journal of Adult Education* 29(11) November, p 3.

————, 1984, Group discussion reports, *Indian Journal of Adult Education*, 45(12) December, p 20-27.

————, 1984, Recommendations, *Indian Journal of Adult Education* 45(12) December, p 29-31.

Bhagat, P., 1981, Evaluation of condensed courses of education for adult women, *Indian Journal of Adult Education* 42 (10) October, p 17-20.

Bhansali, Kamalini, H., 1975, Women and the continuing education, *Journal of Indian Education* 1(4) November, p 18-23.

Chanderasekaran, Raj Kumari, 1980, Designing curriculum and technology for women's adult education programmes, *Indian Journal of Adult Education* 41(4) April, p 19-27.

Chhabra, Rani, 1980, Establishing linkages between women's literacy programmes status issues and access to family planning, *Indian Journal of Adult Education* 41(4) April, p 6-9.

Chinnappa, Padmavati, 1949, The education of women adults, *Education* 28(19) 30 November, p 12-14.

Duncan, Margaret, 1971, Continuing education of women, *Indian Journal of Adult Education* 32(4) April, p 9-12.

Dutta, S.C., 1962, Condensed courses for adult women : A new experiment in adult education, *Indian Journal of Adult Education* 23(8) August, p 3-4.

du Sautey, Peter, 1960, Educating grandmothers, *Indian Journal of Adult*

Education 21(11) November, p 12-14.

Guha, Phulrenu, 1968, Context of literacy for women, *Indian Journal of Adult Education* 29(11) November, p 15-16.

Kaur, A., 1979, Adult education programmes for illiterate women in the age group 15-35, *Indian Journal of Adult Education* 40(12) December, p 19-32.

Kidwai, Mohsina, 1984, Develop unconventional measures of education, *Indian Journal of Adult Education* 45(12) December, p 9-11.

Maitra, S.N., 1972, Women's primary and secondary books, *Indian Journal of Adult Education* 33(6) June, p 14-15.

Mane, M.G., 1984, Educate women to reduce inequalities, *Indian Journal of Adult Education* 45(12) December, p 7-8.

Mukherji, Latika, 1954, Women and adult education, *Indian Journal of Adult Education* 15(3) March, p 13-16.

Nigam, Raghuvir Sahay, 1980, Adult education for women, *Educational Review* 86(3) March, p 49.

Shafi, Rafat S., 1978, Literacy and nutrition education in context of adult education programme for young females, *Indian Journal of Adult Education* 39(2) February, p 17-27, refs.

Seethamma, M.N., 1947, Women and adult education, *Indian Journal of Adult Education* 8(1) January, p 7-9; 8(3) March, p 7-8.

Shahare, M.L., 1984, Eradicating women's illiteracy : A challenge, *Indian Journal of Adult Education* 45(12) December, p 32-38.

Vasudeva Rao, B.S., 1986, Adult Education Programme : A study on women's performance, *Indian Journal of Adult Education* 47(6) June, p 8-12, tabs.

See also
> Functional Literacy
> Non-formal Education
> Social Education

ADULT EDUCATION : AFRICA

Anon, 1960, Access of women to education, *Indian Journal of Adult Education* 21(11) November, p 18.

ADULT EDUCATION : DELHI

See
> Functional Literacy : India : Delhi
> Non-Formal Education : India : Delhi

ADULT EDUCATION : INDIA

Amiruddin, Mir, 1949, Women's role in adult education, *Educational India* 16(5) November, p 138-39.

Anon, 1984, Non-formal adult education for women *Indian Journal of Adult Education* 45(912) December, p 13-19.

Chandra Govind, 1965, Adult education programme for women, *Naya Shikshak* 8(2) October, p 71-75.

Chandrasekaran, Rajkumari, 1977, Role of voluntary organisations in meeting the needs of women in the fields of adult education and female literacy, *Indian Journal of Adult Education* 38(5) May, p 16-24, refs.

Dutta, S.C., 1962, Condensed course for adult women : A new experiment in adult education, *Indian Journal Adult Education* 23(8) August, p 3-4.

Engler, M., 1949, Adult education for women, *Educational India* 16(5) November, p 139.

Gupta, Pushpa and Gupta, Indu, 1984, Sex knowledge of school girls and their mothers, *Progress of Education* 58(6) January, p 138-42.

Gyanchand, Anusuya, 1969, Adult women and the spread of literacy, *Education Quarterly* 21(1) April, p 26-28.

Ida Singh, 1981, Continuing education for women in slums, *Experiments in Education* 9(6) August, p 99-102.

Mehta, Sushila, 1964, Literacy among women, *Indian Journal of Adult Education* 16(5) November, p 11-12.

Misra, Lakshmi, 1980, Adult education programme and women, *Educational Review* 86(3) March, p 41-43.

Nagappa, T.R., 1980, Adult education for women, *Indian Journal of Adult Education* 41(8) August, p 23-25, refs.

See also
    Functional Literacy
    Kasturba National Memorial Trust
    National Adult Education Programme
    Non-formal Education
    Social Education

ADULT EDUCATION : INDIA : DELHI

See
    Functional Literacy : India : Delhi
    Non-formal Education : India : Delhi

ADULT EDUCATION : INDIA : KARNATAKA : MYSORE

Venkata Rao, Lakshmi, 1948, Adult education in the city of Mysore with special reference to education among women, *Indian Journal of Adult Education* 9(1) January, p 21-24.

ADULT EDUCATION : INDIA : MYSORE : CITY

See

Adult Education : India : Karnataka : Mysore

ADULT EDUCATION : INDIA : UTTAR PRADESH

Anon, 1967, U.P. universities urged to set up adult education department, *Indian Journal of Adult Education* 28(5) May, p 4.

ADULT EDUCATION : INDIA : NATIONAL ADULT EDUCATION PROGRAMME

See

National Adult Education Programme : India

ADULT EDUCATION : JAPAN

Nuita, Yoka, 1969, Trends continuing education of women in Japan, *Indian Journal of Adult education* 30(10) October, p 5-7.

ADULT EDUCATION : MYSORE .

See

Adult Education : India : Karnataka : Mysore

ADULT EDUCATION : PHILIPPINES

Atienza, Maria Fe G., 1966, The Philippine Women's University and extramural education for women, *Indian Journal of Adult Education* 27(7) July, p 11-16.

ADULT EDUCATION : TUNISIA

Turkia, Rauni, 1962, Adult education for Tunisian women, *Indian Journal of Adult Education* 23(7) July, p 11-16, 23(9) September, p 4 +

ADULT EDUCATION AND UNIVERSITIES

Anon. 1967, U.P. universities urged to set up adult education department, *Indian Journal of Adult Education* 28(5) May, p 4.

ALAGAPPA UNIVERSITY : CENTRE FOR WOMEN STUDIES
AND RURAL TECHNOLOGY : ROLE

Alagappa University, Centre for Women Studies and Rural Technology, 1989, Seminar on women and development, *University News* 27(2) p 31.

ALEXANDRA GIRLS ENGLISH INSTITUTE, BOMBAY, INDIA

Benjamin, Margret, 1965, Progressive schools : Alexandra Girls English Institute, Bombay, *Indian Education* 4(8-9) July-August, p 36-39.

ALL INDIA ASSOCIATION FOR CHRISTIAN HIGHER
EDUCATION : ROLE

Anon, 1978, Statement and recommendations of the Consultation on "Designing education for tomorrow's women", held at Women's Christian College, Madras, under the auspices of All India Association for Christian Higher Education in December, 1977, *New Frontiers in Education* 8(1) January-March, p 81-84.

ALL INDIA COUNCIL OF WOMEN'S EDUCATION,
1958, NEW DELHI, INDIA

Anon, 1978, Council recast for women's education, *Patriot*, July 3, p 5.
Education (Periodical), 1958, All India Council for Women's Education, *Education* 37(6) June, p 1-3, editorial.

ALL INDIA RADIO : JULLUNDER : TIRANJAN PROGRAMME

Sandhu, D.K. and Shukla, A.N., 1981, Content analysis of Tiranjan programme of AIR Jullunder, *Indian Journal of Extension Education* 17(3-4) September-December, p 7-11, refs.

ARYA KANYA MAHAVIDYALAYA, BARODA, INDIA

Pandit, Pratibha, 1964, Arya Kanya Mahavidyalaya, Baroda, *Indian Education* 3(12) November, p 15-18.

ASSOCIATION OF WOMEN ENTREPRENEURS AND
EXECUTIVES, INDIA : ROLE

S.N.D.T. Women's University and Institute of Marketing and Management, Association of Women Entrepreneurs and Executives, 1989, Seminar on working women challenges ahead, *University News* 27(23), p 31-32.

ATTITUDES

Nirman, Sevante, 1982, Women reluctant to educate daughters, *Indian Express*, November 11, p 3.

Padma, K., 1983, Attitude of literate women of Hyderabad slums, *Experiments in Education* 11(8) October, p 138-40.

Srivastava, R.K. and Rawat, B., 1982, Attitudes of Harijan women towards education : A comparative study of a city and surrounding villages, *Indian Journal of Adult Education* 43(7) July, p 27-31, refs, tabs.

Venkataraman, Leela, 1975, Change of attitudes towards education of women, *Education Quarterly* 27(2) July, p 13-15.

See also

Psychological Aspect of Education

ATTITUDES IN SOCIAL RELATION

Misra, Lakshmi, 1962, The importance of the social attitude in the development of women's education in India, *Shiksha* 14(4) April, p 148-51.

Pandeya, Ram Prasad, 1975, Education : Social attitudes and women's progress, *Educational Review* 81(10) October, p 193-96.

Varma, P.G., and Srivastava, B.K., 1983, A study of attitudes of teachers trainees towards women's participation in social activities and professions, *Asian Journal of Psychology and Education* 11(1), p 21-27.

BARRIERS AGAINST EDUCATION

See

Access to Education

BEDFORD COLLEGE (UNITED KINGDOM)

Hodgkin, Edward, 1949, Women's College celebrates centenary, *Educational India* 15(12) June, p 345-16.

BHARATIYA GRAMEEN MAHILA SANGH, INDIA

Nimbkar, Krishnabai, 1955, Rural women's uplift: The role of the Bharatiya Grameen Mahila Sangh, *Indian Journal of Adult Education* 16(4) December, p 25-29.

BOOK REVIEW

Anon, 1980, (Book review), *Educational Quarterly* 32(2) July, p 46-47; *Indian Education*, March, p 45-47; *Indian Educational Review* 15 (2) February; *Naya Shikshak* 23(1) July-September, p 103; *Teacher Education* 14(10-11) January-April, p 76-77.
Review of the book : Sharma, Savitri, 1980, *Women students in India : Status and Personality*, Concept Publishing Company, New Delhi, 171 p.
————, 1981, (Book review), *Education Quarterly* 33(3) July, p 44-53.
Review of the book : Chandeer, E.M., 1980, *Education of Adolescent girls*, Allen and Unwin, London, 217 p.
————, 1983, (Book review), *New Frontiers in Education* 13(1) January-March, p 72-73.
Review of the book : Chattopadhyaya, Kamladevi, 1983, *Indian Women's Battle for Freedom*, Abhinav Pub., 184 p.
————, 1986, (Book review), *New Frontiers in Education* 16(2) April-June, p 106-08.
Review of the book : Lebra, Joyee, *et al*, 1986, *Women and work in India : Continuity and Change*, Promila, New Delhi, 310 p.
Panda, S.N., 1969, Women's education in India, *Indian Educational Review* 4(2) July, p 151-53.
Review article of the book : Misra, Lakshmi, 1966, *Education of Women in India (1921-66)*, Macmillan.
Wiser, W.H., 1958, The lamplighter : Review of a guide book for development work among rural women, *Indian Journal of Adult Education* 19(2) June, p 25-28.

BOOKS AND READINGS

Chopra, Kamala, 1970, Reading interests of adolescent boys and girls, *Educational India* 37(1) July, p 16-19 +; *Progress of Education* 44(12) July, p 412-18, refs, tabs.
Ghosh, Molina, 1949, Reading interests of high school girls, *Journal of Education and Psychology* 6(4) January, p 182-89.
Maitra, S.N., 1972, Women's primary and supplementary books, *Indian Journal of Adult Education* 33(6) June, p 14-15.

See also
    Text books

BUSINESS EDUCATION

Venkatalakshmi, V., 1960, Women and commercial education, *Educational India*, 27(1) July, p 17-18.

Wells, Inez Ray, 1960, Girls in commercial education in secondary schools, *Teacher Education* 4(2) February, p 19-23.

CAREER EDUCATION

See
Vocational Education

CHILD WELFARE : INDIA

Ravi Kant Singh, 1985, Women's education crucial for child welfare : Children of India, *Patriot*, January 3, p 6 : January 4, p 5.

CITIZENSHIP EDUCATION : INDIA

Anon, 1968, Adult education of women in the changing pattern of society : Seminar working paper, *Indian Journal of Adult Education* 29(10) October, p 6-9.

Dutta, S.C., 1967, Women's education for civic and social responsibility, *Indian Journal of Adult Education* 28(12) December 1967, p 3-4 +.

Misra, Lakshmi, 1961, Democratic India and women's education, *Education Quarterly* 13(50) Summer, p 119-22.

CO-EDUCATION

Hookens, William, Edward, 1949, On co-education, *Education* 28(7) April 15, p 21-22.

Munshi, K.M., 1948, Educational sparks, *Education* 27(19) November 15, p 35-37.

Rai, Kamala, 1984, Problems of girls in co-educational institutions, *National Journal of Education* 7(1) September, p 29-38, refs., tabs.

————, 1985, Adjustment of secondary school girls studying in co-education and segregated institutions in relation to their socio-economic status, *National Journal of Education* 7(2) May, p 46-55.

CO-EDUCATION : INDIA

Choksi, M., 1956, Co-education in India, *Education Quarterly* 8(32) December, p 377-79.

Education Quarterly (Periodical) 1956, Co-education in India, *Education Quarterly* 8(32) p 377-83, special issue.
Contents: M. Choksi p 377-79; Vijay Mulay p 379-81; N.K. Sundaram p 381 82; K.C. Khanna, p 382-83.

Khanna, K.C., 1956, Co-education in India, *Education Quarterly* 8(32)

December, p 382-83.

Labha Singh, 1965, Co-education in India, *Educational Review* 71(11) November, p 246.

Mathur, V.S., 1955, Should boys and girls study together? *Educator* 4(3) July, p 135-37.

Mehta, Hansa, 1969, Co-education : At what stages and why? *Education Quarterly 21* (1) , April, p 22-25.

Mulay, Vijay, 1956, Co-education in India, *Education Quarterly* 8(32) December, p 379-81.

Panda, K.C., 1962, A comparative study of attitudes of students reading in co-educational and single sex institutions towards co-educational practices in India, *Journal of Education and Psychology* 19(4) January, p 190-98, references, tables.

Saksena, Gopala Krishna, 1952, Co-education : The need of the hour, *Educational India* 18(10) April, p 283-86.

Sundaram, N.K., 1956, Co-education in India, *Education Quarterly* 8(32) December, p 381-82.

Uchat, D.A. and Desai, Haribhai G., 1982, Self concept of female students of single sex colleges and co-education colleges, *Journal of Institute of Educational Research* 6(2) May, p 32-36, refs.

Wasi, Muriel, 1978, The case for co-educational college vs women's colleges, *New Frontiers in Education* 8(1) January-March p 42-46.

CO-EDUCATION : INDIA : JAMMU AND KASHMIR

Razdan, Prithvi Nath, 1955, The Kashmir government's educational policy, *Educational India,* 21(1) July, p 8-12

CO-EDUCATION : INDIA : MAHARASHTRA

Jacob, Plamthodathil, S., 1985, Women students programme in co-educational context : A case study, *New Frontiers in Education* 15 (1) January-March, p 77-81

CO-EDUCATION : INDIA : PUBLIC OPINION

Rao, Waman, 1952, Co-education and present Indian opinion, *Educational Review* 58 (12) December, p 230-234

CO-EDUCATION : KASHMIR

See

Co-education : India : Jammu and Kashmir

CO-EDUCATION : UNITED KINGDOM

Anon, 1948, Britain's schools undertake new experiment: Further extension of co-education, *Education* 27 (20) November 30, p 22-23.

CO-EDUCATION : UNITED STATES OF AMERICA

Anon, 1960. Co-education in the United States, *Education* 39 (8) August, p13-15.

COMMERCIAL EDUCATION

See

Business Education

CONSULTATION ON DESIGNING EDUCATION FOR TOMORROW'S WOMEN, 1977, MADRAS

Anon, 1978, Statement and recommendations of the Consultation on "Designing education for tomorrow's women", held at Women's Christian College, Madras, under the auspices of All India Association for Christian Higher Education in December, 1977, *New Frontiers in Education* 8 (1) January-March, p81-84.

CONTINUING EDUCATION

See

Adult Education
Social Education

CORRESPONDENCE EDUCATION

Ranjit Singh and Saini, R.K., 1984, Socio-personal correlates and gain in the knowledge of correspondence course trainees, *Indian Journal of Adult Education* 45 (4) April, p30-33, tabs.

CORRESPONDENCE SCHOOLS AND COURSES

See

Correspondence Education

COST STUDY

See

Economic Aspect of Education.

COURSE OF STUDY

See
Curricula

CURRICULA

Anon, 1977, Statement and recommendations of the Consultations on "Designing education for tomorrow's women", held at Women's Christian College, Madras, under the auspices of All India Association for Christian Higher Education in December, 1977, *New Frontiers in Education* 8 (1) January-March, p81-84.

————, 1984, Job oriented course for women needed, *National Herald*, September 23, p3.

Barnabas, Manorama, 1978, Designing education for tomorrow's women: Curricular aspects, *New Frontiers in Education* 8 (1) January-March p27-41, refs, tabs.

Bhagat, P., 1981, Evaluation of condensed courses of education for adult women, *Indian Journal of Adult Education* 42 (10) October, p17-20, refs.

Chandrasekaran, Rajkumari, 1980, Designing curriculum and technology for women's adult education programmes, *Indian Journal of Adult Education* 41 (4) April, p19-27.

Dutta, S.C., 1962, Condensed course for adult women: A new experiment in adult education, *Indian Journal of Adult Education* 23 (8) August, p3-4.

Jain, Devaki, 1975, Content of education : Its relevance to the status of women, *Education Quarterly* 27 (2) July, p7-9.

Kalia, Narendra Nath, 1984, Changing images of males and females : How of feminist sex role liberation in Indian school text books, *Indian Education* 13 (10-11) January-February, p10-16.

Karlekar, Kalyani,1960, Special curriculum for girls in secondary education, *Teacher Education* 4 (2) February, p33-36.

Maitra, S.N., 1972, Women's primary and secondary books, *Indian Journal of Adult Education* 33 (6) June, p14-15.

Pushpamma, P., 1980, Special curriculum for girls, *Hindu*, October 7, p3.

Robert, Funice Carmichael, 1954, Curricula for women, *Educational Review* 60 (10) October, p196-98.

Sharma, Prabhu Datta, 1973, Women's education : A curricula model for India, *Education Quarterly* 25 (2) July, p12-15.

Varadan, V., 1964, Women: A different education? *Educational Review* 70 (4) April, p75-78.

Vasudeva Rao, B.S., 1986, Adult education programme : A study on women's performance, *Indian Journal of Adult Education* 47 (6) June, p8-12, tabs.

See also
> Books and Reading
> Text Books

CULTURE AND EDUCATION

See

Educational Anthropology

DELINQUENTS

See

Adolescent Girls : Deliquency.

DEMONSTRATION SCHOOLS

See

Demonstration Centres in Education.

DEMONSTRATION CENTRES IN EDUCATION

Anon, 1961, Demonstration home, *Indian Journal of Adult Education* 22 (9) September, p16-18.

DESTITUTES

Razdan, Prithvi Nath, 1953, Educating the destitute, *Educational India* 19 (7) January, p203-07.

Sabha, V.R., 1953, Educating the destitute, *Education* 32 (1) January, p13-19.

DROPOUTS

Anon, 1985, Concern on higher drop-out among girls, *National Herald* April 14, p12.

Pillai, J.K., 1977, A suggested programme for checking the problem of dropouts with special reference to girls, *New Frontiers in Education* 7 (4) October-December, p48-55.

Ravindran Nair, G., 1983, Education : Why do more girls drop out? *Kurukshetra* 31 (15), p14-16.

DROPOUTS: INDIA : DELHI

Khanna, Kailash, 1977, Effectivity of follow-up material for girl dropouts in a slum of Delhi, *Indian Journal of Adult Education* 38 (12) December, p10-16, tabs.

DROPOUTS : INDIA : HARYANA

Surana, M.L., 1985, Girl drop-outs in rural Haryana : A socio-economic analysis, *India Educational Review* 20 (2) April, p109-116.

DURGABAI DESHMUKH COMMITTEE, 1958, NEW DELHI, INDIA

See

National Committee on Women's Education, 1958, New Delhi, India

EWHA UNIVERSITY (KOREA)

Kim, Okgill, 1978, The place of women's colleges : The Korean experience : EWHA University, *New Frontiers in Education* 8 (1) January-March, p47-56, appen.

ECOLOGICAL MOVEMENT

Jain, Shobhita, 1984, Women and peoples ecological movement, *Economic and Political Weekly* 20 (27).

ECONOMIC ASPECT OF EDUCATION : INDIA

Anon, 1980, Education of girls best investment : Reserve Bank of India study, *Economic Times*, October 18, p7.

Gupta, S.L., 1983, A study of private costs of schooling girls at the elementary state, *EPA Quarterly Bulletin* 6 (2) July, p31-40, tabs.

Rana, R.P.S., 1982, Economic aspect of women education, *University News* 20 (23), p719-724.

Wasi, Muriel, 1982, Educated women in India : Ends and means, *Education Quarterly* 34 (4) October, p1-4.

EDUCATION

Adarsh Bala, 1976, Milton's misogyny, *Journal of Indian Education* 1 (5) January, p45-50.

Anon, 1952, Women and education, *Education Quarterly* 4 (14) June, p104-05.

———, 1952, Women education, *Educational India* 19 (1) July, p7-8,

————, 1952, Women and education, *Educational Review* 58 (6) June, p108-09, repr.

————, 1952, Women and education, *Progress of Education* 25(12) July, p335-37.

————, 1952, Women and education, *Shiksha* July, p7-10, repr.

————, 1979, Challenge of women's education, *Hindu*, October 29, p6, November 2, p9.

————, 1981, (Book Review), *Education Quarterly* 33 (3) July, p44-45. Review of the Book : Chandler, E.M., 1980, *Education of Adolescent Girls*, Allen and Unwin, 217 p.

Azmet, Rehana, 1970, A thought on girls education, *Education* 49 (3) March, p12-15.

Basu, Soma, 1989, Can education liberate eve? *Patriot* June 18.

Bodet, Jaimes Torre, 1950, Excerpts from the address to the conference of the International Federation of University Women at Zurich on 12 August 1950, *Education* 29 (15) August 28, p27-29.

Brockway, K.N., 1953, Changes in girls education, 1927-52, *Teaching* 25 (4) June, p143-4.

Chainani, R.S., 1982, Women and her education, *Progress of Education* 57 (4) November, p77-80.

Dutt, U.C., 1956, Women's education, *Shiksha* 9 (2) October, p89-94.

Dutta, S.C., 1967, Women's education for civic and social responsibility, *Indian Journal of Adult Education* 28 (12) December 1967, p3-4 +.

Education (Periodical) 1950, Girls education, *Education* 29 (2) November 25, p3-4, editorial.

Educational Review (Periodical) 1980, Rethinking on women's education, *Educational Review* 70 (9) September, p218, editorial.

Gandhi, T.K., 1951, Girls education, *Shiksha* 3 (3) January, p46-49.

Kashyap, S.S., 1976, Impact of women's education, *Education Quarterly* 28 (2) July, p21-22.

Kurien, Mathew, 1989, Women education and global survival, *Deccan Herald*, July 8.

Mathur, B.S., 1948, Current thought on education, *Education* 27 (18) October 31, p31-32.

Mazumdar, Vina, 1975, Educational development and changes in women's status, *Indian Education* 1 (4) November, p3-7.

Mehta, Sushila, 1961, Where shall we look for leaders? *Indian Journal of Adult Education* 22 (2) February, p9-10.

Menon, Laxmi, 1989, Emancipation of women, *University News* 27 (23) p6-10.

Naik, Chitra, 1970, Social transformation and equal educational opportunity for girls and women, *Naya Shikshak* 13 (1) July-September, p59-66.

Nayar, Usha, 1975, Women, education and work: A review, *Journal of Higher Education*, Autumn, p282-92, refs.

Nanda, Anant, 1951, The school and the adolescent girls, *Educational Forum* 2 (3) July, p27-30.

Ninan, Sevante, 1982, Women reluctant to educate daughter, *Indian Express*, November 11, p3.

Norris, Louis William, 1955, How to educate a woman, *Educational Review* 61 (9) September, p169-71, repr.

Panadikar, Sulabhe, 1969, Imbalances in the progress of girls education, Extent and remedy, *Education Quarterly* 21 (1) April, p9-11.

Pandeya, Ram Prasad, 1975, Education : Social attitudes and women's progress, *Educational Review* 81 (10) October, p193-96.

Patnaik, Narasinga, 1949, Education for women, *Educational Review* 55 (2) February, p28-29.

Pillai, J.K., 1982, The dual role of women, *New Frontiers in Education* 12 (4) October-December, p39-42.

————, 1989, Strategies for empowerment of women, *University News* 27 (23), p1-2.

Rana, R.P.S., 1982, Economic aspect of women education, *University News* 20 (23), p719-724.

Sapra, Ravilal, 1950, Girls education in schools, *Education* 29 (15) August 25, p24-26.

Saraswathi, T.S. and Gupta, Radhika, 1985, Educate women and you educate family, *Perspectives in Education*, 1 (1) January, p49-54, refs, tabs.

Shukla, Sureshchandra, 1981, Perspectives on women's education, *National Journal of Education* 3 (2) March, p7-16.

Srinivasan, K., 1962, Women and we, men, *Educational India* 28 (11-12) May-June, p351-53.

Suman Singh, 1988, Need to define women's education, *Pioneer*, July 6.

Suryakumari, A., 1988, Women's interests, *University News* 26 (45), p1-3.

————, 1989, Strategies for political empowerment of women, *University News*, 27 (23), p17-18.

Tribune (Newspaper), 1988, Educating the daughters, *Tribune*, December 30, editorial.

Tripathi, Madhukanta, 1986, Women's struggle for the new roles, *National Journal of Education* 7 (2) May, p56-60, appendix, refs.

EDUCATION : AFRICA

See

Rural Education : Africa

EDUCATION : ASIA

Mathias, T.A., 1988, Women's education and development : The key to a brighter future in Asia, *New Frontiers in Education* 18 (3), p42-57.

EDUCATION : ASIA : SOUTH

Nayar, Usha, 1986, Women's education in South Asia, *Patriot*, January 16, p4.

EDUCATION : AUSTRALIA

Gill, Betty, 1948, Indian girls study in Australia enjoy student life at domestic college, *Education* 27 (12) 31 July, p6-7.

EDUCATION : BANGLADESH

Anon, 1989, Women's education in Bangladesh, *New Frontiers in Education* 19 (1) January-March, p96-105.

EDUCATION : CEYLON

See

    Education : Sri Lanka

EDUCATION : COSTS

See

    Economic Aspect of Education

EDUCATION : ECONOMIC ASPECT

See

    Economic Aspect of Education

EDUCATION : FINANCE

See

    Economic Aspect of Education

EDUCATION : INDIA

Agarwal, Bina, 1976, Exploitation utilisation of educated women power, *Journal of Higher Education* 2 (92) August, p185-95, refs. tabs.

Agrawal, Mamta, 1981, A study of the impact of education on social, and cultural modernisation of Hindu and Muslim women, *Indian Educational Review* 16 (1) January, p72-77.

Alagappa University, Centre for Women's Studies and Rural Technology 9, 1989, Seminar on women and development, *University News* 27 (2), p31.

Amrik Singh, 1988, Empowerment of women, *Tribune*, July 13.

————, 1988, New deal for women, *Hindustan Times*, June 27.

————, 1989, What happens to brilliant girls? *Tribune*, August 27.

Anklesaria Aiyar, Shahnaz, 1988, Need to improve girls education *Indian Express*, August 13.

Anon, 1950, Girls education, *Shiksha* 3 (1), p26-27; 3 (2) p65-67; 3 (3), p46-49; 3 (4) April, p24-28; 4 (1) July, p105-07; 4 (2) October, p122-24.

————, 1968, Programmes for the promotion of girl education in the new Fourth Plan, *Education Quarterly* 20 (1) April, p32-33.

————, 1977, Statement and recommendations of the Consultation on "Designing education for tomorrow's women" held at Women's Christian College, Madras, under the auspices of all India Association for Christian Higher Education in December 1977, *New Frontiers in Education* 8(1) January-March, p81-84.

————, 1982, Scheme to promote girls education, *Times of India* December 25, p9.

————, 1983, Female education still far from good, 1983, *Hindustan Times*, June 21, p12.

————, 1983, Measures to boost women's education, *Indian Express*, June 14, p4.

————, 1983, Proper education solution to women's problems, *Hindu*, February 6, p13.

————, 1983, States told to make up lag in girls education, *Hindustan Times*, June 17, p4.

————, 1984, Educating women 'crucial', *Patriot*, February 12, p3.

————, 1984, Education plan for girls befits 8,000, *Times of India*, (Bombay), April 9, p4.

————, 1984, Group discussion reports, *Indian Journal of Adult Education* 45 (12) December, p20-27.

————, 1984, Recommendations, *Indian Journal of Adult Education* 45 (12) December, p29-31.

————, 1985, More funds urged for women's education, *Indian Express*, October 1, p7.

————, 1986, Central grants for women's upliftment, *Statesman*, December 20, p8.

————, 1986, Call to promote women's education, *National Herald*, January 14, p6.

————, 1986, Uplift of women through education, *National Herald*, March 12, p5.

————, 1986, Big educational schemes for women proposed, *Patriot*, December 9, p5.

Avadesh Dayal, 1965, Women's education, *Education* 44 (7) July, p31-34.

Bagree, Asha, 1980, Appropriate education for women, *Hindu*, July 9, p5.

Behl, R.K., With women's education? *Tribune*, February 28.

Bhandari, R.K., 1982, Development of women's education, *New Frontiers in Education* 12 (7) October-December, p32-37.

————, 1982, Educational development of women, *Education Quarterly* 34 (3) July, p12-14.

Bhansali, Kamalini, H., 1969, Education of women in modern India : Some achievements and problems, *Education Quarterly* 21 (1) April, p36-43.

Buch, M.B., 1968, Issues and problems in women's education in India *Education Quarterly* 20 (1) April, p34-37.

Chandresekharan, Rajkumari, 1983, Women power must be exploited too, *Hindu*, October 25, p19.

Chandy, Anna, 1962, Problems of women's education, *Educational Review* 68 (5) May, p101-103.

Chari, M.S.V., 1965, Some problems of education, *Education* 44 (5) May, p23-24.

Chattopadhyay, Kamaladevi, 1969, Role of women in modern India, *Education Quarterly* 21 (1) April, p12-14.

Chiplunkar, V.V., 1987, Education and development of women: Project Maher, *Journal of Educational Planning and Administration* 1 (2), p 173-190.

De, S.K., 1959, Progress of women's education in India, *Education* 38 (7) July, p5-11.

Deshmukh, Durgabai, 1960, Expansion of women's education under the Third Plan, *Education Quarterly* 12 (48) Winter, p289-93.

————, 1960, Women's education : A major problem, *Educational India* 27 (3) September, p78-82.

Dey, Chhaya, 1981, Reform entails a predefinition process, *Progress of Education*, 56 (4) November, p85-88.

Education Quarterly (Periodical), 1969, Girls and women's education in India today, *Education Quarterly* 21 (1) April, p1-16, special issue Contents: Education of women in India, Phulrenu Guha, p1-4; Article 45 and primary education of girls, Lakshmi N. Menon, p5-8; Imbalances in the progress of girls education, Sulabha Panandikar, p9-11; Role of women in modern India, Kamaladevi Chattopadhyay, p12-14; Vocational education for women, Rajammal P. Devadas, p15-21; Co-education : At what stages and why, Hansa Mehta, p22-25; Adult women and the spread of literacy, Anusuya Gyanchand, p26-28; Voluntary organisation and women's education, Raksha Saran, p29-32; Towards a new social outlook, Sarojini Mahishi, p33-35; Education of women in modern India : Some achievements and problems, Kamalani Bhansali, p36-13; Education of tribal women and girls, B.H. Mehta, p 44-46.

————, 1969, Reports on the progress of girls and women education in the States, *Education Quarterly* 21 (1) p47-53, special issue.

Contents : Andhra Pradesh, G. Manohar Rao, p47-48; Madhya Pradesh, Vimala Sharma, p48-49; Pondicherry, Lila Indrasen, p49-50; Rajasthan, Prabha Misra, p 50-51; Tamil Nadu, Sarojini Vardappan, p51-53.

Educational India (Periodical) 1948, Women's education, *Educational India* 14 (8) February, p229; 15 (3) September, p97-98, editorial.

————, 1952, The Five Year Plan and women's education, *Education India* 19 (2) August, p 56-59, editorial.

————, 1953, Education of women, *Educational India* 20 (3) September, p91-93, editorial.

————, 1958, Problems in women's education, *Educational India* 25 (2) August, p53-56, editorial.

————, 1959, Education for women, *Educational India* 25 (11-12) May-June, p424-25; 26 (5) November, p154-56, editorial.

————, 1959, Priority for women's education, *Educational India* 25 (8) February, p314-16, editorial.

————, 1964, Education of girls, *Educational India* 30 (8) February, p276-77, editorial

————, 1964, Education of women, *Educational India* 30 (9) March, p307-08.

————, 1966, Women and scientific education, *Educational India* 33 (3) September, p92-93, editorial.

Fernandes, Marjorie, 1984, Development of women's education : Problems and suggestions, *Indian Journal of Adult Education* 45 (9), p4-9.

Gopal Krishna, 1958, Women's education in India, *Educational India* 25 (2) August, p45-48.

Gopalaratnam, D.L., 1947, The educated girl in India, *Educational India* 13 (8) February, p265-266.

Guha, Phulrenu, 1969, Education of women in India : A historical perspective, *Education Quarterly* 21 (1) April, p1-4.

Hooja, G.B.K., 1987, Women's status, family life, education and the media, *University News* 25 (14), p4-6.

Indian Universities Association for Continuing Education, 1989, Empowerment of women: Multi-disciplinary perspectives, *University News* 27 (4) p9-10.

Indira, K., 1988, New vista for Indian girl, *Indian Nation*, October 2.

Israney, S.M., 1989, Status of women in the academic world : Indian context, *University News* 27 (2-3) 11-14.

Jagan Nath, 1988, India hopes to attract more girls to schools, *Indian Nation*, September 8.

Jain, M.K., 1959, Women's education in India, *Educational Review* 65 (5) May, p97-98.

Jain, Shobhita, 1984, Women and peoples ecological movement, *Economic and Political Weekly* 20 (27).

Jacob, A., 1982, Education for women and girls today in cities in India, *Education Quarterly* 34 (4) October, p11-13.

Jaishankar, V., 1979, Role of women's education in India, *Hindu*, October 9, p3.

Jayaraman, Kunthala, 1975, Education for women: A five year plan, *Journal of Higher Education* 1 (2) Autumn, p255-56.

Joshi, Vibha and Menon, Geeta, 1986, Research on women's education in India: A review, *Perspectives in Education* 2 (2) April, p77-79.

Journal of Indian Education (Periodical), 1975, Editorial, *Journal of Indian Education* 1 (4) November, p1-2, editorial.

Kaur, Amrit, 1979, Women education in India today, *Naya Shikshak* 21 (4) April-June, p9-24, tabs.

Kapoor, M., 1978, Women education for national development, *Indian Journal of Adult Education* 39 (7) July, p32-34.

Kapur, H., 1983, Progress in girls education, *National Herald* October 23, p. 2.

Lal, Premchand, 1951, Education of women and girls in India today, *Education* 30 (14) August 31, p7-11.

Leela, R.H., 1968, Stray thoughts on the education of Indian girls, *Educational Review* 74 (5) May, p97-98.

Mehta, Perin H., 1968, The felt needs of female students and their implications for education, *NIE Journal* 3 (1) September, p13-18, refs.

Misra, Lakshmi, 1961, Democratic India and women's education, *Education Quarterly* 13 (50) Summer, p119-22.

Mukherjee, H.B., 1961, Tagore on women's education, *Education Quarterly* 13 (50) Summer, p123-27.

Mukherjee, L., 1956-1957, Education of women in India : Past and present, *Education* 35 (12) December, p5-9; 36 (1) January, p5-10.

Padmanabhan, N.S., 1962, Whither women's education? *Educational Review* 68 (4) April, p90-92.

Panda, S.N., 1969, Women's education in India, *Indian Educational Review* 4 (2) July, 151-53.
Review article of the book, Misra, Lakshmi, 1966, *Education of Women in India* (1921-66), Macmillan.

Pillai, J.K., 1976, Educating women for national development, *Education Quarterly* 27 (4) January, p31-33.

Pande, Mrinal, 1988, Where do the women toppers go? *Hindustan Times*, August 19.

Ravi Kant Singh, 1985, Women's education crucial for child welfare: Children of India, *Patriot*, January 3, p6; January 4, p5.

Saran, Raksha, 1960, Education of women, *Educational India* 26 (8), p263-264.
(Address of Mrs. Raksha Saran at the 29th session of the All India Women's Conference, Madras, 1959).

————, 1962, Expanding women's education in the Third Plan, *Shiksha* 15 (2) October, p50-55.

Satvir Singh, 1975, Women's education in India : A statistical presentation, *Indian Education* 1 (4) November, p34-38.

Shah, Gunvant B., 1975, Genesis of women's education in India, *NIE Journal* 9 (3) January, p1-9, refs. tabs.

Shah, Madhuri R., 1978, The deal is still unfair, *New Frontiers in Education* 8(1) January-March, p 57-59

Shah, Radha Rani, 1932, Education of women in India : Inequalities and bottlenecks, *Education Quarterly* 34 (4) October, p20-27.

Shrimali, K.L. 1959, Future of women's education, *Educational India* 25 (7) January, p248-50.

Varadan, V., 1964, Women : A different education? *Educational Review* 70 (4) April, p75-78.

Venkataraman, Leela, 1975, Change of attitude towards education of women, *Education Quarterly* 27 (2) July, p13-15.

Wasi, Muriel, 1982, Educating women in India : Ends and means, *Education Quarterly* 34 (4) October, p1-4.

EDUCATION : INDIA : ANCIENT

Shamsuddin, 1960, Status of women in ancient India, *Progress of Education* 35 (1) April, p10-12.

EDUCATION : INDIA : ANDHRA PRADESH

Manohar Rao, G., 1969, Reports on the progress of girls and women's education in the States : Andhra Pradesh, *Education Quarterly* 21 (1) April, p47-48.

EDUCATION : INDIA : ASSAM

Das, Lakshahira, 1982, Problem and priorities in the education of women in Assam, *Education Quarterly* 34 (2) April 1982, p22-26.

EDUCATION : INDIA : BIHAR

Jha, J., and Saxena, Bimla, 1983, A study of disadvantages associated with different socio-economic groups of girls studying in secondary schools, *Journal of Education and Psychology* 41 (12) April-July, p12-16.

EDUCATION : INDIA : CENTRAL

Dharam Vir, 1972, Women education : An effort in Central India, *Indian Journal of Adult Education* 33 (8) August, p9.

EDUCATION : INDIA : DELHI

Sharma, S.R., 1989, Delhi tops in women's education, *National Herald*, April 23.

EDUCATION : INDIA: FIVE YEAR PLANS

See

State Aid to Education

EDUCATION : INDIA : GUJARAT

Thanki, Harijiwan, 1968, Gurukul's role in girls' education in Gujarat, *Indian Education* 7 (10-11) September-October, p32-34.

EDUCATION : INDIA : HARYANA

Surana, M.L., 1985, Girl drop-outs in rural Haryana : A socio-economic analysis, *Indian Educational Review* 20 (2) April, p109-16.

EDUCATION : INDIA : JAMMU AND KASHMIR

Razdan, Prithvi Nath, 1955, The Kashmir government's education policy, *Educational India* 22 (1) July, p8-12.

EDUCATION : INDIA : KERALA

Anon, 1984, Kerala gets 1st prize for girls education, *Hindustan Times*, May 25, p4.

EDUCATION : INDIA : MADHYA PRADESH

Shamsuddin, 1976, Developments of women's education in Madhya Pradesh, 1956-1974, *Education Quarterly* 27 (4) January, p34-36.
———, 1977, Development of women's education in new Madhya Pradesh, *Educational India* 43 (7) January, p155-58.
Sharma, Vimla, 1969, Reports on the progress of girls and women education in the states : Madhya Pradesh, *Education Quarterly* 21 (1) April, p48-49.

EDUCATION : INDIA : MADRAS

See

Education : India : Tamil Nadu : Madras

EDUCATION : INDIA : MAHARASHTRA : BOMBAY

Educational India (Periodical), 1948, Women's education, *Educational India* 15 (3) September, p97-98, editorial.

Tawde, Sunanda, S., 1958, Progress in education in rural and urban areas, *Teaching* 31 (2) December, p48-54.

EDUCATION : INDIA : NORTH

Rallia Ram, Mayawanti, 1975, Muslim educated women in North India, *Journal of Higher Education* 1 (2) August, p250.

EDUCATION : INDIA : PONDICHERRY

Indrasen, Lila, 1969, Reports on progress of girls and women's education in the States : Pondicherry, *Education Quarterly* 21 (1) April, p49-50.

EDUCATION : INDIA : PUNJAB

Anand, Kulwant, 1965, Attitudes of Punjab University women students towards marriage and the family, *Indian Journal of Social Work* 26, p87-90.

Kaur, Kuldeep, 1985, Attitudes of the people towards women literacy in Punjab, *Educational Review* 91 (8) August, p126-29.

Mangat, Shavindu K. and Roy, Sumita, 1983, Participation and interest or rural school going girls in household and farm activities, *Indian Journal of Extension Education* 43 (7) July, p2-31, refs, tabs.

EDUCATION : INDIA : RAJASTHAN

Hooja, Meenakshi, 1981-1982, Women of Rajasthan : A demographic profile, *Prasar* 8 (3-4) October, January, p1-17, tabs.

Misra, Prabha, 1969, Reports on the progress of girls and women's education in the States : Rajasthan, *Education Quarterly* 21 (1) April, p50-51.

Saxena, Daya and Bhatnagar, Suman Rani, 1985, A comparative study of time utilisation pattern of tribal and non-tribal women in Rajasthan, *Indian Journal of Extension Education* 21 (1-2) January-June, p83-85, tabs.

EDUCATION : INDIA : TAMIL NADU

Vardappan, Sarojini, 1969, Reports on the progress of girls and women's education in the States : Tamil Nadu, *Education Quarterly* 21 (1) April, p 51-53.

See also

Seethalakshmi Ramaswamy College, Tiruchirappaly.

EDUCATION : INDIA : TAMIL NADU : MADRAS

Brockway, 1953, Changes in girls education, 1927-52, *Teaching* 25 (4) June, p143-44.

EDUCATION : INDIA : UTTAR PRADESH

Anon, 1950, Girls education, *Shiksha* 3 (1) July, p26-27 : 3 (2) October, p65-67.

————, 1951, Girls education, *Shiksha* 3 (3) January, p46-49; 3 (4) April, p24-28; 4 (1) July, p105-107; 4 (2) October, p122-24.

Geldens, Maria, 1956, The Women's Welfare Scheme in Uttar Pradesh *Indian Journal of Adult Education* 17 (9) September, p5-11.

Indian Journal of Adult Education (Periodical), 1966, Welfare project for U.P. women : PRAI's pioneering efforts, *Indian Journal of Adult Education* 27 (4) April, p1-2, editorial.

Sita Ram, 1960, Progress of women's education in Uttar Pradesh, *Shiksha* 12 (3) January, p39-43.

Srivastava, R.K. and Rawat, B., 1982, Attitudes of Harijan women towards education : A comparative study of a city and surrounding villages, *Indian Journal of Adult Education* 43 (7) July, p27-31, refs, tabs.

See also

Government Training College for Women, Allahabad, India

EDUCATION : INDIA : WEST BENGAL

Ghosh, Dhirendra Nath, 1955, Vidyasagar and women's education in Bengal, *Journal of Education* 2 (3-4) Conference Number, p157-63.

EDUCATION : INDONESIA

Santoso, Maria Ulfah, 1948, Brief survey of the Indonesian women's movement, *Education* 27 (5) 15 March, p24-27.

EDUCATION : JAPAN

Castello, Kathleen, 1962, Women's education in Japan, *Educational Review* 68 (4) April, p94.

EDUCATION : KOREA

Kim, Okgill, 1978, The place of women's colleges : The Korean experience : EWHA university, *New Frontiers in Education* 8 (1) January-March, p47-56, appen.

EDUCATION : NEPAL

Basant, Neelam, 1989, Status of women's education in Nepal, *New Frontiers in Education* 19 (1) January-March, p106-109.

Sharma, Jan, 1989, Stress on education of girls in Nepal, *Pioneer* January 13.

EDUCATION : PAKISTAN

Hassan, Masuma, 1980, Women's education in Pakistan, *New Frontiers in Education* 19 (1) January-March, p80-89.

EDUCATION : SRI LANKA

Motwani, Clara, 1961, Education of women in Ceylon, *Education Quarterly* 13 (50) Summer, p175-177.

EDUCATION : UNITED ARAB REPUBLIC

Harby, Mohammed Khairy and Mehrez, Zenab Mohmoud, 1961, Education of women in the U.A.R., *Education Quarterly* 13 (50) Summer, p178-81.

EDUCATION : UNITED KINGDOM

D'Souza, Austin A., 1961, Education of women in the U.K. and the U.S.A., *Education Quarterly* 13 (50) Summer, p182-86.

Murray, A.R., 1956, Women's education at Oxford and Cambridge, *Educational Review* 62 (9) September, p169-70.

See also
  Beford College (UNITED KINGDOM)

EDUCATION : UNITED STATES OF AMERICA

D'Souza, Austin A., 1961, Education of women in the U.K. and the U.S.A., *Education Quarterly* 13 (50) Summer, p182-86.

Norris, Louis, 1955, How to educate a women, *Educational Review* 61 (9) September, p169-71, repr.

Roberts, Funice Carmichael, 1954, Curricula for women, *Educational Review*

60 (10) October, p196-98.

Ury, Glaude, M., Women in U.S., school history textbooks, *Educational Review* 78 (9) September, p197-203.

EDUCATION : UNION OF SOVIET SOCIALIST REPUBLIC

Anon, 1957, Some facts and figures about women in Soviet Russia *Education* 36 (5) May, p26-27.

EDUCATION : WOMEN

See

Education

EDUCATION AND NATIONAL DEVELOPMENT

See

National Development and Education

EDUCATION AND STATE

See

National Policy of Education
State Aid to Education

EDUCATION FOR EQUALITY

Chowdhury, Neerja, 1986, Education for equality, *Statesman*, May 26, p5.
Gore, M.S., 1987, Education for women's equality I & II, *University News* 25 (16), p2-5; 25 (17) p4-7.
Mojumdar, Modhumita, 1988, Education for equality, *Statesman*, June 15.
Mother Teressa Women's University, 1988, Implementation of NEP with special reference to education for women's equality : Report, *University News*, 26 (24), p17.

See also

Educational Equalisation

EDUCATION FOR WOMEN'S EQUALITY

See

Education for Equality
Educational Equalisation

EDUCATION IN CITIES AND TOWNS

Jacob, A., 1982, Education for women and girls today in cities in India, *Education Quarterly* 34 (4) October, p11-13.

Srivastava, R.K., and Rawat, B., 1982, Attitudes of Harijan women towards education : A comparative study of a city and surrounding villages, *Indian Journal of Adult Education* 43 (7) July, p27-31, refs, tabs.

Tawde, Sunanda, S., 1958, Progress in education in rural and urban areas, *Teaching* 31 (2) December, p48-54.

EDUCATION IN URBAN AREAS

See

Education in Cities and Towns.

EDUCATION OF WOMEN

See

Education

EDUCATIONAL ANTHROPOLOGY

Agrawal, Mamta, 1981, A study of the impact of education on social and cultural modernisation of Hindu and Muslim women, *Indian Educational Review* 16 (1) January, p72-77.

EDUCATIONAL BROADCASTING

See

Mass Media

EDUCATIONAL COOPERATION IN HOME AND SCHOOL

See

Home and School

EDUCATIONAL DISCRIMINATION

See

Education for Equality
Educational Equalisation

EDUCATIONAL EQUALISATION

Ahmad, Karuna, 1979, Equality and women's higher education, *Journal of Higher Education* 5 (1) Monsoon, p33-49.

Anon, 1986, Need for women's equality stressed, *Indian Express*, December 21, p3.

Bose, A., 1975, Census figures reveal discrimination against women, *Organiser* 24 (39), p5.

Greenough, Richard, 1963, Barriers against schooling for girls, *Educational Review* 69 (6) June, p130-31.

Mane, M.G., 1984, Educate women to reduce inequalities, *Indian Journal of Adult Education* 45 (12) December, p7-8.

Naik, Chitra, 1970, Social transformation and equal educational opportunity for girls and women, *Naya Shikshak* 13 (1) July-September, p59-66.

Saunders, Fay E., 1980, Discrimination and inequalities between the sexes and school, *Journal of Indian Education* 5 (5) January, p35-42.

Sengupta, M., 1989, Women's status, : What is the concept of equality? *Hindu*, February 7.

Shah, Madhuri R., 1978, The deal is still unfair, *New Frontiers in Education* 8 (1) January-March, p57-59.

Sharma, Radha Rani, 1982, Education of women in India : Inequalities and bottlenecks, *Education Quarterly* 34 (4) October, p20-27, refs, tabs.

Panandikar, Sulabha, 1969, Imbalances in the progress of girls education : Extent and remedy, *Education Quarterly* 21 (1) April, p9-11.

See also
Education for Equality.

EDUCATIONAL FUND RAISING

Anon, 1986, Fund appeal for women's literacy network, *Patriot*, April 30, p3.

EDUCATIONAL LAW AND LEGISLATION

Menon, Lakshmi N., 1969, Article 45 and primary education of girls, *Education Quarterly*, 21 (1) April, p5-8.

EDUCATIONAL PLANNING

Dutt, Sunitee, 1959, National planning and vocations for women in India, *Educational Forum* 4 (1) January, p8-12.

Jayaraman, Kunthala, 1975, Education for women : A five year plan, *Journal of Higher Education* 1 (2) Autumn, p225-56.

EDUCATIONAL RESEARCH : INDIA

Joshi, Vibha and Menon, Geeta, 1986, Research on women's education in India : A review, *Perspectives in Education* 2 (3) April, p77-79.

EDUCATIONAL SOCIOLOGY

Agrawal, Mamta, 1981, A study of the impact of education on social and cultural modernisation of Hindu and Muslim women, *Indian Educational Review* 16 (1) January, p72-77.

Ahmad, Karuna, 1985, The social context of women's education in India, 1921-81 : Tentative formulation, *New Frontiers* 15 (3) p1-36.

Anon, 1968, Adult education of women in the changing pattern of society : Seminar working paper, *Journal of Indian Adult Education* 29 (10), p6-9.

————, 1980, Education of girls best investment : Reserve Bank of India study, *Economic Times*, October 18, p7.

Kurien, Mathew, 1989, Women, education and global survival, *Deccan Herald*, July 8.

Mathias, T.A., 1988, Women's education and development : The key to a brighter future in Asia, *New Frontiers of Education*, July-September 18 (3) p42-57.

Naik, Chitra, 1970, Social transformation and equal educational opportunity for girls and women, *Naya Shikshak* 13 (1) July-September, p59-66.

Pandeya, Ram Prasad, 1975, Education : Social attitudes and women's progress, *Educational Review* 81 (10) October, p193-96

Sharma, Savitri, 1978, A study of the influence of socio-economic backgrounds in regard to the development of different types of values among female college students, *Asian Journal of Psychology and Education* 3 (1) January, 1978, p21-29, refs, tabs.

EDUCATIONAL STATISTICS

Bose, A., 1975, Census figures reveal discrimination against women, *Organiser* 24 (39), p5.

Satvir Singh, 1975, Women's education in India : A statistical presentation, *Indian Education* 1 (4) November, p34-38.

EDUCATIONAL TECHNOLOGY

Chandrasekaran, Raj Kumar, 1980, Designing curriculum and technology for women's adult education programmes, *Indian Journal of Adult Education* 41 (4) April, p19-24.

ELEMENTARY EDUCATION

Gupta, S.L., 1983, Factors influencing the growth of girls education at the elementary stage, *Indian Education Review* 18 (4) October, p77-82.

————, 1983, A study of private costs of schooling girls at the elementary state, *E P A Quarterly Bulletin* 6 (2) July, p31-40, tabs.

EMANCIPATION OF WOMEN

Anon, 1983, (Book review), *New Frontiers in Education* 13 (1) January-March, p72-73.

Review of the book : Chattopadhyaya, Kamladevi, 1983, *Indian Women's Battle for Freedom*, Abhinav Pub., p184.

Basu, Soma, 1980, Can education liberate eve? *Patriot*, June 18.

Dewani, Lakshman, 1989, Nehru and emancipation of Indian women, *Patriot*, December 16.

Menon, Laxmi, 1989, Emancipation of women, *University News* 27 (23).

See also
Educational Sociology
Empowerment of Women.

EMPLOYED WOMEN

See

Working Women

EMPLOYMENT

Agrawal, Bina,1976, Exploitation utilisation of educated women power, *Journal of Higher Education* 2 (2) August, p185-95, refs, tabs.

Agrawal, S.M., 1965, Impact of education on employment of women as career girls, *Education and Psychology Review* 5 (1) January, p34-37.

Anon, 1984, Job oriented course for women needed, *National Herald*, September 23, p3.

————, 1986, (Book review), *New Frontiers in Education* 16 (2) April-June, p106-108.

Review of the book : Lebra, Joyce, *et al.*, 1986, *Women and work in India : Continuity and Change*, Promila, New Delhi, p310.

Banerjee, Nirmala, 1989, Trends in women's employment, 1971-81 : Some macro-level observation, *Economic and Political Weekly* 24 (17) p WS 10-WS 22.

Kapoor, Ranga, 1975, Career opportunities for women, *Education Quarterly* 27 (2) July, p10-12.

Krishnaraj, Maithreyi, 1977, Employment pattern of university educated women and its implications, *Journal of Higher Education* 2 (3), p317-27, appen, refs.

Kumar, Usha A., 1975, Job oriented education for girls : Some practical and theoretical considerations, *Education Quarterly* 27 (3) October, p14-15.

Perin, H. and Mehta, H.P., 1974, Vocational preparation and the employment of women, *Education Quarterly* 26 (2) July, p1-4, refs.

Mitra, Ashok, 1978, Employment of women, *Manpower* 14 (1) p1-29.

Nayar, Usha, 1975, Women, education and work : A review, *Journal of Higher Education* 1 (2) Autumn, p283-92, refs.

Paranjape, S.D., 1974, Problems of graduate employed women: A socio-psychological study and attitude survey, *India Disertation Abstracts* 2 (2) p101-103.

Safaya, Raghunath, 1964, Part-time employment of women teachers *Educational Review* 70 (4) April, p86-87.

Singh, K.P., A comparative study of the attitude of working and non-working women towards women's education and employment, *Interdiscipline* 11 (3), p89-100.

Srivastava, Sumita, 1985, College going girls : Their occupational choices, goals and problems, *Journal of Indian Education* 11 (2) July, p40-44.

Sudha, B.G. and Goetha, S., 1982, Problems of girls as a function of material employment and anxiety, *Journal of Institute of Educational Research* 6 (1) January, p29-37, refs, tabs.

Uplaonkar, U.T., 1983, Occupational aspirations of college students, *Social Change* 13 (2) p16-26.

See also
Working Women

EMPLOYMENT : INDIA

Agrawal, S.M., 1965, Impact of education on employment of career girls, *Education and Psychology Review* 5 (1) January, p34-37.

Anon, 1984, Job oriented course for women needed, *National Herald*, September 23, p3.

Chakrabarti, Ashok Kumar, 1977, Causes of women's unemployment in India, *Economic Affairs* 22 (5), p177-84.

Educational India (Periodical), 1967, Jobless women, *Educational India* 33 (10) April, p345-46, editorial.

Saxena, Usha, 1985, Women in India : Education and employment status, *Economic Times*, May 17, p5.

————, 1985, Women in India : Job opportunities and education, *Economic Times*, May 18, p5.

EMPLOYMENT : PART TIME

See

Part Time Employment

EMPOWERMENT OF WOMEN

Amrik Singh, 1988, Empowerment of women, *Tribune*, July 13.
Indian Universities Association for Continuing Education, 1989. Empowerment of women : Multi-disciplinary perspectives, *University News* 27 (4), p9-10.
Pillai, J.K., 1989, Strategies for empowerment of women, *University News* 27 (23), p1-2.
Suryakumari, A., 1989, A strategies for political empowerment of women, *University News* 27 (23), 17-18.

See also

Educational Sociology
Emancipation of Women

ERADICATION OF ILLITERACY

See

Functional Literacy.

EXCEPTIONAL STUDENT

See

Talented Student

EXTRAMURAL EDUCATION : PHILIPPINES

Atienza, 1966, The Philippine Women's University and extramural education for women, *Indian Journal of Adult Education* 27 (7) July, p11-16.

FAMILY PLANNING

Chhabra, Rami, 1980, Establishing linkages between women's literacy programmes, status issue and access to family planning, *Indian Journal of Adult Education* 41 (4) April, p6-9.

FAMILY PLANNING : INDIA : UTTAR PRADESH

Mulay, Sumati, 1976, Uttar Pradesh literacy and family planning behaviour of rural women, *Indian Journal of Adult Education* 37 (1) January, p9-10, tabs.

FARMER'S EDUCATION

See

Rural Education

FEMALE LITERACY

See

Functional Literacy

FIVE YEAR PLANS : INDIA

See

State Aid to Education

FUNCTIONAL LITERACY

Anon, 1968, Extension of project on farmer's education and functional literacy urged, *Indian Journal of Adult Education* 29 (11) November, 1968, p3.

————, 1984, Female literacy growing, *Patriot*, June 5, p5.

————·, 1986, Female literacy still deemed unnecessary, *Indian Express*, October 13, p4.

————, 1986, Fund appeal for women's literacy network, *Patriot*, April 30, p3.

Bhagat, Bankim Bihari, 1983, Making the other half literate, *Indian Express*, February 26, p6.

Chandrasekaran, Rajkumari, 1977, Role of the voluntary organisations in meeting the needs of women in the fields of adult education and female literacy, *Indian Journal of Adult Education* 38 (5) May, p16-24, refs.

Chhabra, Rami, 1980, Establishing linkages between women's literacy programmes, status issues and access to family planning, *Indian Journal of Adult Education* 41 (4) April, p6-9.

Guha, Phulrenu, 1968, Content of literacy for women, *Indian Journal of Adult Education* 29 (11) November, p15-16.

Gyanchand, Anusuya, 1969, Adult women and the spread of literacy *Education Quarterly* 21 (1) April, p26-28.

Kaur, A., 1979, Adult education programmes for illiterate women in the age group 15-35, *Indian Journal of Adult Education* 40 (12) December, p19-32.

Mehta, Sushila, 1964, Literacy among women, *Indian Journal of Adult Education* 25 (11) November, p11-12.

Mukherji, S., 1985, Benefits we derived from present education, *Yojana* 29 (22), p28-30.

Mulay, Sumati, 1976, Uttar Pradesh literacy and family planning behaviour of rural women, *Indian Journal of Adult Education* 37 (1) January, p9-10, tabs.

Pandey, Balaji, 1985, Eradicating illiteracy among women, *Statesman*, September 11, p6.

Rajan, S. Irudaya, 1988, Progress of female literacy in India, *Yojana* 32(21), p10-12.

Shafi, Rafat S., 1978, Literacy and nutrition education in context of adult education programme for young females, *Indian Journal of Adult Education* 39 (2) February, p17-27, refs.

Shahare, M.L., 1984, Eradicating women's illiteracy : A challenge, *Indian Journal of Adult Education* 45 (12) December, p32-38.

FUNCTIONAL LITERACY : INDIA : DELHI

Seth, M., *et al*, 1983, Group interaction among adult women participating in the functional literacy programme in Delhi, *Indian Journal of Extension Education* 19 (1-2) March-June, p62-68, refs, tabs.

————, 1983, Group intraction among women participants of a functional literacy programme in Delhi : A study, *Indian Journal of Adult Education* 44 (10) October, p24-28, refs, tabs.

FUNCTIONAL LITERACY : INDIA : PUNJAB

Kaur, Kuldeep, 1985, Attitude of the people towards women literacy in Punjab, *Educational Review* 91 (8) August, p126-29.

FUNCTIONAL LITERACY : INDIA : UTTAR PRADESH

Mulay, Sumati, 1976, Uttar Pradesh literacy and family planning behaviour of rural women, *Indian Journal of Adult Education* 37 (1) January, p9-10, tabs.

FUND RAISING

See

Educational Fund Raising

GIFTED STUDENT

See

Talented Student

GIRLS EDUCATION

See
Co-education
Education

GOVERNMENT WOMEN'S PRIMARY TEACHERS TRAINING COLLEGE, PUNE, INDIA

Progress of Education (Periodical), 1970, Centenary of the Government Women's Primary Teachers Training College, Poona, *Progress of Education* 44 (7) February, p578, editorial

GOVERNMENT TRAINING COLLEGE FOR WOMEN, ALLAHABAD, INDIA

Joshi, C.C., 1949, Government Training College for Women, Allahabad, *Shiksha* 1 (3) January, p56-59.

GRAM SEVIKA : INDIA

Devadas, Rajammal P., 1956, Rural women's uplift : Role of the Gram Sevika, *Indian Journal of Adult Education* 17 (1) March, p37-43.

See also
Rural Education

GROUP WORK IN EDUCATION

Anon, 1984, Group discussion reports, *Indian Journal of Adult Education*, 45 (12) December, p20-27.

GURUKUL : INDIA : GUJARAT

Thanki, Harijiwan, 1968, Gurukul's role in girls' education in Gujarat, *Indian Education* 7 (10-11) September-October, p 32-34.

HARIJANS

See
Scheduled Castes and Scheduled Tribes : Harijans

HEALTH AND HYGIENE

Anon, 1981-82, Women and health, *Prasar* 8 (3-4) October-January, p18-25.

HEALTH AND NUTRITION EDUCATION

See
   Nutrition Education

HIGHER EDUCATION

Ahmad, Karuna, 1979, Equity and women's higher education, *Journal of Higher Education* 5 (1) Monsoon, p33-49.

————, 1984, From secondary to higher education : Focus on women, *Journal of Higher Education* 9 (3) Spring, p349-62, refs.

Aneja, Nirmala, 1966, Use of higher education by women, *Social Welfare*, 13, p1-3.

Anon, 1975, Higher education and status of women in India, *Journal of Higher Education* 1 (2) Autumn, p270-72.

Desai, Neera, 1977, Pattern of higher education of women and role of a woman's university, *Journal of Higher Education* 3 (1) Monsoon, p5-19, refs., tabs.

Gopalaratnam, Ranga, 1962, Life in a women's college, *Education Quarterly* 14 (56) December, p267-69.

Inamdar, Hemant V., 1984, A separate university for women, *Progress of Education* 59 (5) December, p90-94 +.

John, Pushpita, 1982, New Approaches to higher education for women, *Education Quarterly* 34 (4) October, p28-30.

Mazumdar, Vina, 1975, Higher education of women in India, *Journal of Higher Education* 1 (2) Autumn, p156-65, tabs.

Murugkar, Lata, 1983, Development goals and women's higher education, *Journal of Higher Education* 8 (3) Spring, p321-26.

Nigam, Raghuvir Sahay, 1970, Universities and female education, *Educational India* 36 (7) January, p233-34 +.

Oak, A.W., 1984, Life-styles of home science graduates, *Research Bulletin* 19 (3-4) September-December, p10-32, tabs.

Padmavati, S., 1975, Higher medical education for women, *Journal of Higher Education* 1 (2) Autumn, p256-58 refs.

Ravindranathan, M.R., 1976, Development of women's education at the university stage, *Journal of Higher Education* 1 (2) Autumn, p258-62, refs, tabs.

Ramachandran Nair, K.R., 1981, Women's education and women's colleges, *University News* 19 (6) March 15, p159-60.

Sharma, Narayan Prasad, 1988, Women and higher education, *Yojana* 32 (21), p6-8.

Sharma, Savitri, 1978, A study of the influence of socio-economic backgrounds in regard to the development of different types of values among female college students, *Asian Journal Psychology and Education* 3 (1) January 1978, p21-29, refs, tabs.

Shastri, Diwakar, 1989, Women's universities or universities for women : Mission of women's institutions in higher education, *University News* 27 (23) p3-5.

Srivastava, Sumita, 1985, College going girls : Their occupational choices, goals and problems, *Journal of Indian Education* 11 (2) July, p40-44.

Uchat, D.A. and Desai, Haribhai, 1982, Self concept of female students of single sex colleges and co-education colleges, *Journal of Institute of Educational Research* 6 (2) May, p32-36, refs.

Wasi, Muriel, 1978, The case for co-educational colleges vs women's colleges, *New Frontiers in Education* 8 (1) January-March, p42-46.

HIGHER EDUCATION : INDIA

Krishnaraj, Maithreyi, 1977, Employment pattern of university educated women and its implications, *Journal of Higher Education* 2 (3) Spring p317-27, appen, refs.

Saxena, Vinodini, 1956, The heroes of adolescent college girls, *Education* 10 (4) October, p313-31, refs.

HIGHER EDUCATION : INDIA : KERALA

Fernandez, Marilyn, 1985, University education for what : The case of Kerala women, *New Frontiers in Education* 15 (1), p82-5.

HIGHER EDUCATION : INDIA : RAJASTHAN

Talesra, Hem Lata, 1986, Higher education among women : An analyses of the situation in a district of India, *Perspective in Education* 2 (2) April, p121-24.

————, 1986, Women's higher education : A feudal background, *Journal of India Education* 11 (6), p66-74.

HIGHER EDUCATION : INDIA : UTTAR PRADESH

Anon, 1967, U.P. universities urged to set up adult education department, *Indian Journal of Adult Education* 28 (5) May, p4.

HIGHER EDUCATION : KOREA

Kim, Okgill, 1978, The place of women's colleges : The Korean experience : EWHA University, *New Frontiers in Education* 8 (1) January-March, p47-56, appen.

HIGHER EDUCATION : PHILIPPINES

Atienza, Maria Fe G., 1966, The Philippine Women's University and extramural education for women, *Indian Journal of Adult Education* 27 (7) July, p11-16.

HIGHER EDUCATION : UNITED KINGDOM

Hodgkim, Edward, 1949, Women's college celebrates Centenary *Educational India*, 15 (12) June, p345-46.

HIGHER EDUCATION OF WOMEN

See

Higher Education

HINDU GIRLS HIGHER SECONDARY SCHOOL, DELHI, INDIA

Anon, 1979, Delhi's grand-old-lady, *Femina*, December 23, p 33.

HOME ECONOMICS

See

Home Science

HOME AND SCHOOL

Sen Gupta, Kamal, 1956, Home and school cooperation as experienced in Lady Irwin School, *Educational Forum* 1 (3) July, p18-20.

HOME SCIENCE

Karlekar, Kalyani, 1960, Special curriculum for girls in secondary education, *Teacher Education* 4 (2) February, p33-36.

Oak, A.W., 1984, Life-style of home science graduates, *Research Bulletin* 19 (3-4) September-December, p10-32, tabs.

Deulkar, Durga, 1960, Place of home science in secondary education for girls, *Teacher Education* 4 (2) February. p29-32.

HUMAN RESOURCE : WOMEN

Agrawal, Bina, 1976, Exploitation utilisation of educated women power, *Journal of Higher Education* 2 (2) August, p185-95, refs, tabs.

Chandresekaran, Raj Kumari, 1983, Women power must be exploited too! *Hindu*, October 25, p19.

Saxena, Daya and Bhatnagar, Suman Devi, 1985, A comparative study of time utilisation pattern of tribal and non-tribal women in Rajasthan, *Indian Journal of Extension Education* 21 (1-2) January-June, p83-85, tabs.

ILLITERACY

See

Functional Literacy.

IMPACT OF EDUCATION

Kashyap, S.S., 1976, Impact of women's education, *Education Quarterly* 28 (2) July, p21-22.

INDIA : NATIONAL COMMITTEE ON WOMEN'S EDUCATION, 1958, NEW DELHI

See

National Committee on Women's Education, 1958, New Delhi India.

INDIAN UNIVERSITIES ASSOCIATION FOR CONTINUING EDUCATION : ROLE

Indian Universities Association for Continuing Education, 1989, Empowerment of women : Multi-disciplinary perspective, *University News* 27 (4), p9-10.

INSTITUTE OF MARKETING AND MANAGEMENT : ROLE

S.N.D.T. Women's University and Institute of Marketing and Management, Association of Women Entrepreneurs and Executives, 1989, Seminar on working women — challenges ahead, *University News* 27 (23), p31-32.

INTERACTION ANALYSIS

Seth, M., 1983, Group interaction among adult women participating in the functional literacy programme in Delhi, *Indian Journal of Extension Education* 9 (1-2) March-June, p62-68, refs, tabs

————, *et al*, 1983, Group intraction among women participates of a functional literacy programme in Delhi : A study, *Indian Journal of Adult Education* 44 (10) October, p24-28, refs, tabs.

See also

Group Work in Education

INTERNATIONAL CONFERENCE ON PUBLIC EDUCATION, 15TH, 1952, GENEVA

Anon, 1952, Women and education, *Shiksha* 5 (1) July, p7-10, repr.
————, 1952, Women's access to education : Geneva Conference examines problem, *Educational India* 19 (3) September, p99.

INTERNATIONAL EDUCATION

Saran, Raksha, 1965, International understanding and cooperation through education — teachers role : A symposium : Women education, *Education Quarterly* 17 (67), September-December, p142-44.

INTERNATIONAL FEDERATION OF UNIVERSITY WOMEN CONFERENCE, AUGUST 12, 1950, ZURICH

Bodet, Jaimes Torre, 1950, Excerpts from the address to the Conference of the International Federation of University Women at Zurich on August 12, 1950, *Education* 29 (15) August, 25, p27-29.

INTERNATIONAL UNDERSTANDING

See

International Education

INTERNATIONAL WOMEN'S YEAR

Chitnis, S., 1975, International Women's Year : Its significance for women in India, *Social Action* 25 (3), p203-220.
Haksar, N.J., 1976, What Women's Year should mean, *Mainstream* 16 (18), p29.
Saradmoni, K., 1975, Waiting for hopeful tomorrow : International Women's Year, *Mainstream* 13 (43), p11-12, 24.

See also

United Nations World Conference of the International Women's Year, 1975, Mexico.

JUVENILE DELINQUENCY

See
    Adolescent Girls : Deliquency

KARVE, ANNASAHAB

See
    Karve, Dhondo Keshav

KARVE, DHONDO KESHAV : ROLE

Divam, Sharada, 1961, S.N.D.T. Women's University : Dr. Karve's experiment, *Educational India* 27 (11-12) May-June, p389-91.

KASTURBA NATIONAL MEMORIAL TRUST : GUJARAT BRANCH : INDIA

Anon, 1964, Activities of Kasturba Trust : Gujarat branch, *Indian Journal of Adult Education* 25 (4) April, p5.

LADY IRWIN SCHOOL: DELHI: INDIA

Sen Gupta, Kamala, 1956, Home and school cooperation as experienced in Lady Irwin School, *Educational Forum* 1 (3) July, p18-20.

LEADERS AND LEADERSHIP

Anon, 1983, Leadership development among rural women, *New Frontiers in Education* 13 (2) April-June, p73-107.

Mehta, Sushila, 1961, Where shall we look for leaders? *Indian Journal of Adult Education* 22 (2) February, p9-10.

LIFE STYLES

Oak, A.W., 1984, Life-styles of home science graduates, *Research Bulletin* 14 (3-4) September-December, p10-32.

LITERACY

See
    Functional Literacy

MALE TEACHERS

Anon, 1979, Ban on male teachers for girls schools held void, *Times of India*, September 1, p3.

MANPOWER

See
Human Resource : Women

MASS MEDIA

Hooja, G.B.K., 1987, Women's status, family life, education and the media, *University News* 25 (14), p4-6.

Sandhu, D.K. and Shukla, A.N., 1981, Content analysis of Tiranjan programme of AIR Jullunder, *Indian Journal of Extension Education* 17 (3-4) September-December, p7-16, refs.

Sharma, Kumud, 1985, Women and media : A case for critical correction, *Indian Journal of Adult Education* 46 (9) September, p27-30.

Singh, R.P., 1969, Wanted a teacheress : A study in newspaper advertisements, *NIE Journal* 4 (1) September, p50-52.

MEDICAL EDUCATION

Padmavati, S., 1975, Higher medical education for women, *Journal of Higher Education* 1 (2) Autumn, p256-58, refs.

MILTON, JOHN : ROLE

Adarsh Bala, 1976, Milton's misogyny, *Journal of Indian Education* 1(5), p45-50.

MOTHERS : ROLE

Hema Kumari, T.A., 1977, Role of the mother and education achievement of the child, *Education Quarterly* 28 (3) October, p16-21.

See also
Role of Women

MOTHER TERESSA WOMEN'S UNIVERSITY : ROLE

Mother Teressa Women's University, 1987, Methodology for women's studies, *University News* 25 (50), p81.

————, 1989, Seminar on women's studies as an academic discipline, *University News* 27 (17), p16.

MUSLIM WOMEN

Agrawal, Mamta, 1981, A study of the impact of education on social and cultural modernisation of Hindu and Muslim women, *Indian Educational Review* 16 (1) January, p72-77.

Beg, Shahnaz Hashmi, 1975, Educational problems of the Muslim women, *Journal of Indian Education* 1 (4) November, p8-13.

Rallia Ram, Mayawani, 1975, Muslim educated women in North India, *Journal of Higher Education* 1 (2) August, p250.

Shavani, Nusrat, 1981, Muslim girls education, *National Herald*, February 21, p 7.

MOTIVATION IN EDUCATION

Kulwinder Singh, 1985-1986, Academic motivation among high school students in relation to academic achievement and sex, *Journal of Education and Psychology* 43 (3-4) October-January, p164-68.

NAEP

See

National Adult Education Programme

NEP

See

National Education Policy

NATIONAL ADULT EDUCATION PROGRAMME : INDIA

Rana, Kamala, 1980, NAEP and the movement of educational women, *Prasar* 7 (1-2) April-July, 39-47.

NATIONAL COMMITTEE ON WOMEN'S EDUCATION, 1958, NEW DELHI: INDIA

Anon, 1959, Measures for rapid expansion of women's education in India : Main recommendations of the Durgabai Deshmukh Committee's report, *Naya Shikshak* 2 (1-2) January-April, p111-117.

NATIONAL DEVELOPMENT AND EDUCATION

Dutt, Sunitee, 1959, National planning and vocations for women *Educational Forum*, 4 (1) January, p8-11.

Kappor, M., 1978, Women's education for nations development, *Indian Journal of Adult Education* 39 (7) July, p32-34.

Mathias, T.A., 1988, Women's education and development : The key to a brighter future in Asia, *New Frontiers in Education* 18 (3), p42-57.

Murugkar, Lata, 1983, Development goals and women's higher education, *Journal of Higher Education* 8 (3), Spring, p321-326.

Pillai, J.K., 1976, Educating women for national development, *Education Quarterly* 27 (4) January, p31-33.

NATIONAL EDUCATION POLICY

Mother Teressa Women's University, 1988, Implementation of NEP with special reference to education for women's equality : Report, *University News* 26 (24), p17.

NEHRU, JAWAHAR LAL VIEWS ON WOMEN'S EDUCATION

Dewani, Lakshman, 1989, Nehru and emancipation of Indian women, *Patriot*, December 16.

NON-FORMAL EDUCATION

Anon, 1984, Non-formal adult education for women, *Indian Journal of Adult Education* 45 (12) p13-19.

Dighe, Anita, 1985, Non-formal education for women, *Social Change* 15 (3), p40-45.

Dutta, S.C., 1985, Develope non-formal structures to educate women, *Indian Journal of Adult Education* 46 (4) April, p11-13.

Haque, Adhila, 1978, Understanding rural school going girls : An implication for non-formal education, *Indian Journal of Adult Education* 39 (4) April, p27-31, tabs.

Jayawera, S., 1979, Programmes of non-formal education for women, *Indian Journal of Adult Education* 40 (12) December, p33-45.

Kidwai, Mohsina, 1984, Develop unconventional measures of education, *Indian Journal of Adult Education* 45 (12) December, p9-11.

Koshy, T.A., 1975, Non-formal education for rural women : An experimental project for the development of the young child, *Indian Journal of Adult Education* 36 (1-2) January-February, p17-19.

Lakshminarayana, M., 1985, Non-formal education for women, *EPA Quarterly Bulletin* 8 (1-2) April-July, p40-44.

Seth, Mridula, 1977, Production centre as venues for non-formal education of women, *Indian Journal of Adult Education* 38 (7), p36-38.

Shah, Gunvant, B., 1976, Non-formal education for women, *Indian Journal of Adult Education* 37, June, p13-15.

Swaminathan, Mina, 1982, Needed two revaluations in one non-formal education for women and girls, *Education Quarterly* 34 (4) October, p5-7.

NUTRITION EDUCATION

Shafi, Rafat, S., 1978, Literacy and nutrition education in the context of adult education programme for young females, *Indian Journal of Adult Education* 39 (2) February, p17-27, refs.

OCCUPATIONAL CHOICES

Srivastava, Sumita, 1985, College going girls : Their occupational choices, goals and problems, *Journal of Indian Education* 11 (2) July, p40-44.

See also
Vocational Education

PRAI

See
Planning, Research and Action Institute, Lucknow, India

PART TIME EMPLOYMENT

Safaya, Raghunath, 1964, Part time employment of women teachers, *Educational Review* 70 (4), p86-87.

PERFORMANCE : ACADEMIC

Vasudeva Rao, B.S., 1986, Adult education programme : A study on women performance, *Indian Journal of Adult Education* 47 (6) June, p8-12, tabs.

See also
Academic Achievement

PHYSICAL EDUCATION AND TRAINING

Abildgaard, Jorgine, 1958, Physical education for girls, *Shiksha* 11 (1) July, p62-65.

PHYSICAL EDUCATION FOR WOMEN

See
Physical Education and Training

PLANNING, RESEARCH AND ACTION INSTITUTE, LUCKNOW : WOMEN SECTION : ROLE

Anon, 1960, The Sangrahalaya : A nucleus for work among women in rural areas, *Indian Journal of Adult Education* 21 (1) January, p13-16.

Indian Journal of Adult Education (Periodical), 1966, Welfare project for U.P. women : PRAI's pioneering efforts, *Indian Journal of Adult Education* 27 (4) April, p1-2, editorial.

PRIMARY EDUCATION

Anon, 1985, New thrust to primary education for girls, *Hindustan Times*, July 9, p10.

Menon, Lakshmi N., 1969, Article 45 and primary education of girls, *Education Quarterly* 21 (1) April, p5-8.

PRODUCTION CENTRES

Seth, Mridula, 1977, Production centre as venues for non-formal education of women, *Indian Journal of Adult Education* 38 (7), p36-38.

PROFESSIONAL EDUCATION

Dutt, Sunitee, 1959, National planning and vocations for women in India, *Education Forum* 4 (1) January, p8-12.

Seddy, S.C., 1983, Trends in professional education among women *Journal of Higher Education* 8 (3) Spring, p327-34.

PROFESSIONS

Dutt, Sunitee, 1959, National planning and vocations for women in India, *Educational Forum* 4 (1) January, p8-11.

Satvir Singh, and Kaur, Harjit, 1976, The relationship of motives, aspiration and anxiety among women teachers at different professional levels, *Asian Journal of Psychology and Education* 1 (2) July p1-11, refs. tabs.

Verma, P.C. and Srivastava, B.K., 1983, A study of attitudes of teachers towards women's participation in social activities and professions, *Asian Journal of Psychology and Education* 11 (1), p21-27.

PROGRESSIVE EDUCATION : INDIA : MAHARASHTRA : BOMBAY

Benjamin, Margaret, 1965, Progressive education : Alexander Girls English Institute, Bombay, *Indian Education* 4 (8-9) July-August, p38-39.

PROGRESSIVE SCHOOLS

See

Progressive Education

PROJECT MAHER : INDIA

Chiplunkar, V.V., 1987, Education and development of women : Project Maher, *Journal of Education and Administration* 1 (2), p173-90.

PSYCHOLOGICAL ASPECT OF EDUCATION

Bhushan, L.I., 1961, Development of women's social freedom scale : A report, *Asian Journal of Psychology and Education* 7 (2) July, p34-38.

Chhabra, Rami, 1980, Establishing linkages between women's literacy programme, status issues and access to family planning, *Indian Journal of Adult Education* 41 (4) April, p6-9.

Christian, J.A., 1980, A correlational study of students performance, *Journal of Institute of Educational Research* 4 (1) January, p16-19, refs.

Gupta, Madhu and Gupta Prabha, 1979, Delinquent tendencies in the adolescent girls at different age levels and the effect on verbal learning, *Asian Journal of Psychology and Education* 4 (3) November, p6-8.

————, 1979, Family problems of adolescent girls as related to problems in other areas and delinquent tendencies, *Journal of Education and Psychology* 37 (1) April, p67-72, refs.

Jha, J. and Saxena, Bimla, 1983, A study of disadvantages associated with different socio-economic groups of girls studying in secondary schools, *Journal of Education and Psychology* 41 (1-2) April-July, p12-16.

Kulwinder Singh, 1985-1986, Academic motivation among high school students in relation to academic achievement and sex, *Journal of Education and Psychology* 43 (3-4) October-January, p164-68.

Paranjape, S.D., 1974, Problem's of graduate employed women : A socio-psychological study and attitude survey, *Indian Dissertation Abstracts* 2 (2) p101-103.

Rai, Kamala, 1985, Adjustment of secondary school girls studying in co-education and regregated institutions in relation to their socio-economic status, *National Journal of Education* 7 (2) May, p46-55.

Ranjit Singh and Saini, R.K., 1984; Socio-personal correlates and gain in the knowledge of correspondance course trainees, *Indian Journal of Adult Education* 45(4) April, p 30-33, tabs.

Santhanam, M.R. and Buch, M.D., 1971, Sex of the teacher as a factor of teacher class room behaviour, *Indian Educational Review* 6 (2) July, p47-68, refs, tabs.

Sehgal, Krishna, 1979, The impact of sex and academic disciplines on the level knowledge of current affairs, *Progress of Education* 53 (12), July, p223-271, tabs.

Sharma, Savitri, 1978, A study of the influence of socio-economic backgrounds in regard to the development of different types of values among female college students, *Asian Journal Psychology and Education* 3 (1) January, 1978, p21-29, refs, tabs.

Sudha, B.G. and Tirath, Lalitha G., 1979, The effect of personality trail variation of the intensity of problems of girls, *Journal of Education and Psychology* 37 (2) July, p103-17, refs.

Sudha, B.G. and Goetha, S., 1982, Problems of girls as a function of material employment and anxiety, *Journal of Institute of Educational Research* 6 (1) January, p27-37, refs, tabs.

Uchat, D.A. and Desai, Haribhai, G., 1982, Self concept of female students of single sex colleges and co-education colleges, *Journal of Institute of Educational Research* 6 (2) May, p32-36, refs.

Venkata Rama Reddy, A. and Balakrishna Reddy, P., 1984, Creativity of adolescent boys and girls in relation to some variables, *Indian Educational Review* 19 (1) January, p60-72.

Zafar Umar, 1979, Acquisition of general information : Role of sex and generally intelligence, *Educational Review*, February, 1979, p25-28, refs, tabs.

See also

RADIO IN EDUCATION

See

RAMASWAMY, SEETHALAKSHMI : ROLE

See

READING INTERESTS

See

> Books and Reading
> Text books

RESEARCH

See

> Educational Research

RESERVE BANK OF INDIA : ROLE

Anon, 1980, Education of girls best investment: Reserve Bank of India study, *Economic Times*, October 18, p 7.

RIGHT OF WOMEN

See

> Women : Legal Status, Laws, etc.

RIGHT TO EDUCATION

Mathur, V.S., 1979, Indian women's right to education, *Education Quarterly* 31 (1) April, p18-20.

ROLE OF WOMEN

Amiruddin, Mir, 1949, Women's role in adult education, *Educational India* 16 (5) November, p138-39.

Chattopadhyay, Kamaladevi, 1969, Role of women in modern India, *Education Quarterly*, 21 (1) April, p12-14.

George, Mary, 1954, Women's role in social education under the community projects, *Indian Journal of Adult Education* 15 (1) March, p17-22.

Pillai, J.K., 1982, The dual role of women, *New Frontiers in Education* 12 (4) October-December, p39-42.

Tripathi, Madhukanta, 1985, Women's struggle for the new roles, *National Journal of Education* 7 (2) May, p56-60, appenx, refs.

RURAL EDUCATION AND RURAL DEVELOPMENT

Acharlu, K.S., 1977, Two hour rural school for small villages *Educational India* 43 (10) April, p223-26.

Anon, 1958, Rural women and community development, *Indian Journal of Adult Education* 19 (2) June, piv-v.

————, 1968, Extension of project on farmer's education and functional literacy urged, *Indian Journal of Adult Education* 29(11) November, p3.

Dubey, V.K. *et al*, 1978, Training rural women for change, *Indian Journal of Adult Education* 39 (7) July, p35-38.

Roy, Sushila, 1959, Women education in villages, *Naya Shikshak* 2 (3) July, p76-79.

Sharma, Premlata, 1984, Study habit and under-achievement among rural girls, *Journal of Education and Psychology* 12 (3), October, p115-18, refs.

Swaminathan, M.S., 1982, Women and rural development, *New Frontiers in Education* 12 (3) July-September, p56-63.

Tawde, Sunanda, S., 1958, Progress in education in rural and urban areas, *Teaching* 31 (2) December, p48-54.

Wiser, W.H., 1958, The lamplighter : Review of a guide book for development work among rural women, *Indian Journal of Adult Education* 19 (2) June, p25-28.

RURAL EDUCATION AND RURAL DEVELOPMENT : AFRICA

Faget, Claire, 1966, African women help in rural education and training, *Educational India* 32 (9) March, p329-30.

RURAL EDUCATION AND RURAL DEVELOPMENT : INDIA

Acharlu, K.S., 1966, Teacher's in rural education, *Educational India* 33 (2) August, p72, letter to editor.

Anon, 1960, The Sangrahalaya : A nucleus for work among women in rural areas, *Indian Journal of Adult Education* 21 (1) January, p13-16.

————, 1983, Leadership development among rural women, *New Frontiers of Education* 13 (2) April-June, p73-107.

Devadas Rajammal, P., 1956, Rural women's uplift : Role of the Gram Sevika, *Indian Journal of Adult Education* 17 (3) March, p 37-42.

Haque, Adhila, 1978, Understanding rural school going girls: An implication for non-formal education, *Indian Journal of Adult Education* 39 (4) April, p27-31, tabs.

Katiyar, S.N., 1962, Modernisation and the rural women, *Teacher Today* 24 (3) January-March, p20-26, tabs.

Kosy, T.A., 1975, Non-formal education for rural women : An experimental project for the development of the young child, *Journal of Indian Adult Education* 36 (1-2) January-February, p17-19.

Mohan Lal, 1961, Problems of girls' education in rural areas, *Education Quarterly* 13 (50) Summer, p167-69.

Nimbkar, Krishnabai, 1955, Rural women's uplift : The role of the Bharatiya Grameena Mahila Sangh, *Indian Journal of Adult Education* 16 (4) December, p25-29.

Rai, S., 1975, Education or our rural women folk, *Education Quarterly* 27 (2) July, p18-19.

————, 1985, More female teachers must in rural schools, *Hindustan Times*, February 6, p20.

Srivastava, K.N., 1961, Women's education in rural communities, *Education Quarterly* 13 (50) Summer, p170-74

————, and Rawat, B., 1982, Attitudes of Harijan women towards education : A comparative study of a city and surrounding villages, *Indian Journal of Adult Education* 43 (7) July, p27-31, refs, tabs.

RURAL EDUCATION AND DEVELOPMENT : INDIA :
ANDHRA PRADESH

Achanta, Laxmi Devi, 1983, Measurement of values of rural women, *Indian Journal of Extension Education* 19 (3-4) September-December, p83-89, refs, tabs.

Rani, Jhansi, and Bhave, Asha M., 1982, Actual and desired type of participation by rural women in selected areas of decision-making, *Indian Journal of Extension Education* 18 (1-2) January, p83-89, tabs.

RURAL EDUCATION AND RURAL DEVELOPMENT :
INDIA : HARYANA

Sharma, S. and Singh, T.R., 1984, Rural women's level of knowledge and persuasion for the acceptance of solar cooker device, *Indian Journal of Extension Education* 20 (1-2) June, p47-51, refs.

Verma, T. and Verma, S., 1985, Training needs of rural women : An action research, *Indian Journal of Extension Education* July-December, p104-07, tabs.

RURAL EDUCATION AND RURAL DEVELOPMENT : INDIA : PUNJAB

Mangal, Shavinder K. and Roy, Sunita, 1983, Participation and interest of rural school going girls in household and farm activities, *Indian Journal of Extension Education* 19 (1-2) March-June, p69-73.

RURAL EDUCATION AND RURAL DEVELOPMENT : INDIA : UTTAR PRADESH

Mulay, Sumati, 1976, Uttar Pradesh literacy and family planning behaviour of rural women, *Indian Journal of Extension Education* 37 (1) January, p9-10, tabs.

S.N.D.T. WOMEN'S UNIVERSITY

See

Shremati Nathibai Damodar Thackersey Women's University, Bombay, India

S.U.P.W.

See

Socially Useful Production Work (Vocational Education)

SANGRAHALAYA, LUCKNOW (INDIA)

See

Planning, Research and Action Institute, Lucknow (India)

SCHEDULED CASTES AND SCHEDULED TRIBES : HARIJANS

Srivastava, R.K. and Rawat, B., 1982, Attitudes of Harijan women towards education : A comparative study of a city and surrounding villages, *Indian Journal of Adult Education* 43 (7) July, p27-31, refs, tabs.

SECONDARY EDUCATION

Anon, 1979, Delhi's grand old lady, *Femina*, December 23, p33.

————, 1985, Free education upto 10 + 2 for girls soon, *Times of India*, February 6, p16.

Brockway, K.N., 1953, Secondary education for Indian girls, *Journal of Education and Psychology* 10 (4) January, p201-04.

Deulkar, Durga, 1960, Place of home science in secondary education for girls, *Teacher Education* 4 (2) February, p29-32.

Ghosh, Molina, 1949, Reading interests of high school girls, *Journal of Education and Psychology* 6 (4) January, p182-89.

Hariani, Kamla, 1970, Educational and vocational aspiration and planning by high school girls, *Journal of Education and Psychology* 28 (3) October, p122-28, refs, tabs.

Jha, J. and Saxena, Bimla, 1983, A study of disadvantages associated with different socio-economic groups of girls studying in secondary schools, *Journal of Education and Psychology* 41 (1-2), April-July, p12-16.

Jacob, Ayseha, 1975, The place of women's education in the ten plus two scheme, *Education Quarterly* 27 (2) July, p16-17.

Karlekar, Kalyani, 1960, Special curriculum for girls in secondary education, *Teacher Education* 4 (2) February, p33-36.

Karve, B.D., 1953, The future of girls' secondary education, *Journal of Education and Psychology* 10 (4) January, p236-40.

Kumar, Rajni, 1982, Secondary education for girls : The what and the how, *Education Quarterly* 34 (4) October, p31-33.

Passi, B.K., 1970, Patterns of vocational aspirations of higher secondary school adolescents in relation to sex and residential back grounds, *Journal of Education and Psychology* 28 (3) October, p57-63 +, tabs.

Rai, Kamala, 1985, Adjustment of secondary school girls studying in co-education and regregated institutions in relation to their socio-economic status, *National Journal of Education* 7 (2) May, p46-55.

Vyas, K.C. and Tripathi, Harish, 1987, Education for high school girls, *Educational India* 3 (10) April, p338-40.

Wills, Inez Ray, 1960, Girls in commercial education in secondary schools, *Teacher Education* 4 (2) February, p19-23.

SEMINAR ON WOMEN AND DEVELOPMENT, 1988

Alagappa University, centre for women's studies and Rural Technology, 1989, seminar on women and development, *University News* 27 (2), p 31.

SEMINAR ON WOMEN'S STUDIES AS AN ACADEMIC DISCIPLINE, 1989

Mother Teressa Women's University, 1989, Seminar on women studies as an academic discipline, *University News* 27 (17), p. 16.

SEMINAR ON WORKING WOMEN — CHALLENGES AHEAD, 1989

S.N.D.T. Women's University and Institute of Marketing and Management, Association of Women Entrepreneurs and Executives, 1989, Seminar on working women — challenges ahead, *University News* 27 (23), p31-32.

SEX EDUCATION

See
Sex Instruction

SEX INSTRUCTION

Gupta, Pushpa and Gupta, Indu, 1984, Sex knowledge of school girls and their mothers, *Progress of Education* 58 (6) January, p138-42.

Saraswat, Renuka, 1974, Sex education : How a college girl looks at it, *Education Quarterly* 26 (1) April, p21-22.

SEX ROLE

Zafar Umar, 1979, Acquisition of general information : Role of sex and general intelligence, *Educational Review* 85 (2) February 1979, p25-28, refs, tabs.

SHREEMATI NATHIBAI DAMODAR THACKERSEY WOMEN'S UNIVERSITY, BOMBAY, INDIA

Divan, Sharada, 1961, S.N.D.T. Women's University : Dr. Karve's experiment, 27 (11-12) May-June, p389-91.

Progress of education (Periodical), 1950, Indian Women's University: S.N.D.T. University, *Progress of Education* 24 (8) March, p312, editorial

SHREEMATI NATHIBAI DAMODAR THACKERSEY WOMEN'S UNIVERSITY, BOMBAY, INDIA : ROLE

S.N.D.T. Women's University and Institute of Marketing and Management, Association of Women Entrepreneurs and Executives, 1989, Seminar on working women — challenges ahead. *University News* 27 (23), p31-32.

SLUMS

Ida Singh, 1981, Continuing education for women in slums, *Experiments in Education* 9 (6) August, p99-102.

Khanna, Kailash, 1977, Effectivity of follow-up material for girl dropouts in a slum of Delhi, *Indian Journal of Adult Education* 38 (12) December, p10-16, tabs.

Padma, K., 1983, Attitudes, of literate women of Hyderabad slums, *Experiments in Education*, 11 (8) October, p138-40.

SOCIAL AND MORAL QUESTIONS

Bhushan, L.I., 1981, Development of women's social freedom scale : A report, *Asian Journal of Psychology and Education* 7 (2) July, p34-38.

See also
Social Education

SOCIAL EDUCATION

Ahmad, Karuna, 1985, The social context of women's education in India, 1921-81: Tentative formulations, *New Frontiers in Education* 15 (3), p1-36

Anon, 1961, Demonstration home, *Indian Journal of Adult Education* 22 (9) September, p16-18.

Bhatnagar, Bimla, 1960, Social education for women, *Education Quarterly* 12 (47) Autumn, p240-41.

Bhushan, L.I., 1981, Development of women's social freedom scale : A report, *Asian Journal of Psychology and Education* 7 (2) July, p34-38.

Dutta, S.C., 1980, Women's education for civic and social responsibilities, *Indian Journal of Adult Education* 28 (12) December, p3-4.

George, Mary, 1954, Women's role in social education under the community projects, *Indian Journal of Adult Education* 15 (1) March, p17-22.

Mahishi, Sarojini, 1969, Towards a new social outlook, *Education Quarterly* 21 (1) April, p33-35.

Misra, Lakshmi, 1962, The importance of the social attitude in the development of women's education in India, *Shiksha* 14 (4) April, p148-51.

Naik, Chitra, 1970, Social transformation and equal educational opportunity for girls and women, *Naya Shikshak* 13 (1) July-September, p59-60.

Padma, K., 1983, Attitude of literate women of Hyderabad slums, *Experiments in Education* 11 (8) October, p138-40.

Pandeya, Ramprasad, 1975, Education : Social attitudes and women's progress, *Educational Review* 81 (10) October, p193-96

Varma, P.C. and Srivastava, B.K., 1983, A study of attitudes of teachers trainees towards women's participation in social activities and professions, *Asian Journal of Psychology and Education* 11 (1) p21-27.

SOCIAL TABOOS

Saran, Raksha, 1965, Teachers role in the eradication of the social taboos in girls' education, *Education Quarterly* 17 (67) September-December, p175-77.

SOCIAL TRANSFORMATION

See

Educational Sociology

SOCIALLY USEFUL PRODUCTIVE WORK

See

Vocational Education

STATE AID TO EDUCATION : INDIA

Anon, 1968, Programme for the promotion of girls education in the Fourth

Plan, *Education Quarterly* 20 (1) April, p32-33.

————, 1984, Education plan for girls, benefits 8,000, *Times of India*, (Bombay), April 9, p4.

————, 1985, More funds urged for women's education, *Indian Express*, October 1, p7.

————, 1986, Central grants for women's upliftment, *Statesman*, December 20, p8.

Deshmukh, Durgabai, 1960, Expansion of women's education under the Third Plan, *Education Quarterly* 12 (48) Winter, p286-93.

Dutt, Sunitee, 1959, National planning and vocations for women, *Educational Forum* 4 (1) January, p8-11.

Educational India (Periodical), 1952, The Five Year Plan and women's education, *Educational India* 19 (2) August, p56-59, editorial.

Saran, Raksha, 1962, Expanding women's education in the Third Plan *Shiksha* 15 (2) October, p50-55.

STATISTICS

See

Educational Statistics

STUDENTS

See

Women Students

STATUS OF WOMEN

Anon, 1975, Higher education and status of women in India, *Journal of Higher Education* 1 (2) Autumn, p270-72.

Chhabra, Rami, 1980, Establishing linkages between women's literacy programmes, status issues and access to family planning, *Indian Journal of Adult Education* 41 (4) April, p6-9.

Hooja, G.B.K., 1987, Women's status, family life, education and the media, *University New* 25 (14), p4-6.

Israney, S.M., 1989, Status of women in the academic world : Indian context, *University News* 27 (23), p11-14.

Jain, Devaki, 1975, Content of education : Its relevance to the status of women, *Education Quarterly* 27 (2) July, p7-9.

Mazumdar, Vina, 1975, Educational development and changes in women's status, *Journal of Indian Education* 1 (4) November, p3-7.

Sengupta, M., 1989, Women's status : What is the concept of equality? *Hindu*, February 7.

Seth, Padma, 1975, The status of women and their legal rights, *Journal of Indian Education* 1 (4) November, p28-33.

Shamsuddin, 1960, Status of women in ancient India, *Progress of Education* 35 (1) April, p10-12.

Verma, Vinod Kumar, 1988, Status of women : Student's views, *Tribune*, August 28.

SYMPOSIUM ON INTERNATIONAL UNDERSTANDING AND COOPERATION THROUGH EDUCATION — TEACHERS ROLE

Saran, Raksha, 1965, International understanding and cooperation through education — teachers role : A symposium : Women education, *Education Quarterly*, September-December, p142-144.

TAGORE, RABINDRANATH : VIEWS ON WOMEN'S EDUCATION

Mukherjee, H.B., 1961, Tagore on women's education, *Education Quarterly* 13 (50) Summer, p123-27.

TALENTED STUDENTS

Pande, Mrinal 1988, Where do the women toppers go? *Hindustan Times*, August 19.

TEACHERS

Acharlu, K.S. 1966, Teachers wife in rural education, *Educational India* 33 (2) August, p72, letter to editor

Anon, 1952, Women and education, *Progress of Education* 25 (12) July, p335-37.

————, 1979, Ban on male teachers for girls school held void, *Times of India*, September 7, p3.

Buch, M.B., 1971, Sex of the teacher as a factor of teacher classroom behaviour, *Indian Educational Review* 6 (2) July, p47-68, refs, tabs.

Mathur, B.S., 1948, Current thoughts on education, *Education* 27 (18) October 31, p31-32.

Rai, S., 1985, More female teachers must in rural schools, *Hindustan Times*, February 6, p20.

Saran, Raksha, 1965, International understanding and cooperation through education teacher role : A symposium : Women education, *Education Quarterly* 17 (67) September, December, p142-44.

————, 1965, Teachers role in the eradication of social taboos in girls education, *Education Quarterly* 17 (67) September-December, p175-77.

Satvir Singh and Kaur, Harjit, 1976, The relationship of motives, aspiration and anxiety among women teachers at different professional levels, *Asian Journal of Psychology and Education* 1 (2) July, p1-11, refs, tabs.

Singh, R.P., 1969, Wanted a teacheress : A study in newspaper advertisements, *NIE Journal* 4 (1) September, p50-52.

TEACHERS : INDIA

Progress of Education (Periodical) 1970, Centenary of the Government Women's Primary Teachers Training College, Poona, *Progress of Education* 44 (7) February, p578, editorial.

Srivastava, Saroj, 1963, Education of women teachers, *Education Quarterly* 15 (57) March, p16-19.

Safaya, Raghunath, 1964, Part time employment of women teachers, *Educational Review* 70 (4) April, p86-87.

TEACHERS : MALE

See
Male Teachers

TEACHER TRAINEES

Verma, P.C., and Srivastava, B.K., 1983, A study of attitudes of teachers trainees towards women's participation in social activities and professions, *Asian Journal of Psychology and Education* 11(1), p21-27.

TEXT BOOKS

Kalia, Narendra Nath, 1984, Changing images of males and females : How of feminist sex role liberation in Indian school text books, *Indian Education* 13 (10-11) January-February, p10-16.

Ury, Glaude M., 1972, Women in U.S. school history textbooks, *Educational Review* 78 (9), p197-203.

See also
Books and Reading
Curricula

TRIBAL EDUCATION

Mehta, B.H., 1969, Education of tribal women and girls, *Education Quarterly* 21 (1) April, p44-46.

Saxena, Daya and Bhatnagar, Suman Rani, 1985, A comparative study of time utilisation pattern of tribal and non-tribal women in Rajasthan, *Indian Journal of Extensions Education* 21 (1-2) January-June, p83-85, tabs.

See also
Scheduled Castes and Scheduled Tribes : Harijans

U.N.

See
United Nations

UNCONVENTIONAL MEASURES OF EDUCATION

Kidwai, Mohsina, 1984, Develop unconventional measures of education, *Indian Journal of Adult Education*, 45 (12) December, p9-11.

See also
Non-formal Education

UNDERACHIEVERS

Sharma, Premlata, 1984, Study habits and underachievement among rural girls, *Journal of Education and Psychology*, 42 (3) October, p115-18, refs.
Vaish, J.D., 1962, Help younger and weaker brothers and sisters, *Educational India* 29 (4) October, p133-35.

See also
Academic Achievement

UNITED NATIONS WORLD CONFERENCE OF THE INTER-NATIONAL WOMEN'S YEAR 1975, MEXICO

Anon, 1975, United Nations World Conference of the International Women's Year, *Journal of Indian Education* 1 (4) November, p43-45.
Ramchandran, Padma, 1975, The World Conference on Women, *Journal of Indian Education* 1 (7) November, p24-27.

See also
International Women's Year

VATSALYADHAM POST-BASIC FOR GIRLS

Kapur, R.K., 1969, Vatsalyadham Post-Basic for Girls, *Educational India* 35 (7) January, p241-42.

VERBAL LEARNING

Gupta, Madhu and Gupta Prabha, 1979, Deliquent tendencies in the adolescent girls at different age levels and their effect on verbal learning, *Asian Journal of Psychology and Education* 4 (3) November, p6-8.

VIDYA SAGAR, ISHWARCHAND : VIEWS ON WOMEN'S EDUCATION

Dhirendranath, Ghosh, 1955, Vidyasagar and women's education in Bengal, *Journal of Education* 2 (3-4) Conference Number, p157-63.

VOCATIONAL EDUCATION

Agarwal, S.M., 1965, Impact of education on career of girls, *Education and Psychology Review* 5 (1) January, p34-37.

Kumar, Usha A., 1975, Job oriented education for girls : Some practical and theoretical considerations, *Education Quarterly* 27 (3) October, p14-15.

Mehta, Perin, H., and Mehta, H.P., 1974, Vocational preparation and the employment of women, *Education Quarterly* 26 (2) July, p1-4, refs.

See also
Business Education
Employment

VOCATIONAL EDUCATION : INDIA

Anon, 1984, New vocational training programme for women, *Statesman*, February 28, p4.

Devadas, Rajammal P., 1969, Vocational education for women, *Education Quarterly* 21 (1) April, p15-21.

Kapur, R.K., 1969, Vatsalyadham Post-Basic for Girls, *Educational India* 35 (7) January, p241-42.

Mehta, Perin, H. and Mehta H.P., 1974, Vocational preparations and the employment of women, *Education Quarterly* 26 (2) July, p1-4, refs.

Venkatalakshmi, V., 1960, Women and commercial education, *Educational India* 27 (1) July, p17-18.

See also
Business Education
Employment

VOCATIONAL GUIDANCE

Ganguly, Shailaja, 1975, Can women manage : Management as a career for women, *Education Quarterly* 27 (2) July, p4-6.

VOCATIONAL INTERESTS

See also
Women's Interests

VOCATIONAL INTERESTS : INDIA : HARYANA

Hariani, Kamala, 1970, Educational and vocational aspirations and planning by high school girls, *Journal of Education and Psychology* 28 (3) October, p 122-128, refs, tabs.

VOCATIONAL INTERESTS : INDIA : PUNJAB

Passi, B.K., 1970, Patterns of vocational aspirations of higher secondary school adolescents in relation to sex and residential background, *Journal of Education and Psychology* 28 (3) October, p57-63 +, tabs.

VOCATIONS

See
Professions

VOLUNTARY ORGANISATIONS : ROLE

Chandrasekaran, Rajkumari, 1977, Role of voluntary organisations in meeting the needs of women in the field of adult education and female literacy, *Indian Journal of Adult Education* 38 (5) May, p 16-24, refs.
Nimlekar, Krishnabai, 1961, voluntary organisations and women's education, *Indian Journal of Adult Education*, 22 (3) March, p5-7.
Saran, Raksha, 1969, Voluntary organisations and women's education, *Education Quarterly* 21 (1) April, p29-32.

WASTAGE IN EDUCATION

See
Dropouts

WOMEN : LEGAL STATUS, LAWS, ETC. : INDIA

Mazumdar, Vina, 1975, Educational development and changes in women's status, *Journal of Indian Education* 1 (4) November, p3-7.

Menon, Lakshmi N., 1969, Article 45 and primary education of girls, *Education Quarterly* 21 (1) April, p5-8.

Seth, Padma, 1975, The status of women and their legal rights, *Journal of India Education* 1 (4) November, p28-33.

WOMEN AND MEDIA

See

Mass Media

WOMEN AND WORK

Anon, 1986, (Book review), *New Frontiers in Education* 16 (2) April-June, p106-08.

Review of the book : Lebra, Joyee, *et al, Woman and Work in India: Continuity and Change*, Promila, New Delhi, 310 p.

WOMEN AS ADMINISTRATORS

Anon, 1983, Leadership development among rural women, *New Frontiers in Education* 13 (2) April-June, p73-104.

Ganguly, Shailaja, 1975, Can women manage : Management as a career for women, *Education Quarterly* 27 (2) July, p4-6.

Mehta, Shushila, 1961, Where shall we look for leaders? *Indian Journal of Adult Education* 22 (2) February, p9-10.

Waston, Leonard E. and Thakkar, Usha, 1989, The management development of women administrators : Some considerations, *University News* 27 (23), p15-16.

WOMEN AS EXECUTIVES

See

Women as Administrators

WOMEN AS MANAGERS

See

Women as Administrators

WOMEN AS SOCIAL WORKERS

George, Mary, 1954, Women's role in social education under the community projects, *Indian Journal of Adult Education* 15 (1) March, p17-22.

Verma, P.C. and Srivastava, B.K., 1983, A study of attitudes of teachers towards women's participation in social activities and professions, *Asian Journal of Psychology and Education* 11 (1), p21-27.

See also
Women in Community Development

WOMEN AS SOCIAL WORKERS : INDIA : UTTAR PRADESH

Geldens, Maria, 1956, The Women's Welfare Scheme in Uttar Pradesh, *Indian Journal of Adult Education* 17 (9) September, p5-11.

See also
Women in Community Development
Women's Welfare Scheme : India : Uttar Pradesh

WOMEN AS TEACHERS

See
Teachers

WOMEN IN COMMUNITY DEVELOPMENT

Anon, 1961, Demonstration home, *Indian Journal of Adult Education* 22 (9) September, p16-18.

Devadas, Rajammal P., 1956, Rural women's uplift : Role of the Gram Sevika, *Indian Journal of Adult Education* 17 (3) March, p37-42.

Mehta, Sushila, 1961, Where shall we look for leaders, *Indian Journal of Adult Education* 22 (2) February, p9-10.

WOMEN IN EDUCATION

See
Teachers

WOMEN IN INDIA

Kalia, Narendra Nath, 1984, Changing images of males and females : How of feminist sex role liberation in Indian school text books, *Indian Education* 13 (10-11) January-February, p10-16.

WOMEN IN LITERATURE

Adarsh Bala, 1976, Million's misogyny, *Journal of Indian Education* 1 (5) January, p45-50.

WOMEN IN SCIENCE AND TECHNOLOGY

Educational India (Periodical), 1966, Women and scientific education, *Educational India* 33 (3) September, p92-93, editorial.

Kumar, Kamla and Khitha, Sadhana, 1982, Women in science and technology, *Education Quarterly* 34 (4) October, p8-10, refs.

Educational India (Periodical), 1966, Women and scientific education, *Educational India* 33 (3) September, p92-93, editorial.

Raman, Usha,1988, Why few women take to science? *Deccan Chronicle*, November 27.

WOMEN IN SOCIAL SERVICE

See
Women as Social worker

WOMEN IN UNITED STATES OF AMERICA

Ury, Glaude, M., 1972, Women in U.S. school history textbooks, *Educational Review* 78 (9) September, p197-203.

WOMEN POWER

See
Human Resource : Women

WOMEN STUDENTS

Anand, Kulwant, 1965, Attitudes of Punjab University women students towards marriage and the family, *Indian Journal of Social Work* 26, p87-90.

Anon, 1980, (Book review) *Education Quarterly* 32 (2) July, p46-47; Indian Education, p. 45-47; *Naya Shikshak* 23 (1) July-September, p103; *Teacher Education* 14(10-11) January-April, p 76-77; *Indian Education* 15 (2); p128-29.

　　Review of the book : Sharma, Savitri, 1980, *Women Students in India : Status and Personality*, Concept Publishing Company, New Delhi, 171 p.

Christian, T.A., 1980, A correlational study of students performance, *Journal of Institution of Educational Research* 4 (1) January, p16-19, refs.

Gill, Betty, 1948, Indian girls study in Australia enjoy student life at domestic college, *Education* 27 (12) 31 July, p6-7.

Gopalaratnam, Ranga, 1962, Life in a women's college, *Education Quarterly* 14 (56) December, p267-69.

Jacob, Planthodathil, S., 1985, Women students programme in co-educational context : A case study, *New Frontiers in Education* 15 (1) January-March, p77-81.

Kulwinder Singh, 1985-1986, Academic motivation among high school students in relation to academic achievement and sex, *Journal of Education and Psychology* 43 (3-4) October-January, p164-68.

Mangat, Shavinder K. and Roy, Sumita, 1983, Participation and interest of rural school going girls in farm activities, *Indian Journal of Extension Education* 43 (7) July, p22-31, refs, tabs.

Mehta, Perin H., 1968, The felt needs of female students and their implications for education, *NIE Journal* 3 (1) September, p13-18, refs.

Oak, A.W., 1984, Life styles of home science graduates, *Research Bulletin* 17 (3-4) September-December, p10-32, tabs.

Panda, K.C., 1962, A comparative study of attitudes of students reading in co-educational and single sex institutions towards co-educational practices in India, *Journal of Education and Psychology* 19 (4) January, p190-98, refs, tabs.

Rai, Kamala, 1984, Problems of girls in co-educational institutions, *National Journal of Education* 7 (1) September, p29-38, refs, tabs.

Saraswati, Renuka, 1974, Sex education : How a college girls looks at it, *Education Quarterly* 26 (1) April, p21-22.

Saxena, Vinodini, 1956, The heroes of adolescent college girls, *Educator* 10 (4) October, p213-31, refs.

Sharma, Savitri, 1978, A study of the influence of socio-economic backgrounds in regard to the development of different types of values among female college students, *Asian Journal of Psychology and Education* 3 (1) January 1978, p21-29, refs, tabs.

Srivastava, Sunita, 1985, College going girls : Their occupational choices, goals and problems, *Journal of Indian Education* 11 (2) July, p40-49.

Uchat, D.A. and Desai, Haribhai G., 1982, Self concept of female students of single sex colleges and co-education colleges, *Journal of Institute of Educational Research* 6(2) May, p 32-36, refs.

Uplaonkar, U.T., 1983, Occupational aspirations of college students, *Social Change* 13(2), p 16-26.

WOMEN'S CHRISTIAN COLLEGE, MADRAS : ROLE

Anon, 1978, Statements and recommendations of the Consultation on "Designing education for tomorrow's women", held at Women's Christian College, Madras, under the auspices of All India Association for Christian

Higher Education, in December, 1977, *New Frontiers in Education* 8 (1) January-March, p81-84.

WOMEN'S COLLEGES

Ramachandran Nair, K.R., 1981, Women's education and women's colleges, *University News* (6) March, p159-60.

Wasi, Muriel, 1978, The case for co-educational colleges vs women's colleges, *New Frontiers in Education* 8 (9) January-March, p42-46.

See also
 Arya Kanya Mahavidyalaya, Baroda, India
 Bedford College (United Kingdom)
 Lady Irwin College, Delhi, India

WOMEN'S COLLEGES : KOREA

Kim, Okgill, 1978, The place of women's colleges : The Korean experience : EWHA University, *New Frontiers in Education* 8 (1) January-March, p47-56, appen.

WOMEN'S COLLEGES : UNITED KINGDOM

Hodgkim, Edward, 1949, Women's college celebrates centenary, *Educational India* 15 (12) June, p345-55.

WOMEN'S EDUCATION

See
Education

WOMEN'S EDUCATION : ROLE

Jaishankar, V., 1979, Role of women's education in India, *Hindu*, October 9, p3.

WOMEN'S EMPLOYMENT

See
Employment

WOMEN'S INTERESTS

Suryakumari, A., 1988, Women's interests, *University News* 26 (45), p1-3.

See also
   Psychological Aspect of Education

WOMEN'S ROLE

See
   Role of Women

WOMEN'S STUDIES

Mazumdar, Vina, 1981, Women's studies : Challenge to educational system, *Economic and Political Weekly* 16, May, p890-92.

Mother Teressa Women's University, 1987, Methodology for women's studies, *University News* 25 (50), p81.

————, 1989, Seminar on women's studies as an academic discipline, *University News* 27 (17), p16.

Yoon, Young Soon, 1983, Women's studies : Is it relevant? *Samya Shakti* 1 (1), p5.

WOMEN'S WELFARE SCHEME : INDIA : UTTAR PRADESH

Geldens, Maria, 1956, The Women's Welfare Scheme in Uttar Pradesh, *Indian Journal of Adult Education* 17 (9) September, p5-11.

See also
   Women as Social Workers

WOMEN'S UNIVERSITIES : ROLE

Desai, Neera, 1977, Pattern of higher education of women and role of a woman's university, *Journal of Higher Education* 3 (1) Monsoon, p5-19, refs, tabs.

Inamdar, Hemant V., 1984, A separate university for women, *Progress of Education* 59 (5) December, p90-94 +.

Nigam, Raghuvir Sahay, 1970, Universities and female education, *Educational India* 36 (7) January, p233-34 +.

Shastri, Diwakar, 1984, Women's universities or universities for women : Mission of women's institutions in higher education, *University News* 27 (23) p3-5.

WORKING WOMEN

Paranjape, S.D., 1974, Problem's of graduate employed women : A socio-psychological study and attitude survey, *Indian Dissertation*

Abstracts 2 (2), p101-103.

S.N.D.T. Women's University and Institute of Marketing and Management, Association of Women Entrepreneurs and Executives, 1989, Seminar on working women — challenges ahead, *University News* 27 (23), p31-32.

See also
Employment

7.3 CHRONOLOGICAL INDEX

1947

Gopalaratnam, D.L., 1947, The educated girl in India, *Educational India* 13 (8) February, p265-66.

Seethamma, M.N., 1947, Women and adult education, *Indian Journal of Adult Education* 8(1) January, p7-9; 8(3) March, p7-8.

1948

Anon, 1948, Britain's schools undertake new experiment: Further extension of co-education, *Education* 27(20) November 30, p 22-23.

Educational India (Periodical), 1948, Women's education, *Educational India* 14 (8) February, p229; 15 (3) September, p97-98, editorial.

Gill, Betty, 1948, Indian girls study in Australia enjoy student life at domestic college, *Education* 27(12) July 31, p 6-7.

Mathur, B.S., 1948, Current thought on education, *Education* 27(18) October 31, p 31-32.

Munshi, K.M., 1948, Educational sparks, *Education* 27(19) November 15, p 35-37.

Santosh, Maria Ulfah, 1948, Brief survey of the Indonesian women's movement, *Education* 27(5) March, p 24-27.

Venkata Rao, Lakshmi, 1948, Adult education in the city of Mysore with special reference to education among women, *Indian Journal of Adult Education* 9(1) January, p 21-24.

1949

Amiruddin, Mir, 1949, Women's role in adult education, *Educational India* 16(5) November, p138-39.

Chinnappa, Padmavati, 1949, The education of women adults, *Education* 28(19) 30 November, p12-14.

Engler, M., 1949, Adult education for women, *Educational India* 16(5) November, p139.

Hookens, William, Edward, 1949, On co-education, *Education* 28(7) April 15, p21-22.

Hodgkin, Edward, 1949, Women's college celebrates centenary, *Educational India* 15(12) June, p345-46.

Patnaik, Narasinga, 1949, Education for women, *Educational Review* 55(2) February, p28-29.

Shukla, M.M., 1949, Sex differences in inducive reasoning during early adolescence, *Journal of Education and Psychology* 6(4) January, p172-76

1950

Anon, 1950, Girls education, *Shiksha* 3(1) July, p26-27; 3(2) October, p65-67

Bodet, Jaimes Torre, 1950, Excerpts form the address to the Conference of the International Federation of University Women at Zurich on 12 August 1950, *Education* 29(15) August 25, p27-29.

Education (Periodical), 1950, Girls education, *Education* 29(21) November 25, p3-4, editorial.

Progress of Education (Periodical), 1950, Indian Women's University: S.N.D.T. University, *Progress of Education*, 24(8) March, p312, editorial.

Sapra, Ramlal, 1950, Girls education in schools, *Education* 29(15) August 25, p24-26.

1951

Anon, 1951, Girls Education, *Shiksha*(3) January, p46-49; 3(4) April, p24-28; 4(1) July, p105-07; 4(2) October, p122-24.

Lal, Prem Chand, 1951, Education of women and girls in India today, *Education* 30(14) August 31, p7-11.

Gandhi, T.K., 1951, Girls education, *Shiksha* 3(3) January, p46-49.

Nanda, Anant, 1951, The school and the adolescent girls, *Educational Forum* 2(3) July, p27-30.

1952

Anon, 1952, Women's access to education: Geneva Conference examines problem, *Educational India* 19(3) September, p99.

————, 1952, Women and education, *Educational India* 19(1) July, p7-8.

————, 1952, Women and education, *Educational Quarterly*, June, p104-05.

————, 1952, Women and education, *Educational Review* 58(6) June, p108-09, repr.

————, 1952, Women and education, *Progress of Education* 25(12) July, p335-37.

————, 1952, Women and education, *Shiksha*, July, p7-10, repr.

Educational India (Periodical), 1952, The Five Year Plan and women's education, 1952, *Educational India* 19(2) August, p56-59, editorial.

Rao, Waman, 1952, Co-education and present Indian opinion, *Educational Review* 58(12) p230-34.

Saksena, Gopala Krishna, 1952, Co-education: The need of the hour, *Educational India* 18(10) April, p283-86.

1953

Brockway, K.N., 1953, Secondary education for Indian girls, *Journal of Education and Psychology* 10(4) January, p201-04.

————, 1953, Changes in girls education, 1927-52, *Teaching* 25(4) June, p143-44.

Educational India (Periodical), 1953, Education of women, *Educational India* 20(3) September, p91-93, editorial.

Karve, B.D., 1953, The future of girls secondary education, *Education and Psychology* 10(4), January, p236-40.

Razdan, Prithvi Nath, 1953, Educating the destitute, *Educational India* 19(7) January, p203-07,

Sabha, V.R., 1953, Educating the destitute, *Education* 32(1) January, p13-19.

1954

George, Mary, 1954, Women's role in social education under the community projects, *Indian Journal of Adult Education* 15(1) March, p17-22.

Mukherji, Latika, 1954, Women and adult education, *Journal of Indian Adult Education* 15(3) March, p13-16.

Roberts, Funics Carmichael, 1954, Curricula for women, *Educational Review* 60(10) October, p196-98.

1955

Ghosh, Dhirendranath, 1955, Vidyasagar and women's education in Bengal, *Journal of Education* 2(3-4) Conference Number, p157-63.

Mathur, V.S., 1955, Should boys and girls study together? *Education* 4(3) July, p135-37.

Nimbkar, Krishnabai, 1955, Rural women's uplift: The role of the Bharatiya Grameen Mahila Sangh, *Indian Journal of Adult Education* 16(4) December, p25-29.

Norris, Louis William, 1955, How to educate a woman, *Educational Review* 61(9) September, p169-71, repr.

Razdan, Prithvi Nath, 1955, The Kashmir government's education policy, *Educational India* 22(1) July, p8-12.

1956

Choksi, M., 1956, Co-education in India, *Education Quarterly* 8(32) December, p377-79.

Devadas, Rajammal, P., 1956, Rural women's uplift: Role of the Gram Sevika, *Indian Journal of Adult Education* 17(1) March, p37-43.

Dutt, U.C., 1956, Women's education, *Shiksha* 9(2) October, p89-94.

Geldens, Maria, 1956, The Women's Welfare Scheme in Uttar Pradesh, *Journal of Indian Adult Education* 17(3) September, p5-11.

Khanna, K.C., 1956, Co-education in India, *Education Quarterly* 8(32) December, p382-83.

Mulay, Vijay, 1956, Co-education in India, *Education Quarterly* 8 (32) December, p379-81.

Murray, A.R. 1956, Women's education at Oxford and Cambridge, *Educational Review* 62(9) September, p169-70

Saxena, Vinodini, 1956, The heroes of adolescent college girls, *Education*, 10(4) October, p213-31, refs.

Sen Gupta, Kamala, 1956, Home and school cooperation as experienced in Lay Irwin School, *Educational Forum* 1(3) July, p18-20.

Sundaram, N.K., 1956, Co-education in India, *Education Quarterly* 8(32) December, p381-82.

1956-57

Mukherjee, L., 1956-57, Education of women in India: Past and Present, *Education* 35(12), December, p5-9; 36(1) January, p5-10.

1957

Anon, 1957, Some facts and figures about women in Soviet Russia, *Education* 36 (5) May, p26-27.

1958

Abildgaard, Jorgine, 1958, Physical education for girls, *Shiksha* 11(1) July, p62-65.

Education (Periodical), 1958, All India Council for Women's Education, *Education* 37(6) June, p1-3, editorial.

Educational India (Periodical), 1958, Problems on women's education, *Educational India*, August 25(2) p53-56, editorial.

Gopal Krishna, 1958, Women's education in India, *Educational India* 25(2), August, p45-48.

Tawde, Sunanda S., 1958, Progress in education in rural and urban areas, *Teaching* 31(2) December, p48-54.

Wiser, W.H., 1958, The Lamplighter: Review of a guide book for development work among rural women, *Indian Journal of Adult Education* 19(2) June, p25-28.

1959

De, S.K., 1959, Progress of women's education in India, *Education* 38(7) July, p5-11.

Dutt, Sunitee, 1959, National planning and vocations for women, *Educational Forum* 4(1) January, p8-11.

Educational India (Periodical), 1959, Education for women, *Educational India* 25(11-12) May-June, p 424-25, editorial.

————, 1959, Priority for women's education, *Educational India* 25 (8) February, p314-16, editorial.

Jain, M.K., 1959, Women's education in Indian, *Educational Review* 65 (5) May, p97-98.

Roy, Shushila, 1959, Women education in villages, *Naya Shikshak* 2(3) July, p 76-79.

Srimali, K.L., 1959, Future of women's education, *Educational India* 25 (7) January, p248-50.

1960

Anon, 1960, Access of women to education, *Indian Journal of Adult Education* 21 (11) November, p18.

————, 1960, Co-education in the United States, *Education* 39 (8) August, p13-15.

————, 1960, The Sangrahalaya : A nucleus for work among women in rural areas, *Indian Journal of Adult Education* 21 (1) January, p13-16.

Bhatnagar, Bimla, 1960, Social education for women, *Education Quarterly* 12 (47) Autumn, p240-41.

Deshmukh, Durgabai, 1960, Expansion of women's education under the Third Plan, *Education Quarterly* 12 (48) Winter, p289-93.

————, 1960, Women's education : A major problem, *Educational India* 27 (3) September, p78-82.

Deulkar, Durga, 1960, Place of home science in secondary education for girls, *Teacher Education* 4 (2) February, p29-32.

du Sautey, Peter, 1960, Educating grandmothers, *Indian Journal of Adult Education* 21 (11) November, p12-14.

Karlekar, Kalyani, 1960, Special curriculum for girls in secondary education, *Teacher Education* 4(2) February, p33-36.

Saran, Raksha, 1960, Education of women, *Educational India* 26 (8) February, p263-64.
(Address of Mrs. Raksha Saran, at the 29th session of the All India

Women's Conference, Madras, 1959).

Shamsuddin, 1960, Status of women in ancient India, *Progress of Education* 35 (1) April, p10-12.

Sita Ram, 1960, Progress of women's education in Uttar Pradesh, *Shiksha* 12 (3) January, p39-43.

Venkatalakshmi, V., 1960, Women and commercial education, *Educational India* 27 (1) July, p17-18.

Wells, Inez Ray, 1960, Girls in commercial education in commerce schools, *Teacher Education* 4 (2) February, p19-23.

1961

Anon, 1961, Demonstration home, *Indian Journal of Adult Education* 22 (9) September, p16-18.

D'Souza, Austin A., 1961, Education of women in the U.K. and the U.S.A., *Education Quarterly* 13 (50) Summer, p182-186.

Divan, Sharada, 1961, S.N.D.T. Women's University : Dr Karve's experiment, *Educational India* 27 (11-12) May-June, p389-91.

Harby, Mohammad Khairy and Mehrez, Zenab Mohmoud, 1961, Education of women in the U.A.R., *Education Quarterly* 13 (50) Summer, p178-81.

Mehta, Sushila, 1961, Where shall we look for leaders? *Indian Journal of Adult Education* 22 (2) February, p9-10.

Misra, Lakshmi,1961, Democratic India and women's education, *Education Quarterly* 13 (50) Summer, p119-22.

Mohan Lal, 1961, Problems of girls education in rural areas, *Education Quarterly* 13 (50) Summer, p167-69.

Motwani, Clara, 1961, Education of women in Ceylon, *Education Quarterly* 13 (50) Summer, p175-77.

Mukherjee, H.B., 1961, Tagore on women's education, *Education Quarterly* 13 (50) Summer, p123-27.

Nimbkar, Krishnabai, 1961, Voluntary organisation and women's education, *Indian Journal of Adult Education* 22 (3) March, p5-7.

Srivastava, K.N., 1961, Women's education in rural communities, *Education Quarterly* 13 (50) Summer, p170-74.

1962

Castello, Kathleen, 1962, Women's education in Japan, *Educational Review* 68 (4) April, p94.

Chandy, Anna, 1962, Problems of women's education, *Educational Review* 68 (5) May, p101-03.

Dutta, S.C., 1962, Condensed course for adult women : A new experiment in adult education, *Indian Journal of Adult Education* 23 (8) August, p3-4.

Gopalaratnam, Ranga, 1962, Life in a women's college, *Education Quarterly*

14 (56) December, p267-69.

Misra, Lakshmi, 1962, The importance of the social attitude in the development of women's education in India, *Shiksha* 14 (4) April, p148-51.

Padmanabhan, N.S., 1962, Wither women's education? *Educational Review* 68 (4) April, p90-92.

Panda, K.C., 1962, A comparative study of attitudes of students reading in co-educational and single sex institutions towards co-educational practices in India, *Journal of Education and Psychology* 19 (4) January, p190-98, refs, tab.

Saran, Raksha, 1962, Expanding women's education in the Third Plan, *Shiksha* 15 (2) October, p50-55.

Srivasan, K., 1962, Women and we, men, *Educational India* 28 (11-12) May-June, p351-53.

Turkia, Rauni, 1962, Adult education for Tunisian women, *Indian Journal of Adult Education* 23(7) July, p 11-16; 23(9) September 62, p 4 +.

Vaish, J.D., 1962, Help younger and weaker brothers and sisters, *Educational India* 29 (4) October, p133-35.

1963

Greenough, Richard, 1963, Barriers against schooling for girls, *Educational Review* 69 (6) June, p130-31.

Srivasan, Saroj, 1963, Education of women teachers, *Education Quarterly* 15 (57) March, p16-19.

1964

Anon, 1964, Activities of Kasturba Trust : Gujarat Branch, *Indian Journal of Adult Education* 25 (4) April, p5.

Educational India (Periodical), 1964, Education of girls, *Educational India* 30 (8) February, p276-77, editorial.

————, 1964, Education of women, *Educational India* 30 (9) March, p307-08, editorial.

Mehta, Sushila, 1964, Literacy among women, *Indian Journal of Adult Education* 25 (11) November, p11-12.

Pandit, Pratibha, 1964, Arya Kanya Mahavidyalaya, Baroda, *Indian Education* 3(12) November, p15-18.

Safaya, Raghunath, 1964, Part time employment of women teachers, *Educational Review* 70 (4) April, p86-87.

Varadan, V., 1964, Women : A different education? *Educational Review* 70 (4) April, p75-78.

1965

Agrawal, S.M., 1965, Impact of education on employment of women as career girls, *Education and Psychology Review* 5 (1) January, p34-37.

Anand, Kulwant, 1965, Attitudes of Punjab University women students towards marriage and the family, *Indian Journal of Social Work*, 26, p 87-90.

Avadhesh Dayal, 1965, Women's education, *Education* 44 (7) July, p31-34.

Benjamin, Margaret, 1965, Progressive schools : Alexander Girls English Institute, Bombay, *Indian Education* 4 (8-9) July-August, p36-37.

Chandra Govind, 1965, Adult education programme for women, *Naya Shikshak* 8 (2) October, p71-75.

Labha Singh, 1965, Co-education in India, *Educational Review* 71 (11) November, p246.

Saran, Raksha, 1965, International understanding and cooperation through education — teachers role : A symposium : Women education, *Education Quarterly* 17 (67) September-December, p142-44.

————, 1965, Teachers role in the eradication of the social taboos in girls education, *Education Quarterly* 17 (67) September-December, p157-77.

1966

Acharlu, K.S., 1966, Teachers wife in rural education, *Educational India* 33 (2) August, p72, letter to editor.

Aneja, Nirmala, 1966, Use of higher education by women, *Social Welfare* 13, p1-3.

Atienza, Maria Fe G. 1966, The Philippine women's university and extramural education for women, *Indian Journal of Adult Education* 27 (7) July, p11-16.

Educational India (Periodical), 1966, Women and scientific education, *Educational India* 33 (3) September, p92-93, editorial.

Faget, Claire, 1966, African women help in rural education and training, *Educational India* 32 (9) March, p329-30.

Indian Journal of Adult Education (Periodical), 1966, Welfare project for U.P. women : PRAI's pioneering efforts, *Indian Journal of Adult Education* 27 (4) p1-2, editorial.

1967

Anon, 1967, U.P. universities urged to set up adult education department, *Indian Journal of Adult Education* 28 (5) May, p4.

Educational India (Periodical), 1967, Jobless women, *Educational India* 33 (10) April, p345-46, editorial.

Vyas, K.C., and Tripathi, Harsh,1967, Education for high school girls, *Educational India* 33(10) April, p338-40.

1968

Anon, 1968, Adult education of women in the changing pattern of society : Seminar working paper, *Indian Journal of Adult Education* 29 (10) October, p6-9.

———, 1968, Programmes for the promotion of girl education in the new Fourth Plan, *Education Quarterly* 20 (1) April, p32-33.

Buch, M.B., 1968, Issues and problems in women's education in India, *Education Quarterly* 20 (1) April, p34-37.

Guha, Phulrenu, 1968, Content of literacy for women, *Indian Journal of Adult Education* 29 (11) November, p15-16.

Leela, R.H., 1968, Stray thoughts on the education of Indian girls, *Educational Review* 74 (5) May, p97-98.

Mehta, Perin, H., 1968, The felt needs of female students and the implication for education, *NIE Journal* 3 (1) September, p13-18, refs.

Thanki, Harijiwan, 1968, Gurukul's role in girl's education in Gujarat, *Indian Education* 7 (10-11) September-October, p32-34.

1969

Bhansali, Kamalini H., 1969, Education of women in modern India : Some achievement and problems, *Education Quarterly* 21 (1) April, p36-43.

Chattopadhyay, Kamaladevi, 1969, Role of women in modern India, *Education Quarterly* 21 (1) April, p12-14.

Devadas, Rajammal P., 1969, Vocational education for women, *Education Quarterly* 21 (1) April, p15-21.

Guha, Phulrenu, 1969, Education of women in India : A historical perspective, *Education Quarterly* 21 (1) April, p1-4.

Gyanchand, Anusuya, 1969, Adult women and the spread of literacy, *Education Quarterly* 21 (1) April, p26-28.

Indrasen, Lila, 1969, Reports on progress of girls and women's education in the States : Pondicherry, *Education Quarterly* 21 (1) April, p49-50.

Kapur, R.K., 1969, Vatsalyadham Post-Basic for Girls, *Educational India* 35 (7) January, p241-42.

Mahishi, Sarojini, 1969, Towards a new social outlook, *Education Quarterly*, 21 (1) April, p33-35.

Manohar Rao, G., 1969, Reports on the progress of girls and women's education in the States : Andhra Pradesh, *Education Quarterly* 21(1) April, p47-48.

Mehta, B.H., 1969, Education of tribal women and girls, *Education Quarterly* 21 (1) April, p44-46.

Mehta, Hansa, 1969, Co-education : At what stages and why? *Education Quarterly* 21 (1) April, p22-25.

Menon, Lakshmi, N., 1969, Article 45 and primary education of girls, *Education Quarterly* 21 (1) April, p5-8.

Misra, Prabha, 1969, Reports on the progress of girls and women's education in the States : Rajasthan, *Education Quarterly* 21 (1) April, p50-51.

Nuita, Yoko, 1969, Trends in continuing education of women in Japan, *Indian Journal of Adult Education* 30 (10) October, p5-7.

Panadikar, Sulabhe, 1969, Imbalances in the progress of girls education : Extent and remedy, *Education Quarterly* 21 (1) April, p9-11.

Panda, S.N., 1969, Women's education in India, *Indian Educational Review* 4(2) July, p151-53.
Review article of the book : Misra, Lakshmi, 1966, *Education of Women in India* (1921-66), Macmillan.

Saran, Raksha, 1969, Voluntary organisations and women's education, *Education Quarterly* 21 (1) April, p29-32.

Sharma, Vimla, 1969, Reports on the progress of girls and women's education in the States : Madhya Pradesh, *Education Quarterly* 21(1) April, p48-49.

Singh, R.P., 1969, Wanted a teachers : A study in newspaper advertisements, *NIE Journal* 4 (1) September, p50-52.

Vardappan, Sarojini, 1969, Reports on the progress of girls and women's education in the states : Tamil Nadu, *Education Quarterly* 21 (1) April, p51-53.

1970

Anon, 1970, Advancement of women through access to education, *Education Quarterly* 22 (3) October, p49-55.

Azmat, Rehana, 1970, A thought on girls education, *Education* 49 (3) March, p12-15.

Chopra, Kamala, 1970, Reading interests of adolescent boys and girls, *Educational India* 37 (1) July, p16-19 +; *Progress of Education* 44(12) July, p412-18, refs, tabs.

Hariani, Kamala, 1970, Educational and vocational aspirations and planning by high school girls, *Journal of Education and Psychology* 28 (3) October, p122-28, refs, tabs.

Naik, Chitra, 1970, Social transformation and equal educational opportunity for girls and women, *Naya Shikshak* 13 (1) July-September, p59-66.

Nigam, Raghuvir Sahay, 1970, Universities and female education, *Educational India* 36 (7) January, p233-34 +

Passi, B.K., 1970, Patterns of vocational aspirations of higher secondary school adolescents in relation to sex and residential background, *Journal of Education and Psychology* 28 (3) October, p57-63 +, tabs.

1971

Duncan, Margaret, 1971, Continuing education of women, *Indian Journal of Adult Education* 32 (4) April, p9-12.

Santhanam, M.R., and Buch, M.B., 1971, Sex of the teacher as a factor of Teacher classroom behaviour, *Indian Educational Review* 6 (2) July, p47-68, refs, tabs.

1972

Dharam Vir, 1972, Women education : An effort in Central India, *Indian Journal of Adult Education* 33 (8) August, p9.

Maitra, S.N., 1972, Women's primary and supplementary books, *Indian Journal of Adult Education* 33 (6) June, p14-15.

Ury, Glaude, M., 1972, Women in U.S. school history textbooks, *Educational Review* 78 (9) September, p 197-203.

1973

Sharma, Parabhu Datta, 1973, Women's education : A curricle model for India, *Education Quarterly* 25(2) July, p 12-15.

1974

Perin H. and Mehta, H.P., 1974, Vocational preparation, and the employment of women, *Education Quarterly* 26 (2) July, p1-4, refs.

Paranjape, S.D., 1974, Problem's of graduate employed women : A socio-psychological study and attitude survey, *Indian Dissertations Abstracts* 2 (2), p101-103.

Saraswat, Renuka, 1974, Sex education : How a college girl looks at it, *Education Quarterly*, 26 (1) April, p21-22.

Singh, K.P., 1974, A comparative study of the attitude of working and non-working women towards women's education and employment, *Interdiscipline* 11 (3), p89-100.

1975

Anon, 1975, United Nations World Conference of the International Women's Year, *Journal of Indian Education* 1 (4) November, p43-45.

Beg, Shahnaz Hashmi, 1975, Educational problems of the Muslim women, *Indian Journal Education* 1 (4) p8-13.

Bhansali, Kamalini, H., 1975, Women and the continuing education, *Journal of Indian Education* 1 (4) November, p18-23.

Bose, A., 1975, Census figures reveal discrimination against women, *Organiser* 24 (39), p5.

Chitnis, S., 1975, International Women's Year : Its significance for women in India, *Social Action* 25 (3), p203-220.

Ganguly, Shailaja, 1975, Can women manage : Management as a career for women, *Education Quarterly* 27 (2) July, p4-6.

Jacob, Ayesha, 1975, The place of women education in the ten plus two scheme, *Education Quarterly* 27 (2) July, p16-17.

Jain, Devaki, 1975, Content of education : Its relevance to the status of women, *Education Quarterly* 27 (2) July, p7-9.

Jayaraman, Kunthala, 1975, Education for women : A five year plan, *Journal of Higher Education* 1 (2) Autumn, p255-56.

Journal of Indian Education (Periodical), 1975, (Editorial), *Journal of Indian Education* 1 (4) November, p1-2, editorial.

Kapoor, Ranga, 1975, Career opportunities for women, *Education Quarterly* 27 (2) July, p10-12.

Koshy, T.A., 1975, Non-formal education for rural women : An experimental project for the development of the young child, *Indian Journal of Adult Education* 36 (1-2), January-February, p17-19.

Kumar, Usha A., 1975, Job oriented education for girls : Some practical and theoretical consideration, *Education Quarterly* 27 (3) October, p14-15.

Mazumdar, Vina, 1975, Educational development and changes in women's status, *Journal of Indian Education* 1 (4) November, p3-7.

——, 1975, Higher education of women in India, *Journal of Higher Education* 1 (2) Autumn, p156-65, tabs.

Nayar, Usha, 1975, Women, education and work : A review, *Journal of Higher Education* 1 (2) Autumn, p283-92, refs.

Padmavati, S., 1975, Higher medical education for women, *Journal of Higher Education* 1 (2) Autumn, p256-58, refs.

Pandeya, Ram Prasad, 1975, Education : Social attitudes and women's progress, *Educational Review* 81 (10) October, p193-96.

Rabindranathan, M.R., 1975, Development of women's education at the university stage, *Journal of Higher Education* 1 (2) Autumn, p258-62, refs, tabs.

Rai, S., 1975, Education of our rural women folk, *Education Quarterly* 27 (2) July, p18-19.

Rallia Ram, Mayawanti, 1975, Muslim educated women in North India, *Journal of Higher Education* 1 (2) Autumn, p250.

Ramachandran, Padma, 1975, The World Conference on Women, *Journal of Indian Education* 1 (2) November, p24-27.

United Nations World Conference of the International Women's Year, 1975, Mexico.

Saradmoni, K., 1975, Waiting for hopeful tomorrow : International Women's Year, *Mainstream* 13 (43), p11-12, 24.

Satvir Singh, 1975, Women's education in India : A statistical presentation, *Journal of Indian Education* 1 (4) November, p34-38.

Seth, Padma, 1975, The status of women and their legal rights, *Journal of Indian Education* 1 (4) November, p28-33.

Shah Gunvant, B., 1975, Genesis of women's education in India, *NIE Journal* 9 (3) January, p1-9, refs. tabs.

Venkataraman, Leela, 1975, Change of attitude towards education of women, *Education Quarterly* 27 (2) July, p13-15.

1976

Adarsh Bala, 1976, Milton's misogyny, *Journal of Indian Education* 1(5) January, p45-50.

Agrawal, Bina, 1976, Exploitation utilisation of educated women power, *Journal of Higher Education* 2 (2) August, p185-95, refs, tabs.

Haksar, N.J., 1976, What Women's Year should mean, *Mainstream* 16(18) p29.

Kashyap, S.S., 1976, Impact of women's education, *Education Quarterly* 28 (2) July, p21-22.

Mulay, Sumati, 1976, Uttar Pradesh literacy and family planning behaviour of rural women, *Indian Journal of Adult Education* 37(1) January, p9-10, tabs.

Pillai, J.K., 1976, Educating women for national development, *Education Quarterly* 27 (4) January, p31-33.

Satvir Singh and Kaur, Harjit, 1976, The relationship of motives, aspiration and anxiety among women teacher at different professional levels, *Asian Journal of Psychology and Education* 1(2) July, p1-11, refs, tabs.

Shah, Gunvant, B., 1976, Non-formal education for women, *Indian Journal of Adult Education* 37, June, p13-15.

Shamsuddin, 1976, Developments of women's education in Madhya Pradesh, 1956-1974, *Education Quarterly* 27 (4) January, p34-36.

1977

Acharlu, K.S., 1977, Two hour rural school for small villages, *Education India* 43 (10) April, p223-26.

Chakrabarti, Ashok Kumar, 1977, Causes of women's unemployment in India, *Economic Affairs* 22 (5), p177-84.

Chandrasekaran, Rajkumari, 1977, Role of voluntary organisations in meeting the needs of women in the fields of adult education and female literacy, *Indian Journal of Adult Education* 38 (5) May, p15-24, refs.

Decusker, Mahesh, 1977, A study into the correlation between the scholistic achievements and the achievement in co-curriculum activities of girl students of higher secondary schools of Sagar town, *Progress of Education* 51 (12) July, p221-25, refs, tabs.

Desai, Neera, 1977, Pattern of higher education of women and role of women's university, *Journal of Higher Education* 3 (1) Monsoon, p5-19, refs. tabs.

Hema Kumari, T.A., 1977, Role of the mother and education achievement of the child, *Education Quarterly* 28 (3) October, p16-21.

Khanna, Kailash, 1977, Effectivity of follow-up material for girl dropouts in a slum of Delhi, *Indian Journal of Adult Education* 38(12) December, p10-16, tabs.

Krishnaraj, Maithreyi, 1977, Employment pattern of university educated women and its implications, *Journal of Higher Education* 2 (3) Spring, p317-27, appen, refs.

Pillai, J.K., 1977, Suggested programme for checking problems of dropouts with special reference to girls, *New Frontiers in Education* 7 (4) October-December, p48-55.

Seth, Mridula, 1977, Production centres as venues for non-formal education of women, *Indian Journal of Adult Education* 38 (7) p36-38.

Shamsuddin, 1977, Development of women's education in new Madhya Pradesh, *Educational India* 43 (7) January, p155-58.

1978

Anon, 1978, Council recast for women's education, *Patriot*, July 3, p5.

———, 1978, Statement and recommendations of the Consultation on "Designing education for tomorrow's women", held at Women's Christian College, Madras, under the auspices of All India Association for Christian Higher Education in December, 1977, *New Frontiers in Education* 8 (1) January-March, p81-84.

Barnabas, Manorama, 1978, Designing education for tomorrow's woman : Curricular aspects, *New Frontiers in Education* 8 (1) January-March, p27-41, refs. tabs.

Dubey, V.K., *et al*, 1978, Training rural women for change, *Indian Journal of Adult Education* 39 (7) July, p35-38.

Haque, Adhila, 1978, Needs of rural school going girls : Implication for non-formal education, *Indian Journal of Adult Education* 39 (10) october, p9-13, tabs.

———, 1978, Understanding rural school going girls : An implication for non-formal education, *Indian Journal of Adult Education* 39 (4) April, p27-31, tabs.

Kapoor, M., 1978, Women's education for national development, *Indian Journal of Adult Education* 39 (7) July, p32-34.

Kim, Okgill, 1978, The place of women's colleges : The Korean experience : EWHA University, *New Frontiers in Education* 8 (1) January-March, p47-56, appen.

Mitra, Ashok, 1978, Employment of women, *Manpower* 14 (1), p1-29.

Shaji, Rafat S., 1978, Literacy and nutrition education in the context of adult education programme for young females, *Indian Journal of Adult Education* 39 (2) February, p17-27, refs.

Shah, Madhuri R., 1978, The deal is still unfair, *New Frontiers in Education* 8 (1) January-March, p57-59.

Sharma, Savitri, 1978, A study of the influence of socio-economic backgrounds in regard to the development of different types of values among female college students, *Asian Journal of Psychology and Education* 3 (1) January, 1978, p21-29, refs. tabs.

Wasi, Muriel, 1978, The case for co-educational colleges vs women's college, *New Frontiers in Education* 8 (1) January-March, p42-46.

1979

Ahmad, Karuna, 1979, Equity and women's higher education, *Journal of Higher Education* 5 (1) Monsoon, p33-49.

Anon, 1979, Ban on male teachers for girls schools held void, *Times of India*, September 1, p3.

————, 1979, Challenge of women's education, *Hindu*, October 29, p6; November 2, p9.

————, 1979, Delhi's grand old lady, *Femina*, December 23, p 33. Hindu Girls Higher Secondary School, Delhi.

Gupta, Madhu and Gupta Prabha, 1979, Delinquent tendencies in the adolescent girls at different age levels and the effect on verbal learning, *Asian Journal of Psychology and Education*, 4 (3) November, p6-8.

————, 1979, Family problems of adolescent girls as related to problems in other areas and delinquent tendencies, *Journal of Education and Psychology* 37 (1) April, p62-72, refs.

Jaishankar, V., 1979, Role of women's education in India, *Hindu*, October 9, p3.

Jayaweera, S., 1979, Programmes of non-formal education for women, *Indian Journal of Adult Education* 40 (12) December, p33-45.

Kaur, A., 1979, Adult Education programmes for illiterate women in the age group 15-35, *Indian Journal of Adult Education* 40 (12) December, p19-32.

Kaur, Amrit, 1979, Women education in India today, *Naya Shikshak* 21 (4) April-June, p9-24, tabs.

Mathur, V.S., 1979, Indian women's right to education, *Education Quarterly* 31 (1) April, p18-20.

Sehgal, Krishna, 1979, The impact of sex and academic discipline on the level knowledge of current affairs, *Progress of Education* 53 (12) July, p223-271, tabs.

Sudha, B.G., and Tirath, Lalith G., 1979, The effect of personality trail variation on the intensity of problems of girls, *journal of Education and*

Psychology 37 (2) July, p103-17, refs.
Zafar Umar, 1979, Acquisition of general information : Role of sex and general intelligence, *Educational Review* 85 (2) February 1979, p25-28, refs, tabs.

1980

Anon, 1980, (Book review), *Educational Quarterly* 32 (2) July, p46-47; *Indian Education*, March, p45-47; *Indian Educational Review* 15 (2) February; *Naya Shikshak* 23 (1) July-September, p103; *Teacher Education* 14 (10-11) January-April, p76-77.
Review of the book : Sharma, Savitri, 1980, *Women Students in India : Status and personality*, Concept Publishing Company, New Delhi, 171 p.
————, 1980, Education of girls best investment : Resrve Bank of India study, *Economic Times*, October 18, p 7.
Asha, 1980, Appropriate education for women, *Hindu*, July 9, p5.
Chandrasekaran, Rajkumari, 1980, Designing curriculum and technology for women's adult education programmes, *Indian Journal of Adult Education* 41 (4) April, p19-24.
Chhabra, Rami, 1980, Establishing linkages between women's literacy programmes, status issues and access to family planning, *Indian Journal of Adult Education* 41 (4) April, p6-7.
Christian, J.A., 1980, A correlational study of students performance, *Journal of Institute of Educational Research* 4 (1) January, p16-19, refs.
Dutta, S.C., 1980, Women's education for civic and social responsibilities, *Indian Journal of Adult Education* 28 (12) December, p3-4 +
Educational Review (Periodical) 1980, Re-thinking on women's education, *Educational Review* 70 (9) September, p218, editorial.
Misra, Lakshmi, 1980, Adult education programme and women, *Educational Review* 86 (3) March, p41-43.
Nagappan, T.R., 1980, Adult education for women, *Indian Journal of Adult Education* 41 (8) August, p23-25, refs.
Nigam, Raghuvir Sahay, 1980, Adult education for women, *Educational Review* 86 (3) March, p49.
Pushpamma, P., 1980, Special curriculum for girls, *Hindu*, October 7, p3.
Rana, Kamala, 1980, NAEP and the movement of educational women, *Prasar* 7 (1-2) April-July, p39-47.
Saunders, Fay E., 1980, Discrimination and inequalities between the sexes and school, *Journal of Indian Education* 5 (5) January, p35-42.

1981

Agrawal, Mamta, 1981, A study of the impact of education on social and cultural modernisation of Hindu and Muslim women, *Indian Educational*

Review 16 (2) January, p72-77.

Anon, 1981, (Book review), *Education Quarterly* 33 (3) July, p44-53. Review of the book : Chandler, E.M., 1980, *Education of Adolescent Girls*, Allen and Unwin, London, 217 p.

Bhagat, P., 1981, Evaluation of condensed courses of education for adult women, *Indian Journal of Adult Education* 42 (10) October, p17-20, refs.

Bhushan, L.I., 1981, Development of women's social freedom scale : A report, *Asian Journal of Psychology and Education* 7 (2) July, p34-38.

Dey, Chhaya, 1981, Reform entails a predefinition process, *Progress of Education* 56 (4) November, p85-88.

Ida Singh, 1981, Continuing education for women in slums, *Experiments in Education* 9 (6) August, p99-102.

Mazumdar, Vina, 1981, Women's studies : Challenge to educational system, *Economic and Political Weekly*, May 16, p890-92.

Ramachandran Nair, K.R., 1981, Women's education and women's college, *University News* 19 (6) March, p159-60.

Sandhu, D.K., and Shukla, A.N., 1981, Content analysis of Tiranjan programme of AIR Jullunder, *Indian Journal of Extension* 17 (3-4) July-December, p7-16, refs.

Shervani, Nusrat, 1981, Muslim girls education, *National Herald*, February 21, p7.

Shukla, Sureshchandra, 1981, Perspectives on women's education, *National Journal of Education* 3 (2) March, p7-16.

1981-82

Anon, 1981-1982, Women and health, *Prasar* 8 (3-4) October-January, p18-25.

Hooja, Meenakshi, 1981-1982, Women of Rajasthan : A demographic profile, *Prasar* 8 (3-4) October-January, p1-17, tabs.

1982

Anon, 1982, Scheme to promote girls education, *Times of India*, December 25, p9.

Bhandari, R.K., 1982, Development of women's education, *New Frontiers in Education* 12 (4) October-December, p32-34.

——, 1982, Educational development of women, *Education Quarterly* 34 (3) July, p12-14.

Chainani, R.S., 1982, Woman and the education, *Progress of Education* 57 (4) November, p77-80.

Jacob, A., 1982, Education for women and girls today in cities in India, *Education Quarterly* 34 (4) October, p11-13.

John, Pushpita, 1982, New approaches to higher education for women, *Education Quarterly* 34 (4) October, p28-30.

Katiyar, S.N., 1982, Modernisation and the rural women, *Teacher Today* 24 (3) January-March, p20-26, refs.

Kumar, Kamla and Khitha, Sadhana, 1982, Women in science and technology, *Education Quarterly* 34 (4) October, p8-10, refs.

Kumar, Rajani, 1982, Secondary education for girls : The what and the how, *Education Quarterly* 34 (4) October, p31-33.

Ninan, Sevanti, 1982, Women reluctant to educate daughters, *Indian Express*, November 11, p3.

Pillai, J.K., 1982, The dual role of women, *New Frontiers in Education* 12 (4) October-December, p39-42.

Rana, R.P.S., 1982, Economic aspect of women education, *University News* 20 (23), p 719-724.

Rani, Jhansi and Bhave, Asha M., 1982, Actual and desired type of participation by rural women in selected areas of decision making, *Indian Journal of Extension Education* 18 (1-2), January-June, p83-89, tabs.

Sharma, Radha Rani, 1982, Education of women in India : Inequalities and bottlenecks, *Education Quarterly* 34 (4), October, p20-27, refs, tabs.

Srivastava, R.K. and Rawat, B., 1982, Attitudes of Harijan women towards education : A comparative study of a city and surrounding villages, *Indian Journal of Adult Education* 43(7), July, p27-31, refs, tabs.

Sudha, B.G., and Goetha, S., 1982, Problems of girls as a function of material employment and anxiety, *Journal of Institute of Educational Research* 6 (1), January, p27-37, refs, tabs.

Swaminathan, M.S., 1982, Women and rural development, *New Frontiers in Education* 12(3), July-September, p56-63.

Swaminathan, Mina, 1982, Needed two revaluations in one non-formal education for women and girls, *Education Quarterly* 34(4), October, p5-7.

Uchat, D.A., and Desai, Haribhai G., 1982, Self concept of female students of single sex colleges and co-education colleges, *Journal of Institute of Educational Research* 6(2), May, p32-36, refs.

Wasi, Muriel, 1982, Educating women in India : Ends and means, *Education Quarterly* 34(4), October, p1-4.

1983

Achanta, Laxmi Devi, 1983, Measurement of Values of rural women, *Indian Journal of Extension Education* 19(3-4), July-December, p83-89, refs, tabs.

Anon, 1983, (Book Review), *New Frontiers in Education* 13(1), January-March, p72-73.

————, 1983, Female education still far from good, *Hindustan Times*, June 21, p12.

————, 1983, Leadership development among rural women, *New Frontiers in Education* 13(2), April-June, p73-107.

————, 1983, Measures to boost women's education, *Indian Express*, June 14, p4.

————, 1983, Proper education solution to women's problems, *Hindu*, February 6, p13.

————, 1983, States told to make up lag in girls education, *Hindustan Times*, June 17, p4.

Bhagat, Bankim Bihari, 1983, Making the other half literate. *Indian Express*, February 26, p6.

Chandrasekaran, Raj Kumari, 1983, Women power must be exploited too, *Hindu*, October 25, p19.

Gupta, S.L., 1983, Factors influencing the growth of girls education at the elementary stage, *Indian Educational Review* 18(4), October, p77-92.

Gupta, S.L., 1983, A study of private costs of schooling girls at the elementary state, *EPA Quarterly Bulletin* 6(2), July, p31-40, tabs.

Jha, J., and Saxena, Bimla, 1983, A study of disadvantages associated with different socio-economic groups of girls studying in secondary schools, *Journal of Education and Psychology* 41(1-2), April-July, p12-16.

Kapar, H.L., 1983, Progress in girls education, *National Herald*, October 23, p2.

Mangal, Shavinder K. and Roy, Sunita, 1983, Participation and interest of rural school going girls in household and farm activities, *Indian Journal of Extension Education*, 19(1-2), January-June, p69-73.

Murugkar, Lata, 1983, Development goals and women's higher education, *Journal of Higher Education* 8(3), Spring, p321-26, refs.

Padma, K., 1983, Attitude of literate women of Hyderabad slums, *Experiments in Education* 11(8), October, p138-40.

Ravindran Nair, G., 1983, Education : Why do more girls drop out? *Kurukshetra*, 31(15), p14-16.

Seddy, S.C., 1983, Trends in professional education among women, *Journal of Higher Education* 8(3), Spring, p327-30

Seth, M., et al., 1983, Group interaction among adult women participating in the functional literacy programmes in Delhi, *Indian Journal of Extension Education* 19(1-2), January-June, p62-68, refs, tabs.

————, 1983, Group intraction among women participants of a functional literacy programme in Delhi : A Study, *Indian Journal of Adult Education* 44(10), October, p24-28, refs, tabs.

Uplaonkar, U.T., 1983, Occupational aspirations of college students, *Social Change* 13(2), p16-26.

Varma, P.C. and Srivastava, B.K., 1983, A study of attitudes of teachers trainees towards women's participation in social activities and profession,

Asian Journal of Psychology and Education 11(1), p 21-27.

Yoon, Young Soon, 1983, Women's studies : Is it Relevant: *Samya Shakti*, 1(1), p 5.

1984

Ahmad, Karuna, 1984, From secondary to higher education : Focus on women, *Journal of Higher Education* 9(3), Spring, p349-62, refs.

Anon, 1984, Educating women 'crucial', *Patriot*, February 12, p3.

————, 1984, Education plan for girls benefits 8,000, *Times of India*, (Bombay) April 9, p4.

————, 1984, Female literacy growing, *Patriot*, June 5, p5.

————, 1984, Group discussion reports, *Indian Journal of Adult Education* 45(12), December, p20-27.

————, 1984, Job oriented course for women needed, *National Herald*, September 23, p3.

————, 1984, New vocational training programme for women, *Statesman*, February 28, p4.

————, 1984, Non-formal adult education for women, *Indian Journal of Adult Education* 45(12), p13-19.

————, 1984, Recommendation, *Indian Journal of Adult Education* 45(12), December, p29-31.

Fernandes, Marjorie, 1984, Development of women's education : Problems and suggestions, *Indian Journal of Adult Education* 45(9), p4-9.

Inamdar, Hemant V., 1984, A separate university for women, *Progress of Education* 59(5), December, p90-94+.

Jain, Shobhita, 1984, Women and peoples ecological movement, *Economic and Political Weekly* 20 (27).

Kalia, Narendra Nath, 1984, Changing images of males and females : How of feminist sex role liberation in Indian school text books, *Indian Education* 13(10-11), January-February, p10-16.

Kidwai, Mohsina, 1984, Develop unconventional measures of education, *Indian Journal of Adult Education* 45(12), December, p9-11.

Mane, M.G., 1984, Educate women to reduce inequalities, *Indian Journal of Adult Education* 45(12), December, p7-8.

Oak, A.W., 1984, Life-styles of home science graduates, *Research Bulletin*, 14(3-4), September-December, p10-32, tabs.

Rai, Kamala, 1984, Problems of girls in co-educational institutions, *National Journal of Education* 7(1), September, p29-38, refs. tabs.

Ranjit singh and Saini, R.K., 1984, Socio-personal correlates and gain in the knowledge of correspondence course trainees, *Indian Journal of Adult Education* 45(4), April, p30-33, tabs.

Shahare, M.L., 1984, Eradicating women's illiteracy : A challenge, *Indian Journal of Adult Education* 45(12), December, p32-38.

Sharma, Premlata, 1984, Study habits and underachievement among rural girls, *Journal of Education and Psychology* 42(3), October, p115-18, refs.

Sharma, S. and Singh, T.R., 1984, Rural women's level of knowledge and persuation for the acceptance of solar cooker device, *Indian Journal of Extension Education* 20(1-2), January-June, p 47-51, refs.

Venkata Rama Reddy, A. and Balakrishna Reddy, P., 1984, Creativity of adolescent boys and girls in relation to some variables, *Indian Educational Review* 19(1), January, p60-72.

1985

Ahmad, Karuna, 1985, The social context of women's education in India, 1921-81 : Tentative formulations, *New Frontiers in Education* 15(3), p1-36.

Anon, 1985, Concern on higher drop-out among girls, *National Herald*, April, 14, p12

————, 1985, Free education upto 10 + 2 for girls soon, *Times of India*, February 6, p16.

————, 1985, More funds urged for women's education, *Indian Express*, October 1, p7.

————, 1985, New thrust to primary education for girls, *Hindustan Times*, July 9, p10.

Dighe, Anita, 1985, Non-formal education for women, *Social Change* 15(3), p40-45.

Dutta, S.C., 1985, Development of non-formal structure to educate women, *Indian Journal of Adult Education* 46(4), April, p11-13.

Fernandez, Marilyn, 1985, University education for what : The case of Kerala women, *New Frontiers in Education* 15(1), p82-85.

Jacob, Planthodathil S., 1985, Women students programme in co-educational context : A case study, *New Frontiers in Education* 15(1), January-March, p77-81.

Lakshminarayana M., 1985, Non-formal education for women, *EPA Quarterly Bulletin* 8(1-2), April-July, p40-44.

Mukherji, S., 1985, Benefits we derived from present education, *Yojana* 29(22), p28-30.

Pandey, Balaji, 1985, Eradicating illiteracy among women, *Statesman*, September 11, p6.

Rai, Kamala, 1985, Adjustment of secondary school girls studying in co-education and regregated institutions in relations to their socio-economic status, *National Journal of Education* 7(2), May, p46-55.

Rai, S., 1985, More female teachers must in rural schools, *Hindustan Times*, February 6, p20.

Ravi Kant Singh, 1985, Women's education crucial for child welfare : Children of India, *Patriot*, January 3, p6; January 4, p5.

Saraswathi, T.S., and Gupta, Radhika, 1985, Educate women and you educate family, *Perspectives in Education* 1(1), January, p49-54, refs, tabs.

Saxena, Daya and Bhatnagar, Suma Rani, 1985, A comparative study of time utilisation pattern of tribal and non-tribal women in Rajasthan, *Indian Journal of Extension Education* 21(1-2), January-June, p83-85, tabs.

Saxena, Usha, 1985, Women in India : Education and employment status, *Economic Times*, May 17, p5.

——, 1985, Women in India : Job opportunities and education, *Economic Times*, May 18, p5.

Sharma, Kumud, 1985, Women and media : A case for critical correction, *Indian Journal of Adult Education* 46(9), September, p27-30

Srivastava, Sumita, 1985, College going girls : Their occupational choices goals and problems, *Journal of Indian Education* 11(2), July, p40-14.

Surana, M.L., 1985, Girl dropouts in rural Haryana, *Indian Educational Review* 20(2), April, p109-116.

Tripathi, Madhukanta, 1985, Women's struggle for the new roles, *National Journal of Education* 7(2), May, p56-60, appendix, refs.

Verma, T., and Verma, S., 1985, Training needs of rural women : An action research, *Indian Journal of Extension Education* 21(3-4), July-December, p104-107, tabs.

1985-86

Kulwinder Singh, 1985-86, Academic motivation among high school students in relation to academic achievement and sex, *Journal of Education and Psychology* 43(3-4), October-January, p164-68.

1986

Anon, 1986, (Book Review), *New Frontiers in Education* 16(2), April-June, p106-08.
Review of the book : Lebra, Joyee, *et al, Women and work in India: Continuity and Change*, Promila, New Delhi, 310 p.

Anon, 1986, Call to promote women's education, *National Herald*, January 14, p6.

——, 1986, Central grants for women's upliftment, *Statesmen*, December 20, p8.

——, 1986, Female literacy still deemed unnecessary, *Indian Express*, October 13, p4.

——, 1986, Fund appeal for women's literacy network, *Patriot*, April 30, p3.

——, 1986, Need for women's equality stressed, *Indian Express*, December 21, p3.

————, 1986, Uplift of women through education, *National Herald*, March 12, p5.

Chowdhury, Neerja, 1986, Education for equality, *Statesman*, May 26, p5.

Joshi, Vibha and Menon, Geeta, 1986, Research on women's education in India : A review, *Perspectives in Education* 2(2), April, p77-79.

Nayar, Usha, 1986, Women's education in South Asia, *Patriot*, January 16, p4.

Talesra, Hemlata, 1986, Higher education among women: An analyses of the situation in a district of India, *Perspectives in Education* 2(2), April, p121-25.

————, 1986, Women's higher education : A feudal background, *Journal of Indian Education* 11(6), p66-74.

Vasudeva Rao, B.S., 1986, Adult education programme : A study on women's performance, *Indian Journal of Adult Education* 47(6), June, p8-12, tabs.

1987

Anon, 1987, Big educational schemes for women proposed, *Patriot*, December 9, p5.

Chiplunkar, V.V., 1987, Education and development of women : Project Maher, *Journal of Educational Planning and Administration* 1(2), p173-90.

Gore, M.S., 1987, Education for women's equality I & II, *University News* 25(16), p2-5; 25(17), p4-7.

Hooja, G.B.K., 1987, Women's status, family life, education and the media, *University News* 25(14) p 4-6.

Mother Teresa Women's University, 1987, Methodology for women's studies, *University News* 25(50), p 81.

1988

Amrik Singh, 1988, Empowerment of women, *Tribune*, July 13.

————, 1988, New deal for women? *Hindustan Times*, June 27.

————, 1988, What happens to brilliant girls? *Tribune*, August 27.

Anklesaria Aiyar, Shahnaz, 1988, Need to improve girls education, *Indian Express*, August 13.

Behl, R.K., 1988, Whither women's education? *Tribune*, February 28.

Indira, K., 1988, New vista for Indian girl, *Indian Nation*, October 2.

Jagan Nath, 1988, India hopes to attract more girls to schools, *Indian Nation*, September 8.

Mathias, T.A., 1988, Women's education and development : The key to a brighter future in Asia, *New Frontiers in Education* 18(3), p42-57.

Mojumdar, Modhumita, 1988, Education for equality, *Statesman*, June 15.

Mother Teressa Women's University, 1988, Implementation of NEP with special reference to education for women's equality : Report, *University News* 26(24), p17.

Pande, Mrinal, 1988, Where do the women toppers go? *Hindustan Times*, August 19.

Rajan, S. Irudaya, 1988, Progress of female literacy in India, *Yojana*, 32(21), p10-12.

Ramana, Usha, 1988, Why few women take to Science? *Deccan Chronicle*, November 27.

Sharma, Narayan Prasad, 1988, Women and higher education, *Yojana* 32(21), p6-8.

Suman Singh, 1988, Need to define women's education, *Pioneer*, July 6.

Suryakumari, A., 1988, Women's interests, *University News* 26(45), p1-3.

Tribune (Newspaper), 1988, Educating the daughters, *Tribune*, December 30, editorial.

Verma, Vinod Kumar, 1988, Status of women : Student's views, *Tribune*, August 28.

1989

Alagappa University, Centre for Women's Studies and Rural Technology, 1989, Seminar on women and development, *University News* 27(2), p31.

Anon, 1989, Women's education in Bangladesh, *New Frontiers in Education* 19(1), January-March, p96-105.

Banerjee, Nirmala, 1989, Trends in women's employment, 1971-81 : Some macro-level observations, *Economic and Political Weekly* 24(17), pWS 10-WS 22.

Basnet, Neelam, 1989, Status of women's education in Nepal, *New Frontiers in Education* 19(1), January-March, p106-09.

Basu, Soma, 1989, Can education liberate eve? *Patriot*, June 18.

Dewani, Lakshman, 1989, Nehru and emancipation of Indian women, *Patriot*, December 16.

Hasan, Masuma, 1989, Women's education in Pakistan, *New Frontiers in Education* 19(1), January-March, p80-89.

Indian University Association for Continuing Education, 1989, Empowerment of women : Multi-disciplinary perspectives, *University News* 27(4), p9-10.

Israney, S.M., 1989, Status of women in the academic world : Indian context, *University News* 27(23), p11-14.

Kurien, Mathew, 1989, Women, education and global survival, *Deccan Herald*, July 8.

Menon, Laxmi, 1989, Emancipation of women, *University News* 27(23), p6-10.

Mother Teressa Women's University 1989, Seminar on women's studies as an academic discipline, *University News* 27(17), p16.

Pillai, J.K., 1989, Strategies for empowerment of women, *University News* 27(23), p1-2.

S.N.D.T. Women's University and Institute of Marketing and Management, Association of Women Entrepreneurs and Executives, 1989, Seminar on working women's challenges ahead, *University News* 27(23), p31-32.

Sengupta, M., 1989, Women's status : What is the concept of equality? *Hindu*, February 7.

Sharma, Jan, 1989, Stress on education of girls in Nepal, *Pioneer*, January 13.

Sharma, S.R., 1989, Delhi tops in women's education, *National Herald*, April 23.

Shastri, Diwakar, 1989, Women's universities or universities for women : Mission of women's institutions in higher education, *University News* 27(23), p3-5.

Suryakumar, A., 1989, Strategies for political empowerment of women, *University News* 27(23), p17-18.

Watson, Leonard E. and Thakkar, Usha, 1989, The management development of women administrators : Some considerations, *University News* 27(23), p15-16.

Anon, 1989, Women's education in Bangladesh, *New Frontiers in Education* 19(1), p96-105.

7.4 LIST OF JOURNALS SCANNED

EDUCATION

Asian Journal of Psychology and
    Education (Tri-A)
Agra Psychological Research Cell
Tiwari Kothi, Belanganj
Agra
Uttar Pradesh-282 004.

Audio-Visual Education (Q)
Ministry of Education and Social
    Welfare
(*Now* Ministry of Human Resource
    Development)
Government of India
Room No. 52, 'C' Wing
Shastri Bhavan
New Delhi-110 001.

Bharatiya Shiksha Shodh Patrika
    (Bi-A)
Indian Institute of Educational
    Research
Sarawati Kunj, Nirala Nagar
Lucknow
Uttar Pradesh 262 001

Bulletin of Non-formal Education
    (Q)
National Council of Educational
    Research and Training
N.I.E.Campus
Sri Aurobindo Marg
New Delhi-110 016

E.P.A. Quarterly Bulletin
(Educational Planning and
     Administration Bulletin) (Q)
National Institute of Educational
     Planning and Administration
17-B, Sri Aurobindo Marg
New Delhi-110 016

Education (M)
Teacher's Cooperative Education
     Journals and Publications Ltd.
Kanyakubja College
10 Staff Colony
Lucknow
Uttar Pradesh-226 001

Education and Psychology Review
     (Q)
Faculty of Education and Psychology
Maharaja Sayajirao University of
     Baroda
Fatechganj
Baroda
Gujarat- 390 001.

Education Quarterly (Q)
Ministry of Human Resources
     Development
Department of Education
Government of India
Room No. 503, C Wing
Shastri Bhavan
New Delhi-110 001

Educational Forum (Q)
Alumni Association
Central Institute of Education
33, Chhatra Marg
Delhi-110 007

Educational India (M)
Hindu Press
Machlipatnam
Tamil Nadu-521 001

Educational Miscellany (Q)
Publication Unit
Directorate of Education
Government of Tripura
Agartala
Tripura-799 001

Educational Review (M)
41, Sankuwar Street
Triplicane, Madras
Tamil Nadu-600 005

Educator (Q)
University Training College
Nagpur
Maharashtra-440 001.

Experiments in Education (M)
SITU Council of Educational
     Research
No. 3, Trust Link Street
Mandavelipakkam, Madras
Tamil Nadu-600 028.

Indian Education (M)
All India Federation of Educational
     Associations
(V.P. Raghvachari)
2-1-108/3, University Road
Nallakunta, Hyderabad
Andhra Pradesh-500 044.

Indian Educational Review (H.Y.)
National Council of Educational
     Research and Training
NIE Campus, Sri Aurobindo Marg
New Delhi-110 016.

Indian Institute of Education Bulletin
     (A)
28/2 Kothrud, Karve Road
Pune
Maharashtra-411 029

Perspective in Education (Q)
Society for Educational Research and
    Development
40, Harinagar, Gotil Road
Baroda
Gujarat-390 007.

Prasar (Q)
Department of Adult Education
University of Jaipur
Jaipur
Rajasthan-302004.

Primary Teacher (Q)
National Council of Educational
    Research and Training
N. I.E. Campus
Sri Aurobindo Marg
New Delhi-110 016.

Progress of Education (M)
Pune Vidyarthi Griha Prakashan
186, Sadashiv Peth
Pune
Maharashtra-411 030

Quest in Education (Q)
Indian Council of Basic Education
Gandhi Shikshan Bhavan, Juhu
Bombay
Maharashtra-400 049.

Rajasthan Board Journal of
    Education (Q)
Evaluation and Academic
    Programmes
Board of Secondary Education
Government of Rajasthan
Ajmer
Rajasthan-305 001.

Research Bulletin (Q)
Maharashtra State Council of
    Educational Research & Training
Pune
Maharashtra-411 030.

Shiksha (Q)
Education Department
Government of Uttar Pradesh
Lucknow
Uttar Pradesh-226 001.

Student Action (M)
AISF, 417, Asaf Ali Road
New Delhi-110 002.

Teacher Education (Q)
Directorate of Extension Programme
    for Secondary Education
National Council of Educational
    Research and Training
N.I.E. Campus
Sri Aurobindo Marg
New Delhi-110 016.

Teacher Today/Naya Shikshak *(Q)
Directorate of Primary and
    Secondary Education
Government of Rajasthan
Bikaner
Rajasthan-334 001.

Teaching (Q)
Oxford University Press
Post Box-31
Bombay-400 001.

University Administration (Bi-A)
OUB/L-29, Osmania University
    Campus
Hyderabad
Andhra Pradesh-500 007.

University News (F)
Association of Indian Universities
16, Kotla Marg
New Delhi-110 002.

OTHER JOURNALS/NEWS PAPERS*

Deccan Chronicle (D)
Sarojini Devi Road
Sikandrabad.

Deccan Herald (D)
66, M.G. Road
Bangalore
Karnataka.

Economic Affairs (Q)
BC/144, Sector 1, Salt lake City
Calcutta
West Bengal-700 064.

Economic and Political Weekly
Samiksha Trust
Skylarke
284, Shahid Bhagat Singh Road
Bombay
Maharashtra-400 038.

Economic Times (D)
7, Bahadur Shah Zafar Marg
New Delhi-110 002.

Femina (W)
Times of India Press
Dr. D.N. Road
Bombay
Maharashtra.

Hindu (D)
No. 5, I.E.N.S. Building
Rafi Marg
New Delhi-110 001.

Hindustan Times (D)
Hindustan Times Building
Kasturba Gandhi Marg
New Delhi-110 001.

Indian Dissertation Abstracts (Q)
Indian Council of Social Science
    Research
35, Ferozeshah Road
New Delhi-110 001.

Indian Express (D)
Bahadur Shah Zafar Marg
New Delhi-110 002.

Indian Journal of Social Work (Q)
Tata Institute of Social Science
Deonar
Bombay
Maharashtra-400 088.

Indian Nation (M)
Mazharul Haque Path
Patna
Bihar.

Interdiscipline (HY)
(Contd. from *Social Science
    Abstracts*)
Gandhian Institute of Studies
Box 166, Rajghat
Varanasi
Uttar Pradesh-221 001.

Kurukshetra (M)
Publications Division
Patiala House
New Delhi-110 001.

Mainstream (W)
F-24, Bhagat Singh Market
New Delhi- 110 001.

Manpower (Q)
Institute of Applied Manpower
    Research
Indraprastha Estate, Ring Road
New Delhi-110 002.

National Herald (D)
Herald House
Bahadur Shah Zafar Marg
New Delhi-110 002.

Organiser (W)
Bharat Prakashan Ltd.
29, Rani Jhansi Marg
New Delhi-110 055.

Patriot (D)
Link House
Bahadur Shah Zafar Marg
New Delhi-110 002.

Pioneer (D)
20 A-1, Vidhan Sabha Marg
Lucknow
Uttar Pradesh

Samya Shakti (Bi-A)
Centre for Women's Development
    Studies
B-43, Panchsheel Enclave
New Delhi-110 017.

Social Action (Q)
Indian Social Institute
Institutional Area
Lodhi Road
New Delhi-110 003.

Social Change (Q)
Council for Social Development
Sangha Rachana
53, Lodhi Estate
New Delhi-110 003.

Social Welfare (M)
Central Social Welfare Board
Jeewan Deep
Parliament Street
New Delhi-110 001.

Statesman (D)
Statesman House
Cannaught Circus
New Delhi-110 001.

Times of India (D)
Bahadur Shah Zafar Marg
New Delhi-110 002.

Tribune (D)
Chandigarh- 160 020.

Yojana (F)
Publications Division
Government of India
Patiala House
New Delhi-110 001.

ABBREVIATIONS AND SIGNS

A	: Annual		Q	: Quarterly
appen	: Appendix		refs	: References/
Bi-A	: Bi-Annual			Bibliography
Bi-M	: Bi-Monthly		repr	: Reproduced
D	: Daily		Rev	: Review
Ed	: Edited/Editor		tabs	: Tables
F	: Fortnightly		Tr	: Translated/Translator
ftns	: Footnotes		Tri-A	: Tri Annual
HY	: Half Yearly		W	: Weekly
illus	: Illustrations		+	: Continued on later pages
M	: Monthly			in the same issue
p	: Pages			* Stray issues scanned

PART IV

SELECT BIBLIOGRAPHIES ON WOMEN'S EDUCATION AND ALLIED TOPICS

8

SELECT BIBLIOGRAPHIES ON WOMEN'S EDUCATION AND ALLIED TOPICS

8.1 INDIAN DOCTORAL DISSERTATIONS

Agarwal, Neeraj, Mohini, 1988, *Role of sex in dynamics of classroom teaching behaviour flow pattern*, Meerut.

Agrawal, Rekha, Rani, 1988, *A study of psychological characteristics of the disadvantaged female learners*, B.H.U.

Ahmad, Karuna, 1969, *Social background of the women under-graduates of Delhi University*, Delhi.

Ahmad Shadbano *see* Shadbano, Ahmad

Akhtar, H.Nazeem, 1989, *A study of the non-formal educational needs of the muslim women in the city of Madras and developing an appropriate non-formal educational curriculum*, Madras.

Ashalata, 1984, *Modernity among educated working women in Bihar*, Bhagalpur.

Aurangabadkar, Nalini Jeevan, 1976, *Sociological analysis of adjustment problems among working women*, Osmania.

Babel, Manjula, 1988, *Adjustments of foreign students studying in the Universities of Rajasthan*, Sukhadia.

Banerjee, Gauri Rani, 1943, *Some aspects of the position of women in India*, Allahabad.

Banoo Shamima *see* Shamima, Banoo.

Basu, Uma, 1975, *Female education in Bihar from 1904 A.D. to the present day*, Patna.

Bhai, P. Nirmala, 1982, *Status dynamics among Harijan women in Kerala*, Kerala.

Bhandari, Usha, Kiran, 1983, *Modernisation among female students in Kumaun*, Kumaun.

Bhatia, Pratima, 1977, *Role conflict among working women*, Lucknow.

Chanana, Karuna *see* Ahmad, Karuna

Chandrabai, M., 1979, *Changes in status, attitude choice and aspirations of Hindu urban women*, Madras.

Chandramani, Indra, 1988, *A study of occupation and career perceptions of the various nursing personnel working in the training institutions of nursing in the city of Greater Bombay*, S.N.D.T.

Chandrasekaran, Premila, 1983, *Attitudes of rural women of Tamil Nadu towards formal education of women*, Madras.

Chithra, M.N., 1971, *The social background of some undergraduate women students in Mysore city*, Delhi.

Chitra, Sharda, 1984, *Changing status and life pattern of educated employed women in urban communities of Moradabad Division*, Rohilkhand.

Chittema, M., 1978, *An experimental non-formal nutrition programme for rural women*, Madras.

Chopra, Meenakshi, 1978, *Sex differences in social structure and dynamics of educational institutions at the secondary level*, Jammu.

Darbari, Priti, 1960, *Changing social attitudes among modern educated Hindu women*, Agra.

Das, Rosy, 1979, *Women's education in Assam in the post independence period, 1947-71 and its impact on the social life of the state*, Gauhati.

Dave, Javendra Kakubhai, 1972, *A study of evolution of female education in Gujarat till independence*, Sardar Patel.

Desai, C.D., 1976, *Girls access to school education in Gujarat State : A study of factors and problems in historical perspective*, Bombay.

Devi, B. Rama *see* Rama Devi, B.

Devi, V. Lalitha *see* Lalitha Devi, V.

Dutta, Indranee, 1988, *Self-concept and personality adjustment of girls through pubescence*, Gauhati.

Fareeda Khatoon, 1989, *A study of mathematical aptitude among boys and girls and its relationship with interests and vocational preferences at secondary level*, Osmania.

Fatma, Nikhat *see* Nikhat Fatma

Gandhi, Yogini R., 1978, *Development of women's education in Greater Bombay, 1961-74*, SNDT.

Gondhalekar, Asha Y., 1975, *Objectives of women's education as perceived by the students and their parents in Maharashtra with special reference to Poona*, SNDT.

Gupta, Rajeshwar Nath, 1980, *Influence of socio-economic characteristics of the household on female work participation rate : A case study of Gujarat, 1972-73*, JNU.

Gupta, Uma, 1979, *Status and role of educated working women of Agra*, Agra.

Gurbaxami, Kamal Ramchand, 1989, *A critical study of the curricula and materials in the school final year with a view to judging their relevance to the changing roles and responsibilities of educated women*, Osmania.

Hate, Chandrakala, 1947, *A Social position of Hindu women*, Bomday.

Indukumari, M.,1976, *Education and social status of Muslim women in Kerala*, Kerala.

Jaiswal, Rajendra Prasad, 1989, *Professional status of women : A comparative study of women and men scientists and engineers*, JNU.

Johri, Prema, 1970, *Status of working women*, Lucknow.

Joshi, Malati M., 1982, *Socio-economic conditions of women working in cotton textile mills in Greater Bombay*, SNDT.

Kakar, Ved Kumari, 1985, *A study of job satisfaction in relation to attitudes, job values and vocational interests of women*, Bhopal.

Kapur, Promilla, 1960, *Socio-psychological study of the change in attitudes of young educated Hindu women*, Agra.

Kaur, Malkit *see* Malkit Kaur.

Kaur, Prabhjot *see* Prabhjot Kaur.

Khare, Prabhakar Narayan, 1964, *A study of the family life of women earners of Indore city*, Vikram.

Khatoon, Fareeda *see* Fareeda Khatoon.

Kumari, M.Indu *see* Indukumari, M.

Kumari, Shyam *see* Shyam Kumari.

Lahkar, Bina, 1976, *The progress of women's education in Assam from 1874 to 1970*, Gauhati.

Lata, Asha *see* Asha Lata.

Lalitha Devi, U.,1980, *Changing status of employed women in Kerala*, Kerala.

Liankhuma, J., 1989, *A study of the development of women's education in Mizoram*, NEHU.

Mahajan, Amarjit, 1978, *Police women in the states of Punjab, Himachal Pradesh and Union Territory of Chandigarh : A sociological study of a new role*, Punjab.

Maitreyi, Krishna Raj, 1980, *Women scientists, their families and their work*, SNDT.

Malkit Kaur, 1982, *Emerging status, role of rural women in the context of changing technology in Haryana*, Haryana Agrl.

Manju Swarup *see* Swarup, Manju.

Mehta, J.D., 1978, *Beyond the household walls : A study of women executives at work and at home*, TISS.

Misra, Lakshmi, 1960, *Education of women in India during the period 1921 to 1956*, Saugar.

Mithilesh Singh, 1988, *Constraints effecting Indian women's participation in games and sports*, Banasthali.

Mohanty, Pratime, 1981, *Family background and career orientation among the women students of Utkal University*, Utkal.

Mullatti, L.L., 1979, *Impact of virashaivism on the status of women*, Poona.

Naidu Varlami *see* Varlami, Naidu.

Naik, Chitrarekha Harischandra, 1979, *The education of women in the province of Bombay : A retrospect and a prospect*, Bombay.

Negi, V.S., 1980, *Changing behavioural indicators and social outlook of women graduates of Uttarakhand*, Agra.

Nikhat Fatma, 1972-75, *Attitude of Muslim women of Aligarh Muslim University : Relations and adjustments,* Aligarh.

Nirmala Bhai, P. *see* Bhai, P Nirmala.

Prabhakar, Annemme, 1989, *Nurse tutor's preparation, perception and performance of their role in diploma schools of nursing in Maharashtra,* SNDT.

Prabhjot Kaur, 1977, *A career pattern study of higher secondary girls of Delhi with reference to a career planning programme for them,* Delhi.

Raghunanda Reddy, C., 1985, *The changinng status of educated working women in India : A case study of Rayalaseema,* Sri Venkateswara.

Rajwade, Krishna, 1980, *Status of Muslim women in Indore city,* Indore.

Rajalakshmi, R., 1985, *A study of the social, economic and political aspects of the growth of higher educaton of women in the Madras presidency, 1921-47,* JNU.

Rama Devi, B., 1963, *Women's education and traditional values,* Madras.

Ramanamma, 1969, *Position of women in India with special reference to Poona,* Poona.

Rao Sakuntala, 1953, *Indian womanhood through ages,* Calcutta (D.Litt).

Reddy, C. Raghunanda *see* Raghunanda Reddy, C.

Roy, Shibani, 1969-76, *Status of Muslim women in North India : A study in the dynamics of change,* Delhi.

Sakhare, Seema Trimbak, 1977, *A sample survey of women's opinion and behaviour relating to family life as correlates of educational status,* Nagpur.

Samant, Prema A., 1976, *A critical study of the professional, familial and economic conditions of women primary teachers working under the Bombay Municipal Corporation,* SNDT.

Sareen, Shakuntala, 1959, *Women's education in Uttar Pradesh : A sociological study,* Agra.

Seth, Jeevan Jyoti, 1985, *The role of United Nations in improving the status of women : Political, civil, economic and social, 1947-75,* Delhi.

Shadbano, Ahmad, 1978, *Changing social status of women among Muslims of Aligarh,* Aligarh.

Shah, Beena, 1982, *A sociological study of educational development of graduate students of Kumaun University with special reference to caste,* Kumaun.

Shah, Kalpana Ghanshyambhai, 1976-80, *Voluntary organisation and women's liberation : A case study of Akhil Hind Mahila Parishad,* South Gujarat.

Shah, Sulochana M., 1977, *Social and political progress of women in India, 1828-1972,* SNDT.

Shakuntala Rao *see* Rao, Shakuntala.

Shamima, Banoo, 1982, *Sex differences in parental press at several socio-economic levels,* Jammu.

Shantha, N., 1983, *Study of the returns from education to employed in Bangalore city*, Mysore.

Sharma, Ashok Kumar, 1983, *Changing status and employment pattern of educated women with reference to role conflict*, Roorkee.

Sharma, Sushila, 1966, *Role and response of women in planned change*, Saugar.

Shukla, Premlata, 1979, *Sociological study of problems and aspirations of women teachers in Rewa District*, Awadhesh Pratap.

Shyam Kumari, 1979, *Problems of women education and their impact on its progress in east U.P. at the secondary level since 1947*, Gorakhpur.

Singh, *see* under full name.

Srivastava, Deepa Rani, 1988, *A study of prospective professional women : Psychological and environmental*, B.H.U.

Solomen, Savitri, 1979, *A study of educated ladies in Greater Bombay in respect of utilization of their talents in various walks of life on honorary basis*, Bombay.

Sood, S.M., 1970, *Attitude of rural women in Delhi territory towards selected aspects of educational programmes for improvement in nutrition and extent of adoption of these practices*, IARI., (M.Sc. Dissertation).

Srivastava, Vinita, 1972, *Employment of educated married women, its causes and consequences : with reference to Chandigarh*, Punjab University.

Subbaiah, Rekha, 1975-79, *The career women : A sociological analysis of the problems and changing role*, Mysore.

Sushma, 1989, *Effectiveness of concept attainment and biological science inquiry models for teaching biological sciences to VIII class students*, B.H.U.

Swarup, Manju, 1985, *Development of girls education in U.P. from 1950-75*, Kanpur.

Talesra, Hem Lata, 1985, *Higher education among women : An analysis of the situation of higher education at a district level*, Baroda.

Tandon, S.D., 1959, *Changing attitudes and culture patterns among educated earning women in U.P.*, Agra.

Tayal, Satyabala, 1980, *A sociological study of the educated scheduled caste women of Vidarabha*, Nagpur.

Thakker, Pravinabalen Natwarlal, 1970, *Development of women's education in Gujarat since Independence*, Gujarat Vidyapith, (Gujrati).

Tribhuvan, U.D., 1978, *A study of educated scheduled caste women in an urban setting*, Poona.

Tripathi, Pratibha, 1988, *A comparative study of the correlates of academic attainments of pupil of junior high school*, Avadh.

Usha Rani, 1970, *Attitude of working women towards others and vice-versa in West Bengal* , Calcutta.

Vakil, Vidya Vanraj, 1956-67, *Girls' education in modern India with special reference to its expansion in the state of Bombay*, Bombay.

Varlami, Naidu, 1974, *Career orientation and professional preparation among the women teacher trainees of the colleges of education in Madhya Pradesh,* Ravishankar.

Yasin, Yasmin *see* Yasmin Yasin.

Yasmin Yasin, 1985, *A study of vocational interests of girls as related to their level of intelligence, parental education and socio-economic status,* Kashmir.

8.2 BOOKS PUBLISHED IN INDIA

Adiseshiah, Malcolm S., 1984, *Science and technology for women,* Affliated East-West Press, Madras.

Agrawal, Anju and Arora, D.R., 1989, *Women in rural society,* Vohra Publishers, Allahabad, 85 p.

Aggarwal, J.C., 1987, *Indian women : Education and status,* Arya, Delhi.

Ahmad, Karuna *see* Chanana, Karuna.

Arora, D.R., jt. author *see* Agarwal, Anju and Arora, D.R.

Ashok Kumar, 1989, *Indian women towards 21st century,* Criterion Publications, New Delhi.

Asthana Pratima, 1974, *Women's movement in India,* Vikas, New Delhi.

Bagal, Jogesh Chandra, 1956, *Women's education in Eastern India : The first phase,* The World Press Pvt Ltd., Calcutta.

Baig, Tara Ali, ed., 1958, *Women of India,* Publications Division, New Delhi.

————, 1976, *Women power of India,* Sultan Chand and Sons, New Delhi.

Bhagat, Rekha and Mathur, P.N., 1989, *Mass media and farm women,* Intellectual Publications, New Delhi, 100p.

Bhandari, R.K., 1982, *Educational development of women in India,* Ministry of Education and Culture, New Delhi.

Blumberg, Rhoda Lois and Dwaraki, Leela, 1980, *India's educated women : Options and constraints,* Hindustan Publishing Corporation, Delhi.

Chachra, Meenu, jt. author, *see* Vyas, Anju and Chachra, Meenu.

Chanana, Karuna, ed., 1988, *Socialisation education and women : Explorations in gender identity,* Orient Longman, New Delhi.

Chandra, Lokesh *see* Lokesh Chandra.

Dandekar, Kumini, 1983, *Employment Guarantee Scheme : An employment opportunity for women,* Orient Longman, New Delhi.

De Reincourt, Amaury *see* Reincourt, Amaury de.

Desai, Neera, 1985, *A Decade of women's movement in India : Review of achievements and issues—Theme for discussion.* SNDT, Bombay, (National Seminar by Research Unit on Women's Studies).

————, and Krishnaraj Matthreyi, 1987, *Women and society in India,* Ajanta, Delhi.

————, and Patel, Vibhuti, 1985, *Indian women : Change and challenge in the international decade 1975-85*, Popular, Bombay.

De Souza, Alfred, ed., 1975, *Women in contemporary India: traditional images and changing roles*, Manohar, Delhi.

Dhingra, O.P., 1972, *Women in Employment*—Report of field investigation into the problems of professionally trained employed women in India. Shri Ram Centre of Industrial Relations and Human Resources, New Delhi.

Dhruvarajan, Vanaja, 1989, *Hindu women and the power of ideology*, Sage Publications, New Delhi, 164p.

Garg, Pulin K., jt. author *see* Parikh, Indira and Garg, Pulin K.

Ghosh, S.K., 1989, *Indian women through the ages*, Ashish Publishing House, New Delhi, 341p.

Hate, Chandrakala A., 1969, *Changing status of woman in post-independence India*, Allied, Bombay.

Hem Lata, 1989, *Higher education among women*, National, New Delhi.

India, Ministry of Education and Social Welfare, Department of Education, 1977, *Misconceptions influencing non-formal education for women*, Directorate of Non-formal (Adult) Education, New Delhi.

————, 1978, *Adult education programmes for women* —Report of the committee appointed by the Ministry of Education and Social Welfare, New Delhi.

————, Department of Social Welfare, 1974, *Towards Equality*, Report of the Committee on the Status of Women in India, New Delhi.

————, 1975, *The scheme of functional literacy for adult women*, New Delhi.

India, Ministry of Education and Youth Services, 1970, *Spread of girls' education in Mehsana district : A sample survey*, New Delhi.

India, Ministry of Human Resource Development, 1987, *Muslim female education in metropolitan city of Calcutta : A perspective study of an urban minority (1971-81)*, New Delhi.

————, 1988, *National perspective plan for women 1988-2000 A.D.*, New Delhi.

Indian Adult Education Association, 1956, *Grameen mahilayen aur vikas carya*—Report of Regional Seminar Organised at Alipore (Delhi), New Delhi.

————, 1977, *Curriculum construction for non-formal education of women*, New Delhi.

————, 1980, *New trends in adult education for women* – Report of the National Seminar, New Delhi.

Indian Council of Social Science, Research, 1977, *Critical issues on the status of women* : Suggested priorities for action, New Delhi.

————, 1977, *Programme of women's studies*, New Delhi.

————, 1978, *Status of women in India* : A synopsis of the report of the National Committee, Allied Publishers India, New Delhi.

Indian Social Studies Trust, 1985, *The study of utilization and wastage of training programme of national and regional vocational training institutes for women*, New Delhi.

Indira, R., 1989, *Women in technical education : A sociological study*, Sharada Prakashan, Delhi.

Jain, Devaki and Banerjee, Nirmala, ed., 1985, *Women in poverty : The tyranny of the household*, Vikas, New Delhi.

Jain, S.D. and Reddy, V. Krishnamurthy, 1979, *Role of women in rural development: A study of Mahila Mandals*, National Institute of Rural Development, Hyderabad.

Jesudasan, Victor, *et al*, 1981, *Non-formal education for rural women and development of the young child*, Allied Publishers, New Delhi.

Jha, K.N., 1985, *Women towards modernization*, Janaki Prakashan, Patna.

Kapoor, Manindra, 1986, *Women and family life education in India*, Printwell Publishers, Jaipur.

Kapur, Promilla, 1970, *Marriage and the working women in India*, Vikas, Delhi.

———, 1974, *Changing status of the working woman in India*, Vikas, Delhi.

Karkal, Malini and Pandey, Divya, 1989, *Studies on women and population*, Himalaya Publishing House, Delhi, 106 p.

Krishnamurthy, J., 1989, *Women in colonial India: Essays on survival work and the state*, Oxford University Press, Delhi, 242, p.

Krishnaraj, Maitreyi, 1983, *Research on women and work in the seventies*, Research Unit on Women's Studies, Women's University, Bombay.

———, 1984, *Why study women : Sociology of women*, Lesson I, SNDT Open University Programme.

———, and Mehta, Madhavi, 1982, *Unemployed Post-graduate degree holders in science in Bombay*. Research Centre for Women's Studies and Council of Scientific and Industrial Research, Bombay.

Kumari, Ranjana *see* Ranjana Kumari.

Lakshmi, C.S., 1983, Non-textual methods of research in women's studies. Research Unit on Women's studies, SNDT Women's University, Bombay, Seminar abstract, memeo.

Lahkar, Bina, 1987, *Development in women education : Study of Assam*, Omsons, Guwahati.

Lokesh Chandra, 1989, *Women in Delhi Sultanate*, Vohra Publishers, Allahabad, 188p.

Mann, K.,1987, *Tribal women in a changing society*, Mittal Publications, Delhi

Mathew, P.M., and Nair, M.S.,1986, *Women's organisations and women's interests*, Ashish Publishing House, New Delhi, 175p.

Mathur, P.N., jt. author, *see* Bhagat, Rekha and Mathur, P.N.

Mathur, Y.B., 1973, *Women's education in India 1813-1966*. Asia, Bombay.

Maurya, R.D., 1988, *Women in India*, Chugh Publications, Allahabad, 235p.

Mazumdar, Vina, 1978, *Role of rural women in development* : Report of an International seminar, U.K., 1977, Allied, Delhi.

————, 1988, *National specialised agencies and women's equality* : *NCERT*, Centre for Women's Developmennt Studies, New Delhi, 149 p.

————, 1988, *National specialised agencies and women's equality* : *khadi and Village Industries*, Centre for Women's Development Studies, New Delhi, 191p.

————, and Pandey, Balaji, 1985, *Perspective on women's education, 1971-81*. Centre for Women's Development Studies, New Delhi, Unpublished paper.

Mehra, Rekha and Saradamoni, K., 1983, *Women and rural transformation*, Concept Publishing Company, New Delhi.

Mehta, Vimla, 1979, *Attitude of educated women towards social issues*, National, Delhi.

Misra, Lakshmi, 1966, *Education of women in India, 1921-66*. Macmillan, New Delhi.

Mitra, Asok, 1979, *Status of women literacy and employment*, Allied, Bombay.

————, *et al*, 1979, *Status of women : Household and non-household activity*, Allied, Bombay.

Mother Teresa Women's University, Kodaikanal, 1982, *Towards equal status*, Madras.

————, 1984, *National seminar on education and employment for women in India*, Kodaikanal.

————, 1985, *Education and employment for women in India* : Report of the National Seminar, Kodaikanal.

————, 1986, *Development of women through education* : Report of the Workshop, Madras, Kodaikanal.

————, 1986, *Report* of Expert Committee on Women's University, 1986 Kodaikanal, Chairman : Malcolm S.Adiseshiah.

Mukherji, Anindita and Verma, Neelam, 1987, *Socio-economic backwardness in women*, Ashish Publishing House, 68p.

Murli Manohar, K., ed., 1984, *Women's status and development in India*, Society for Women's Studies and Development, Warangal.

Nair, M.S., jt. author *see* Mathew, P.M. and Nair, M.S.

Nanda, B.R., 1970, *Indian women from purdah to modernity*, Vikas, New Delhi.

Narayan, S., 1989, *Development through women programme*, Inter-India Publication, Delhi, 95p.

National Council for Education Research and Training, 1982, *Status of women through curriculum*, Elementary teahcer's handbook, New Delhi.

————, 1984, *Status of women through curriculum* : *Secondary and senior secondary stages*, New Delhi.

————, 1984, *Status of women through teaching of Mathematics*, Tecahers handbook, New Delhi.

Nimbkar, Krishna, Bai, 1958, *Development work among rural women : A guide book,* Indian Adult Education Association, Delhi.

Oak, A.W., 1988, *Status of women in education.* Indian Publications, Ambala cantt.

Panandikar, Sulabha, *et al.* ed., 1975, *Future trends in women's higher education and the role of the SNDT Women's University* : Report of the round table discussion, 1973, Bombay.

Pandey, Divya, jt. author, *see* Karkal, Malini and Pandey, Divya.

Pandey, Rekha, 1988, *Women from subjection to liberation,* Mittal Publications, New Delhi, 232p.

Parikh, Indira and Garg, Pulin K., 1989, *Indian women : An inner dialogue,* Sage Publications, New Delhi, 224p.

Patwa, Subhadra, 1985, *Women's studies centres in India,* Research Centre on Women's Studies Bombay.

Ranjana Kumari, 1989, *Women-headed household in rural India,* Radiant Publishers, New Delhi, 111p.

Reincourt, Amaury de, 1989, *Women and power in history,* Sterling Pulishers, New Delhi, 467p.

SNDT Women's University, 1981, *Report of the First National Conference on Women's Studies,* Bombay.

Sakhare, Seema, 1985, *Our fight for socio-legal justice for women in India,* National Seminar on "Decade of Women's Movement in India " A review of achievements and issues . Research Unit of Women's Studies, SNDT Women's University, Bombay.

Sapru, R.K., 1989, *Women and development,* Ashish Publishing House, 355p.

Sarkar, Lotika, 1988, *National specialised agencies and women's equality: Law Commission of India,* Centre for Women's Development Studies, New Delhi, 118p.

Sen, Gita and Crown, Caren, 1985, *Development crisis and alternative vision : Third world women's perspective,* DAWN, New Delhi,.

Sengupta, Padmini, 1964, *Women in India,* Ministry of Information and Broadcasting, New Delhi.

Sharma, Kumud, 1988, *National specialised agencies and women's equality,* Centre for Women's, Development Studies, New Delhi, 149p.

Sharma, Savitri, 1979, *Women students in India : Status and personality,* Concept Publishing Company, New Delhi.

Sheikh Abdulla, K.B., 1933, *League to promote girls' education,* AMU Press, Aligarh.

————, 1938, *An appeal to members of the Court of the Muslim University, Aligarh for financial help to Muslim Girls' College,* AMU Press, Aligarh.

Shridevi, S., 1968, *A century of Indian womanhood,* Rao and Raghavan, Mysore.

Srinavasa, M.N., 1978, *The changing position of Indian women,* Oxford University Press, Bombay.

Srivastava, Ginny, *et al, Links for the chain,* A report of non-formal education involving women in South Asia—Programme and Problems, Seva Mandir, International Council for Adult Education, The International Development Research Unit, Women's Development Unit, Udaibur.

Talesra, Hem Lata, 1989, *Higher education among women,* National Publishing House, New Delhi.

Usmani, Meena, jt. author *see* Vyas, Anju and Usmani, Meena.

Verma, Neelam, jt. author *see* Mukherji, Anindita and Verma, Neelam.

Vohra, Roopa and Sen, Arun K., 1986, *Status education and problems of Indian women,* Akshat Publication, Delhi.

Vyas, Anju and Chachra, Meenu, 1989, *Women : An annotated bibliography of directories and statistical resources,* Centre for Women's Development Studies, New Delhi, 32p.

Vyas, Anju and Usmani, Meena, 1989, *Women : An annotated bibliography of bibliographies,* Centre for Women's Development Studies, New Delhi, 27p.

Wasi, Muriel, 1971, *The educated woman in Indian society today,* Tata McGraw-Hill Publishing Ltd., Bombay.

8.3 BOOKS PUBLISHED ABROAD

Acker, Sandra, *et el,* 1984, ed, *Women and education,* World yearbook of education, 1964, Kegan Paul, London.

Agarwal, Bina, 1983, *Report on the current status and needed priorities of women's studies in Asia and the Pacific,* APDC, Kuala Lumpur.

Association of Southeast Asian Institutions of Higher Learning, Bangkok, 1976, *Role of women in development,* Bangkok.

Barnes, Mildred J., *et al,* 1966, *Sports activities for girls and women,* Meredith Corporation, New York.

Blue, Adrianne, 1987, *Grace under pressure : The emergence of women in sport,* Sidgwick and Jackson, London.

Boserup, E., 1970, *Women's role in economic development,* George Allen & Unwin, London.

Burstyn Joan N., 1980, *Victorian education and the ideal of womanhood,* Croom Helm, London.

Chandler, E.M., 1980, *Educating adolescent girls,* George Allen & Unwin, London.

Deem, Rosemary, 1979, *Women and schooling,* Routedge and Kegan Paul, London.

Fidell, Linda S. and Delamater, John, ed, 1971, *Women in the profession : What's all the fuss about,* Sage, London.

Howe, Florence, 1970, *Seven years later—Women's studies programmes,* 1976, National Advisory Council on Women's Educational Programme.

Huston, Perdita, 1979, *Third world women speak out*, Praeger, New York.

Jeffrey, Patricia, Jeffery, Roger and Lyon, Andrew, 1989, *Labour pains and labour power : Women and childbearing in India*, Zed Books, New Jersey, 292p.

Jeffery, Roger, jt. author *see* Jeffery, Patricia, Jeffery, Roger and Lyon Andrew.

Lyon, Andrew, jt. author *see* Jeffery, Patricia, Jeffery, Roger and Lyon, Andrew.

Martin, Jane Roland, 1885, *Reclaiming a conversation : The ideal of the educated woman*, Yale University Press, New Haven.

McWilliams-Tulberg, Rita, 1975, *Women at Cambridge : A men's university though of a mixed type*, Victor Gollanez, London.

Mehta, Rama, 1970, *The western educated Hindu woman*, Asia Publishing Co., New York.

Philips, Paul and Phillips, Erin, 1983, *Women and work : Inequality in the labour market*, James Lorimer & Company, Toronto.

Report of the sub-committee on the status of academic women on the Berkeley campus, 1970, University of California, Academic Senate Berkeley Division, Berkeley.

Seal, K.C., 1981, *Women in the labour force: A statistical profile in women in the labour force*, Asian Regional Employment and Training Programme, ILO, Geneva.

Sen, Gita, 1985, *Women and agriculture,* World employment programme, ILO, Geneva.

United Nations Commission on the Status of women, 1966, *Resources available to Member States for the advancement of women*, New York.

————, *The role of women in the economic and social development of their countries*, Report of the Secretary General, New York.

8.4 UNESCO PUBLICATIONS

Analysis of some aspects of the action undertaken since 1975 by the Section of equality of educational opportunity for girls and women to promote equality of educational opportunity for girls and women, Paris, Unesco, 1985, 51 p. ED-85/WS/24.

Aseskog, Birgitta, *A study on some activities implemented in Sweden to promote equality of opportunity for girls in technical and vocational education,* Paris, Unesco, 1987, 55 p. ED-87/WS/30.

Asian Regional Seminar on Access of Girls to Primary Education, Kathmandu, Nepal, 2-6 October 1978, *Final report,* Paris, Unesco, 1978, 37 p. S.A. 22.2

Bergarra, R., *Promotion of girls' and women's access to technical and vocational education : Examples of action,* Paris, Unesco, 1986, 79 p. ED-86/WS/103.

Best, F., *Women's right to education,* International symposium, Paris, Unesco, 14-18 September 1987, Reference document No. 2, Paris, Unesco, 1987, 40 p. Ed-87/Conf.809/COL,1.

Borclle, Germaine, *Jobs for women : a plea for equality of opportunity,* Paris, Unesco, 1985, 165 p.

Comparative report on the role of working mothers in early childhood education in five countries, Paris, Unesco, 1978, 82 p. ED-78/WS/71.

Education, training and employment opportunities for women in Sierra Leone, Paris, Unesco, 1974, 186 p.

Eliminating sex stereotyping in schools, A regional guide for educators in North America and Western Europe, Paris, Unesco, 1984, 182 p. ED-84/WS/51.

Equality of educational opportunity for girls and women, Paris, Unesco, 1983, 62 p. Ed-83/WS/55.

Identification and elimination of sex stereotypes in and from school textbooks, Some suggestions for action in the Arab world, Paris, Unesco, 1983, 59 p. Ed-84/WS/31.

Identification and elimination of sex stereotypes in and from school textbooks, Some suggestions for action in Asia and the Pacific, Paris, Unesco, 1985, 37 p. ED-85/WS/58.

International Congress on the situation of women in technical and vocational education, Bonn, Federal Republic of Germany, 9-12 June 1980, *Final document,* Paris, Unesco, 1980, 5 p. S.A. 23.8.

International expert meeting on the role of women in the education of young people for peace, mutual understanding and respect for human rights, New Delhi, India, 7-11 December 1981, *Summary record of discussions,* Paris, Unesco, 1982, 35 p. + annexes Ed-82/CONF. 609/4

International seminar on opening-up to women of vocational training and jobs traditionally occupied by men, Frankfurt, 11-13 November 1980, *Summary record of discussions,* Paris, Unesco, 1981, 64 p. ED-80/CONF.708/COL.2.

International seminar on women's education, training and employment, in developed countries, Tokyo, Japan, 2-6 December 1980, *Summary record of discussions,* Paris, Unesco, 1980,83 p. ED-80/CONF.710/4.

International symposium on the right of women to education with a view to their access to employment, Paris, Unesco, 14-18 September 1987, *Final report,* Paris, Unesco, 1987, 20 p. ED-87/CONF.809

International symposium on the right of women to education with a view to their acess to employment, Paris, Unesco, 14-18 September 1987, *Reference document No. 1,* Paris, Unesco, 1987. 56 p. ED-87/Conf.809/COL.2

Inventory on the results of experience of Japan in developing successful approaches to improving the status of women, Paris, Unesco, 1976, 87 p.

Jaarsma, Ria, *Long way . . . A study on some activities implemented in the Netherlands to promote equality of opportunity for girls and women in scientific, technical and vocational education,* Paris, Unesco, 1987, 95 p. ED-87/WS/42; S.A. 23.61

Langkau-Hermann, Monica, *Education and training of professional women with a view to enabling them to resume their interrupted activities or to take up a new career,* Working document of international seminar on women's education, training and employment in developed countries, Tokyo, Japan, 2-6 December 1980, Paris, Unesco, 1980, 83 p.

Literacy for women, A development priority, Paris, Unesco, S.A. 27.13

Mac Donald, Doris, *Measures to provide the access of girls and women to secondary technical and vocational education in New Zealand,* A report on policies and selected activities, Paris, Unesco,1987, 47 p.+ annexes, Ed-87/WS/40; S.A. 23.62.

National inventory on the status of women in Brazil, Paris, Unesco 1977, 52 p.

National inventory on the status of women in Ghana, Paris, Unesco, 1977, 62 p.

National inventory on the status of women in Tunisian society, Paris, Unesco, 1976, 80 p.

National inventory on the status of women in the United Kingdom, Paris, Unesco,1976, 51 p.

National inventory on the status of women in the USA, Paris, Unesco, 1976,78 p.

National inventory on the status of women in the USSR, Paris, Unesco, 1977, 25 p.

A National survey on sex biases in Zambian textbooks in primary and junior secondary schools and their implications for education in Zambia, Paris, Unesco, 1984, 43 p. ED-84/ws/25.

Poole, Millicent, *School leavers in Australia,* Paris, Unesco, 1978, 188 p

Purgand, W., *et al, Measures to promote the equality of opportunity for girls and women in vocational education in the German Democratic Republic,* by W. Purgand with the co-operation of B. Gericke and G. Pogodda, Paris, Unesco, 1987, 44 p. ED-87/ws/38.

Report on the relationship between educational opportunities and employment opportunities for women, Paris, Unesco, 1975, 144 p. Ed-74/WS/56.

The Role of working mothers in early childhood education in Arab Republic of Egypt, Paris, Unesco, 1978, 31 p.

The Role of working mothers in early childhood education in Hungarian People's Republic, Paris, Unesco, 1977, 77 p.

The Role of working mothers in early childhood education in India, Paris, Unesco, 1977, 200 p.

The Role of working mothers in early childhood education in Nigeria, Paris, Unesco, 1978, 68 p.

The Role of working mothers in early childhood education in Trinidad and Tabago, Paris, Unesco, 1978, 123 p.

School curricula and standards of education and training in Madagascar, Paris, Unesco, 1978, 79 p.

School curricula and standards of education and training in Portugal, Paris, Unesco, 1979, 77 p.

Standardisation of education and curricula for boys and girls in general education, vocational and teacher-training schools in the Mongolian People's Republic, Paris, Unesco, 1979, 49 p. S.A. 31.9.

Status of girls in primary education in some Asian countries and prospects, Working document of Asian regional seminar on access of girls to primary education, Paris, Unesco, 1978, 37 p. S.A.22.12

A Study of the portrayal of women and men in school textbooks and children's literature in France, Paris, Unesco, 1983, 66 p. ED-83/WS/118.

Study on access of women to science education and training and associated careers in Malaysia, Paris, Unesco, 1983, 77 p. ED-83/Ws/107.

Study on curricula and standards of education and training for boys and girls in secondary schools and teacher-training institutes in Jamaica, Paris, Unesco, 1979, 99 p. S.A. 31.10

Study on curricula and standards of education and training for boys and girls in secondary schools and teacher-training institutes in Jordan, Paris, Unesco, 1978, 63 p. S.A. 31.11.

A Study on the differences between the educational programmes of young girls and young boys in Turkey, Paris, Unesco, 1979, 44 p. S.A. 31.12.

Study on the differences of curricula for girls and boys in Afghanistan, Paris, Unesco, 1978, 87 p. S.A. 31.13.

A Study on educational opportunities and employment oportunities open to women in Sri Lanka, Paris, Unesco, 1974, 73 p.

Study on portrayal of men and women in Chinese school textbooks and children's literature, Paris, Unesco, 1983, 69 p. ED-83/WS/22.

Study on portrayal on men and women in school textbooks and children's literature in Norway, Paris, Unesco, 1983, 108 p. ED-83/WS/45.

Study on portrayal of men and women in school textbooks and childrens' literature in the Ukrainian Soviet Socialist Republic, Paris, Unesco, 1982, 56 p. ED-82/Ws/109.

Survey on the representation of women in higher education research, educational planning, administration and management, carried out with the assistance of the International Federation of University Women, Paris, Unesco, 1987, 173 p. ED-87/WS/8.

Unesco's contribution towards improving the status of women, Report by the Director-General, Paris, Unesco, 1978, 20 C/17.

Women and development : Indicators of their changing roles, Paris Unesco, 1981: (Socio-economic studies, 3).

Women's studies and social sciences in Asia: Report of a meeting of experts, Bangkok, Unesco, 1983.

APPENDICES

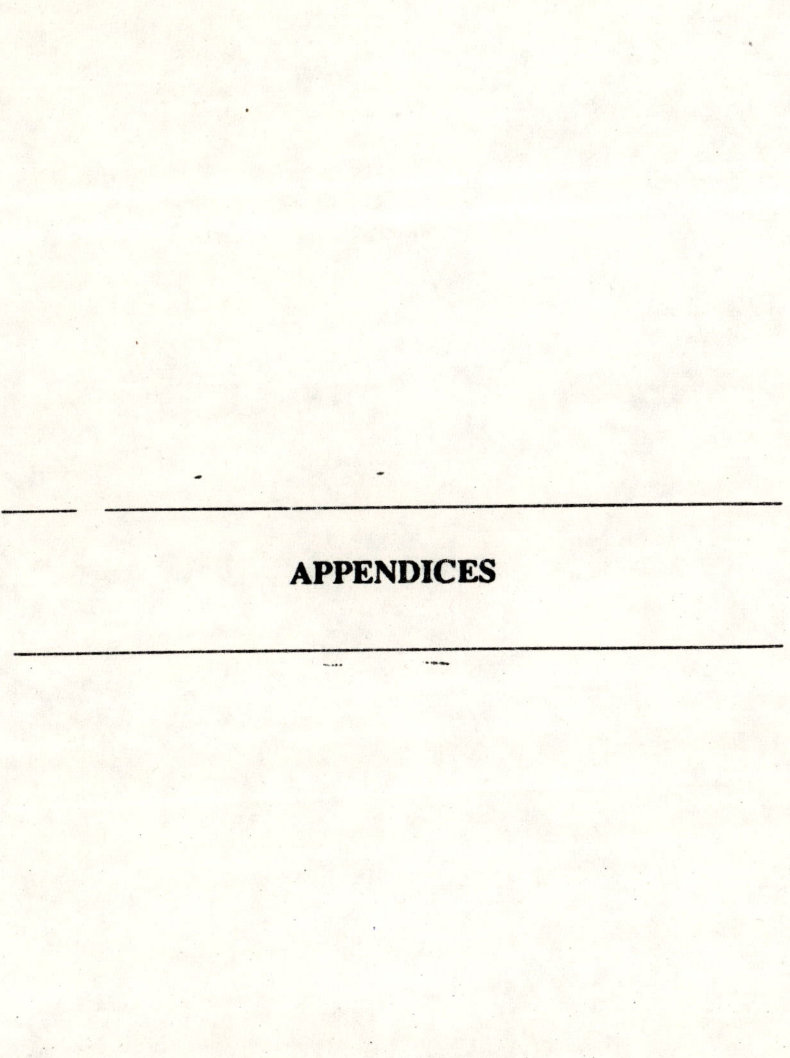

UN Declaration on Elimination of Discrimination Against Women*

Premable

The Preamble to the Declaration sets forth the underlying convictions and concerns of the United Nations in regard to discrimination against women:

The General Assembly,

Considering that the peoples of the United Nations have, in the Charter, reaffirmed their faith in fundamental human rights, in the dignity and worth of the human person and in the equal rights of men and women.

Considering that the Universal Declaration of Human Rights asserts the principle of non-discrimination and proclaims that all human beings are born free and equal in dignity and rights and that everyone is entitled to all the rights and freedoms set forth therein, without distinction of any kind, including any distinction as to sex.

Taking into account the resolutions, declarations, conventions and recommendations of the United Nations and the specialized agencies designed to eliminate all forms of discrimination and to promote equal rights to men and women.

Concerned that despite the Charter of the United Nations, the Universal Declaration of Human Rights, the International Convenants on Human Rights and other instruments of the United Nations and the specialized agencies and despite the progress made in the matter of equality of rights, there continues to exist considerable discrimination against women.

Considering that discrimination against women is incompatible with human dignity and with the welfare of the family and society,

---

* General Assembly Resolution adopted on 7th November 1967.

prevents their participation, on equal terms with men in the political, social, economic and cultural life of their countries and is an obstacle to the full development of the potentialities of women in the service of their countries and of humanity.

Bearing in mind the great contribution made by women to social, political, economic and cultural life and the part they play in the family and particularly in the rearing of children.

Convinced that the full and complete development of a country, the welfare of the world and the cause of peace require the maximum participation of women as well as men in all fields.

Considering that it is necessary to ensure the universal recognition in law and in the face of the principle of equality of men and women.

Solemnly proclaims this Declaration.....

The Preamble emphasizes not only that discrimination against women is unjust, and incompatible with human dignity and with the welfare of the family and of society, but that women's full services and talents are needed, alongside those of men, for the full and complete development of a country, the welfare of the world and the cause of peace. The Assembly proclaims the Declaration "to ensure the Universal recognition in law and in face of the principle of equality of men and women".

Article 1

Discrimination against women, denying or limiting as it does their equality of rights with men, is fundamentally unjust and constitutes an offence against human dignity.

Article 2

All appropriate measures shall be taken to abolish existing laws, customs, regulations and practices which are discriminatory against women, and to establish adequate legal protection for equal rights of men and women, in particular:

(a) The principle of equality of rights shall be embodied in the constitution or otherwise guaranteed by law;
(b) The international instruments of the United Nations and the specialised agencies relating to the elimination of

discrimination against women shall be ratified or acceded to and fully implemented as soon as practicable.

Article 3

All appropriate measures shall be taken to educate public opinion and to direct national aspirations towards the eradication of prejudice and the abolition of customary and all other practices which are based on the idea of the inferiority of women.

Article 4

All appropriate measures shall be taken to ensure to women on equal terms with men, without any discrimination;

  (a) The right to vote in all elections and be eligible for election to all publicly-elected bodies.
  (b) The right to vote in all public referenda.
  (c) The right to hold public office and to exercise all public functions. Such rights shall be guaranteed by legislation.

Article 5

Women shall have the same rights as men to acquire change or retain their nationality. Marriage to an alien shall not automatically affect the nationality of the wife either by rendering her stateless or by forcing upon her the nationality of her husband.

Article 6

  1. Without prejudice to the safeguarding of the unity and the harmony of the family, which remains the basic unit of any society, all appropriate measures, particularly legislative measures, shall be taken to women, married or unmarried, equal rights with men in the field of civil law and in particular:

  (a) The right to acquire, administer, enjoy, dispose of and inherit property, including property acquired during marriage.
  (b) The right to equality in legal capacity and the exercise

thereof.
(c) The same rights as men with regard to law on the movement of persons.

2. All appropriate measures shall be taken to enqure the principle of equality of status of the husband and wife, and in particular;

(a) Women shall have the same right as men to free choice of a spouse and to enter into marriage only with their free and full consent.

(b) Women shall have equal rights with men during marriage and at its dissolution. In all cases the interest of the children shall be paramount.

(c) Parents shall have equal rights and duties in matters relating to their children. In all cases the interest of the children shall be paramount.

3. Child marriage and the betrothal of young girls before puberty shall be prohibited, and effective action, including legislation, shall be taken to specify minimum age for marriage and to make the registration of marriages in an official register compulsory.

Article 7

All provisions of penal codes which constitute discrimination against women shall be repealed.

Article 8

All appropriate measures, including legislation, shall be taken to combat all forms of traffic in women and exploitation of women.

Article 9

All appropriate measures shall be taken to ensure to girls and women, married or unmarried, equal rights with men in education at all levels, and in particular:

(a) Equal conditions of access to, and study in educational

institutions of all types, including universities and vocational, technical and professional schools;

(b) The same choice of curricula, the same exminations, teaching staff with qualifications of the same standard and school premises and equipment of the same quality, whether the institutions are co-educational or not;

(c) Equal opportunities to benefit from scholarships and other study grants;

(d) Equal opportunities for access to programmes of continuing education, including adult literacy programmes;

(e) Access to educational information to help in ensuring the health and well-being of families.

Article 10

1. All appropriate measures shall be taken to ensure to women, married or unmarried; equal rights with men in the field of economic and social life, and in particular:

   (a) The right, without discrimination on grounds of marital status, or any other grounds, to receive vocational training to work, to free choice of profession and employment and to professional and vocational advancement;

   (b) The right to equal remuneration with men and equality of treatment in respect of work of equal value;

   (c) The right to leave with pay, retirement privileges and provision for security in respect of unemployment, sickness, old age or other incapacity to work;

   (d) The right to receive family allowance on equal terms with men.

2. In order to prevent discrimination against women on account of marriage or maternity and to ensure their effective right to work, measures shall be taken to prevent their dismissal in the event of marriage or maternity and to provide paid maternity leave, with the guarantee of returning to former employment, and to provide the necessary social services, including child-care facilities.

3. Measures taken to protect women in certain types of work, for reasons inherent in their physical nature, shall not be regarded

as discriminatory.

Article 11

1. The principle of equality of rights of men and women demands implementation in all States in accordance with the principles of the Charter of the United Nations and of the Universal Declaration of Human Rights.
2. Governments, non-governmental organizations and individuals are urged, therefore, to do all in their power to promote the implementation of the principles contained in this Declaration.

Selective Extracts on Women's Education
from Some Significant Documents
(Not Included in the Main Text)*

Extracts from Wood's Despatch, 1884

The importance of female education in India **cannot be overrated**; and we have observed with pleasure the evidence **which is now afforded** of an increased desire on the part of many of **the natives of India to give a** good education to their daughters. **By this means a far greater** proportional impulse is imparted to the educational and moral tone of the people than by the education of men. We have already observed that schools for females are included among those to which grants in-aid may be given and we cannot refrain from expressing our cordial sympathy with the efforts which **are** being made in this direction. Our Governor-General in Council has decided in a communication to the Government of Bengal that the Government ought to give to natives female education in India its frank and cordial support; in this we heartily concur.

*Important recommendation of Indian Education Commission, 1882-83.***

Women education

It will have been seen that female education is still in an extremely backward condition, and that it needs to be fostered in every legitimate way. . . . Hence we think it expedient to recommend, that public funds of all kinds — local, municipal and provincial — should be chargeable in an equitable proportion for the support of girls' schools as well as

---

* *Selections from the Educational Records, Part II*, 1840-1859, Richey, National Archives of India, New Delhi. Paragraph numbered according to the document.

** *Report of the Indian Education Commission*, Government Printing, Calcutta.

for boys' schools.

*Extracts from the Government Resolution on Educational Policy 1913.**

Recommendations

(5) For the education of women, there should be special curriculum of practical utility for girls and too much importance should not be attached to their examinations.

*Extracts from the Calcutta University Commision, 1917-19***

Female education

Purdah schools should be organised for Hindu and Muslim girls whose parents are willing to extend their education to 15 or 16; a special Board of women's education should be established in the Calcutta University and should be empowered to propose special courses of study more particularly suited for women, and to organise co-operative arrangements for teaching in the women's colleges, more particularly for the training of teachers and in preparation for medical courses.

Major Recommendation

6. Special attention was to be paid to women's education and a Board constituted for the purpose.

*Extracts from the report on the Post-War Educational Development, 1944****

Whatever is needed for boy and men, not less will be required for girls and women.

---

* The Government passed the Resolution in Educational Policy on February 27, 1913.

** The Government appointed Calcutta Univerity Commission under Dr. Michael Sadler, the Vice-Chancellor of Leeds University as chairman for holding an enquiry of very comprehensive nature into the problems of Calcutta University.

*** headed by John Sargent.

(In any modern community it is even more important for the mothers to be educated than the fathers and consequently all educational facilities, *matatis mutandis* — and the differences are by no means so fundamental in the old fashioned imagine — should be equally available for both sexes.)

Report by the Central Advisory Board of Education, January 1944, Ministry of Education, Government of India, 1964. Commonly known as Sargent Report.

Extracts for the Proceedings of the State Education Ministers, Third Conference, 20th and 21st September 1957 at New Delhi

Item 6. Girls' education. The Conference approved the following recommendations of the Panel on Education with regard to Girls' education :

(a) Provision for free accommodation for women teachers.
(b) Appointment of school mothers in rural areas to give encouragement to co-education.
(c) Award of stipend to women teachers for training at the undergraduate level.
(d) Organisation of condensed or special courses of general education and teachers' training for adult women.
(e) Organisation of refresher courses for trained women teachers.
(f) Award of stipends for girls studying in classes VII to XI provided the recepients undertake to adopt teaching profession for a period of five years at least.

Extracts from the Report of the Committee of Members of Parliament on Education : National Policy on Education, 1967 [7]

B. Equalization of educational opportunities

8. Education of girls : There is still wide gap in the enrolment of boys and girls at all stages. It is necessary to eliminate this gap at the primary stage, and to narrow it at the other stages.

---

7. * Published by the Ministry of Education, Government of India, New Delhi, 1967.

Extracts from the Proceedings of the Central Advisory Board of Education. Thirty-Third Meeting, 22nd and 23rd August 1967, at New Delhi.

Education of Girls

35. The education of girls should, therefore, receive special emphasis and funds, required for its advancement, particularly for the implementation of its special programmes, should be provided on a priority basis. The funds for girls education and its special programmes should be earmarked so that there is no possibility of their being diverted into other uses.

35(a) While it is recognised that the gap between the enrolment of boys and girls is being bridged in the field of general education, it is noticed that the gap is actually widening in the field of vocational education for lack of adequate facilities of vocational education for girls. It is urgently necessary to expand and improve the programme of vocational education for girls by organising ITIs and Polytechnic for women offering suitable coures leading to jos or to self-employment.

35(b) Condensed courses for adult women should be organised on a large   scale and it should be ensured through proper coordination among different agencies and Government departments that women who complete the courses are suitably employed. This is one important way of meeting the present shortage of women personnel.

Thirty-ninth Meeting, 6th and 7th June 1983 at New Delhi

Women's Education

Special efforts are required for accelerating the pace of education of girls/women.

First Five Year Plan, 1951-52 to 1955-56*

Chapter XXXIII Education

8. Women's Education

The general purpose and objective of women's education cannot, of

---

* Published by the Planning Commission, Government of India, New Delhi, 1952.

course be different from the purpose and objectives of men's education. There are, however, vital differences in the way in which this purpose has to be realised.

The problem of women's education in India is above all the problem of the education of grown-up women. Generally women cannot always be educated in the same continuous fashion as men. Unlike boys, girls are forced to suspend their studies in the early teens due to a variety of reasons and take up wider responsibilities of the home. Arrangement should, therefore be made to facilitate resumption of studies by women at a time when they have leisure.

Second Five Year Plan, 1956-57 to 1960-61**

Chapter XXIII Education

Secondary Education (Girls Education)

At the secondary stage, the education of girls lags seriously behind. At present out of total population of 12 million girls in the age group 14-17 years, about 3 per cent are attending schools. Plans of states do not provide in sufficient measure for the education of girls, for the number of high schools for girls is expected to increase from 1,500 to 1,700 only by the end of the Second Plan.

Third Five Year Plan 1961-62 to 1965-66*

Chapter XXIX Education

Elementary Education (Girls Education)

A very large gap still exists between the proportion of boys and girls attending school. . . . The National Counsel for Women's Education carefully considered the special measures needed for promoting the education of girls at the primary, middle and secondary stages and made a series of recommendations. These include the provision of

---

** Published by the Planning Commission, Government of India, New Delhi, 1958.

* Published by the Planning Commission, Government of India, New Delhi, 1961.

quarters for women teachers, special allowances for women teachers working in rural areas, condensed educational courses for adult women so as to enlarge the supply of women teachers, stipend for women teacher trainees, attendance prizes and scholarships, appointment of school mothers in co-educational institutions and provision of necessary amenities. To some extent proposals on these levels have been embodied in the plans of the states.

Girls Education

Over the past decade, while the additional number of boys enrolled in schools was 13.2 million, in the case of girls, the addional enrolment was only 6.8 million. The census of 1961 has shown that, as against a literacy rate of 34 per cent for men, only about 13 per cent of the women are literate. Consequently, by far the most important objective in the field of education during the Third Plan must be to expand facilities for the education of girls at various stages. According to the programmes which have been formulated taking age-group 6-14, the proportion of girls at schools increase to 46 per cent, compared to 73 per cent for boys. Out of about 20.4 million additional children to be enrolled in schools during the Third Plan in the various age-groups, about 10.3 million are expected to be girls, their proportion in the lowest age-group being 56 per cent. At the end of Third Plan, the disparity between boys and girls, although somewhat reduced, will still be considerable.

It is estimated that, of the resources available under the Plan for the development of education, about Rs. 175 crores will be devoted to the education of girls, of which about 114 crores are for education at the primary and middle school stages.

Fourth Five Year Plan, 1969-70 to 1973-74*

Chapter XVI Education and Manpower

Girls Education

Sustained efforts to extend education among girls have been made

---

* Published by the Planning Commission, Government of India, New Delhi, 1970.

from the First Plan period. Girls students, as a percentage of their population in the relevant age-group, increased from 25 in 1950-51 to 1959 in 1968-69 in classes IX-XI. The gap between the enrolment of boys and girls is still considerable. During the Fourth Plan, the enrolment of girls will be further increased through the organisation of special programmes the nature of which will vary from state to state.

Women's Studies Centres/Cells in Indian Universities/Colleges
(Up to March, 1989)

Women Studies Cell

1. Women Studies Cell, B.N.K.B. (P.G.) College Akbarpur Faizabad, U.P.
   Mr. R. K. Tripathi, Principal.
2. Women Studies Cell, Sociology Department, Bhopal University, Bhopal, M.P.
   Dr. I. S. Chauhan, Prof. and Head.
3. Dr. D.K. Lal Das, Head, College of Social Work Hyderabad, A.P.
4. Women Studies Cell, Sociology Department Jodhpur University, Jodhpur.
   Prof. Sheo Kumar Lal, Head
5. Women Studies Cell, Principal A.N.D.M.M. College, Kanpur,
   Dr. Hemlata Swarup, Principal.
6. Women Studies Cell, S.D. College, Muzaffarnagar, U.P.
   Dr. L.N. Mittal, Principal.
7. Women Studies Cell, Home Science Department, College for Women, Trivandrum
   Prof. Chandravally Thampuran, Head.

Centre for Women's Studies

1. Women's Studies Centre, Andhra University, Waltair, Andhra Pradesh.
   Prof. Ila Rao, Director.
2. Women's Studies Centre, Berhampur University, Berhampur, Orissa.
   Dr. Bibekananda Das, Director.
3. Women' Studies Centre, Banaras Hindu University, Varanasi.
   Dr. Surinder Jetley Hony. Director.

4. Centre for Women's Studies, Calcutta University, Calcutta.
   Dr. Bharati Roy, Director.

5. Women's Studies Centre, University of Delhi, Delhi
   Dr. Susheela Kaushik, Director.

6. Women's Studies Centre, Punjab University, Chandigarh.
   Dr. Pam Rajpur, Director.

7. Centre for Women's Studies, Gauhati University, Guwahati.
   Dr. Renu Debi, Director.

8. Women's Studies Centre, Goa University, Bombolin, Goa.
   Mr. S.R.Phal, Director.

9. Centre for Women's Studies, Gulbarga University, Gulbarga,
   Karnataka
   Dr. Ujwala Patil, Director.

10. Centre for Women's Studies, Jadavpur University, Calcutta
    Ms. Jasodhara Bagachi, Director.

11. Women's Studies Centre, Karnataka University, Dharward.
    Dr. Veena Shanteshwar, Director.

12. Women's Studies Centre, Kerala University, Karyavattom,
    Trivandrum.
    Dr. P.K.B. Nair, Director.

13. Centre for Women's Studies, Kurekshetra University,
    Kurekshetra
    Dr. C.L. Kundu

14. Women's Studies Centre, Nagarjuna University, Guntur,
    Andhra Pradesh
    Prof. T. Nirmala, Director.

15. Women's Studies Centre, Poona University, Pune,
    Prof. A. Ramanama, Director.

16. Women's Studies Centre, Punjab University, Chandigarh
    Dr. Pam Rajput, Director.

17. Women's Studies Centre, Rajasthan University, Jaipur
    Dr. Pratibha Jain, Director.

18. Women's Studies Centre, Rani Durgawati Vishwavidyalaya,
    Jabalpur
    Dr. Sheela Shukla, Hony. Director.

19. Women's Studies Centre, S.N.D.T. Women's University, Santa
    Cruz (W), Bombay.
    Prof. Maithreyi Krishan Raj, Director.

20. Women's Studies Centre, Sri Padmavathi Mahila
    Vishwavidyalaya, Tirupati
    Dr. S.A.T. Adilakshmi, Director.

International Workshop on Women's Studies, Trivandrum (26 to 29 April 1989)

The ICSSR sponsored the International Workshop on Women's Studies at the Institute of Management in Government, Trivandrum, from 26 to 29 April, 1989. The workshop aimed developing a network and linkages within the neighbouring countries to discuss the important issues pertaining to women's development and to share the experience gained through the regional and national workshops conducted earlier.

The workshop was attended by foreign delegates from Bangladesh, Bangkok, Malaysia, Singapore and Turkey and Indian participants from all over the country.

In all 24 papers were presented at the workshop. The workshop was divided into eight sessions, each consisting of one sub-theme as under: (i) Women's studies: an overview; (ii) Women and the household; (iii) Education and health; (iv) Minorities; (v) Women and work; (vi) Special issues; (vii) Women and justice; (viii) Others.

The workshop made the following important recommendations;

I. There is a need to develop more active networks within each region for dissemination of knowledge of the research findings as well as details of action taken on new problems and policy issues.

II. In future the following imperatives would be kept in mind while undertaking feminist activities:-

(a) Emphasis should be given to working out casual links between apparently related aspects;

(b) Within each discipline the knowledge acquired through women's studies should be systematically incorporated in standard models so as to modify existing theses on a consistent basis;

(c) Themes like ethnicity, communalism, violence etc., should be re-examined from the point of view of women's studies; and

(d) There were new groups like the newly prosperous peasantry emerging which should be studied to understand the dynamics of Indian women's situations.

III. Following. suggestions were made in evolving methodologies, viz. (i) more intensive micro-studies for establishing casual links; (ii) focus on the dynamics of issues examined and therefore, on a more historical perspective; (iii) a better understanding of the limits imposed by discipline-wise studies; (iv) a methodology in investigating the lives of ordinary people whereby the researchers could also gain some knowledge and insights.

IV. The workshop made the following suggestions for action:

(1) The ICSSR should organize workshops on methodology on women's studies where the links between the discipline-wise studies and inter-disciplinary work would be thoroughly explored.

(2) Studies conducted on stock-taking of the work done so far should be published.

(3) Training courses should be organised for handling of data and research material.

(4) A specialist group should be set up to deal with the national data system from the point of view of women's studies.

(5) In each study the points of intervention by policy makers should be highlighted.

(6) The ICSSR may provide scholarships and fellowships to the people who do not fulfil the normal rigid criteria of selection of such fellowships to encourage scholars who had dropped out temporarily for household duties and now returning to academic work. This should also include the activists looking at particular theoretical points or researchers using unusual methods such as oral history, participatory research, etc.

(7) It was indicated that in such gatherings all the areas should be adequately represented.

(8) Greater efforts should be made to disseminate existing and newly acquired knowedge among the students, teachers, trade-unions and workers associations.

V. The workshop identified the following priority areas of research in the area of womens' studies:

(1) Casual links between infant mortality and fertility.

(2) The relative impact of home and school on children.

(3) Role of teachers in education.

(4) Relative impact on girls' education of lack of facilities and of social barriers.

(5) The casual relations between education, work, and autonomy for women.

(6) Evaluation of the performance of government policies for women.

(7) The role of the media.

(8) The ideology of family and the policies of power and control over women.

(9) The impact of technological changes on women.

(10) Research on women's traditional knowledge systems about health, etc., mainly in terms of indigenous categories.

(11) Oral history of women participating in earlier movements.

(12) Studies of women's literature and women in literature.

World Overview of Women's Education

Female Adult Illiteracy[1] : General Trends and Situation

During the period 1960 to 1985, the world adult (15 years of age and over) illiteracy rate for both sexes is estimated to have decreased by 11.6 percentage points, from 39.3 per cent to 27.7 per cent. The total number of illiterates increased, however, owing to a considerable increase in population during the same period. Out of the 735 million illiterates in 1960, 428 million (58 per cent) were women. In 1985, an estimated 561 million women were illiterate, and they represented nearly two-thirds of the total number of illiterates (889 million). Two facts emerge: (a) from 1960 to 1985, while the total number of female illiterates increased, the total number of male illiterates remained practically unchanged, i.e., 328 million in 1985 versus 307 million in 1960; (b) the female illiteracy rate decreased from 45 per cent to 35 per cent during the same period, but since nearly all the female illiterates are concentrated in developing countries, nearly half of the adult women in developing countries were still illiterate in 1985 (49 per cent). The evolution of female illiteracy from 1960 to 1985 is shown in Table 1.

The highest decline was in developing countries, where the rate for women illiteracy dropped by 20 percentage points, from 68.9 per cent to 48.9 per cent, while in developed countries where the illiteracy rate was already low in 1960, the rate for women declined by 3.6 percentage points, from 6.2 per cent to 2.6 per cent. In the developing countries, the female illiteracy rate in 1985 was at about the same level as the male rate in 1960. Furthermore, it should be noted that the illiteracy rate for males also dropped by 20 percentage points during the same period in developing countries. Since this rate started at a lower level than that of women in 1960, the relative decline has been greater for males than for females.

At the regional level in 1985, the highest adult rate of female illiteracy is found in Africa, where nearly two adult women out of three are illiterate (64.5 per cent), followed by Asia where nearly one woman out of two is illiterate (47.4 per cent). Owing to the size of its population, the greatest number of female illiterates is found in Asia (427 million in 1985), which accounts for about 76 per cent of the world total of female illiterates. In Latin America, the percentage of female illiterates is significantly lower (19.2 per cent), and a number of countries in that region have eradicated illiteracy (e.g., Argentina, Costa Rica, Cuba, Trinidad and Tobago).

TABLE 1:   Estimates of Adult Illiteracy in the World and Selected Major Regions by Sex, 1960-1985

(In millions and percentage)

Region		1960		1985	
		Male	Female	Male	Female
World total	Illiterates	307	428	328	561
	Illiteracy %	33.5	44.9	20.5	34.9
Developed countries	Illiterates	12	22	7	12
	Illiteracy %	3.6	6.2	1.7	2.6
Developing countries	Illiterates	295	406	321	549
	Illiteracy %	49.6	68.9	27.9	48.9
Africa	Illiterates	56	68	64	98
	Illiteracy %	73.4	88.5	43.3	64.5
Asia	Illiterates	224	318	238	427
	Illiteracy %	45.3	65.1	25.6	47.4
Latin America/	Illiterates	17	23	19.2	24.3
Caribbean	Illiteracy %	28.4	36.6	15.3	19.2
Europe and USSR	Illiterates	17	17	4.5	9.4
	Illiteracy %	4.6	6.7	1.6	3.0

Note: Persons 15 years of age and above

Despite the progress made, there is much to be done before female illiteracy can be eradicated worldwide. While developed countries are close to the goal, developing countries, with the exception of Latin America and Oceania, are still far from it. Furthermore, the 36 least developed countries have the highest female illiteracy rate, i.e., 78 per cent. The most disturbing fact is that the number of female illiterates is increasing not only in absolute terms but also in relation to males. Access to employment, especially in the formal sector, and access to many forms of participation are made difficult, if not impossible, through illiteracy. The costs of illiteracy are not only borne by the women themselves; the standard of living and quality of life of their families is also affected. In fact, illiteracy has implications for society itself, since human resources that could be more fruitfully invested in development are wasted or minimized. Clearly, the progress made has not been important enough. Indeed, although illiteracy rates are expected to continue to decline in the near future, the projected increase in the total adult population would result in an increase in the total illiterate population. For example, if there were a drop of 5 points in the world female illiteracy rate between 1985 and 2000 (it dropped by 3.5 points between 1960 and 1970), i.e., to a level of 29.9 per cent, the total number of female illiterates could then be expected to be roughly 637 million (an increase of 76 million over 1985). It can also be seen that without special efforts to reduce the gap between male and female illiteracy it will take many years before that gap disappears thus *de facto* discrimination will continue for several decades in this critical area.

Urban-rural Differences

UNESCO has data on illiteracy by country that were collected through national census or surveys. Such data are available by age group, sex and rural and urban categories for a few countries. They indicate, *inter alia*, that the rate of illiteracy is considerably higher in older generations, which attests to the efforts made by countries in recent decades.

In Table 2, data are presented for the group aged 15-19 years. These data are of particular interest because illiteracy at that age is generally permanent. The data were collected between 1978 and 1982. The people covered are now between 22 and 30 years old and are fully involved in productive and reproductive life; their illiteracy can thus be expected to continue to handicap their future and their contribution to society will into the twenty-first century.

In most of the countries for which data are available, female illiteracy rates are considerably higher than those of males in both urban and rural areas, with the exception of Brazil and the Philippines. The differences between the urban and rural rates are generally much greater for females: young rural women are not only less literate than their urban sisters but the gap between them is generally greater than between urban and rural men. This should be considered in light of the importance or women in agricultural and rural development in many countries.

TABLE 2:   Illiteracy Rates for the 15-19 Age Group in Urban and Rural Areas

(Percentage)

Region		Female illiteracy		Male illiteracy	
		Urban	Rural	Urban	Rural
Africa	Benin	59.0	92.1	31.4	68.3
	Togo	34.3	66.4	9.2	28.7
	United Republic of				
	Tanzania	21.2	43.5	7.1	18.4
Latin America	Brazil	7.6	29.4	9.4	37.3
	Ecuador	2.4	10.6	1.6	7.8
Asia	Afghanistan	56.4	93.8	31.4	55.7
	Bangladesh	52.1	74.6	42.1	60.9
	China	3.2	16.6	1.4	4.7
	India	29.2	66.3	17.9	39.6
	Indonesia	7.0	19.6	3.3	12.2
	Nepal	46.5	85.2	27.0	53.8
	Pakistan	45.9	86.9	36.7	63.8
	Philippines	2.9	10.1	3.2	12.0
	Sri Lanka	5.6	11.2	4.8	10.6

Note: Data were collected through censuses or surveys from 1978 to 1982.

Enrolment of Girls in First – and Second-level Education[2]

Female enrolment has increased from 1970 to 1984 as quickly is as male enrolment, but the proportion of females out of the total is remarkably stable. The only noticeable increase at the secondary level in development countries (from 37 to 40 per cent).

The period 1970-1984[3] has seen a significant numerical growth in enrolment of girls in first and second level education, from 261 million in 1970 to 374 million in 1984. The enrolment of girls represented approximately 44 per cent of the total enrolment in both 1970 and 1984. These aggregates hide a certain diversity, however.

Female Enrolment in First-level Education

Female enrolment in first-level education has seen the greatest increase in absolute numbers, as 261 million girls were enrolled in 1984 compared to 193 million in 1970. The ratio world-wide of girls to boys in education at the first level has hardly increased: from 80.4 girls to

100 boys in 1970 to 81.6 girls to 100 boys in 1984. This represents a deficit of over 59 million girls compared to the number there would be if girls had the same enrolment rates as boys. In 1984, there were still rather wide differences between regions, from near parity in the developed regions and in Latin America and the Caribbean to large differences in Asia and Africa (Table 3). It should also be noted that between 1970 and 1984 in Asia and Latin America and the Caribbean no progress was observed in the girls enrolment ratios relative to boys enrolment ratios.

Another way of looking at the situation is by taking gross enrolment figures, i.e., the enrolment at each level, regardless of the age of pupils, compared to the population which, according to national regulations, should be enrolled at each level (Table 4). In this case, there is parity in the developed countries, and the difference between the male and female ratios is fairly low in Latin America and the Caribbean, although the difference increased from 2 to 4 percentage points from 1970 to 1984. In 1984, the difference between male and female gross enrolment ratios was greatest in Asia and Africa, with 21 and 18 percentage points, respectively. In the case of Africa, this represented a 4 point improvement over 1970. Considerable progress was observed in this period in the Arab States: the difference in percentage points in gross enrolment ratios between boys and girls fell from 32 to 13.

It is clear that greater efforts are necessary in most developing regions if the gap between the chances of girls compared to boys to go to school at the 1st level is to be closed and if female illiteracy is to be eradicated in the twenty-first century.

In developed regions all children go to primary school. The numbers of girls enrolled has decreased although the gross ratio remains unchanged; the decrease in numbers is related to a decrease in the number of births.

It is of interest to note that the percentage of repeaters[4] of a grade was higher among boys than girls in 66 out of the 90 countries studied by UNESCO around 1980, although in most cases the differences were rather small. Girls repeated less than boys in Europe and Latin America and the Caribbean. Africa and Asia and Oceania present a more unfavourable situation for girls in this respect.

TABLE 3:   Standardized Total and Female Enrolment in First and Second Levels of Education in 1970 and 1984 in millions

	First level			Second level		
	Total	Female	Percentage of females	Total	Female	Percentage of females
World						
1970	433	193	45	160	68	43
1984	581	261	45	261	113	43
Developed countries						
1970	123	60	49	81	39	48
1984	114	55	48	88	43	49
Developing countries						
1970	310	133	43	79	29	38
1984	466	206	44	173	70	41
Africa						
1970	33	13	39	5	2	29
1984	76	34	45	23	9	39
Latin America and the Caribbean						
1970	47	23	49	8	4	50
1984	70	34	49	21	11	52
Asia						
1970	243	103	42	75	28	37
1984	337	146	43	141	56	40

Notes: i.   Figures have been rounded.
          ii. "Standardized enrolment means that the data have been standardized to reflect the structure of education existing in 1984. This has been done by reclassifying the enrolment data by grade for this period to align them with the number of grades presently corresponding to first and second level general education", UNESCO, *A Summary Statistical Review of Education in the World, 1970-1984*, Paris, 1986, para. 3.2.

TABLE 4:   Difference Between Male and Female Gross Enrolment Ratios in Percentage Points

Region	First level		Second level	
	1970	1984	1970	1984
Developed countries	1	1	2	−2
Developing countries	19	19	11	13
Africa	22	18	8	14
Latin America and the Caribbean	2	4	2	−2
Asia	20	21	12	14
Arab States*	32	13	16	15

*   Data for the Arab States are also included in Africa and Area.

Female Enrolment in Second-level Education

The increase in absolute numbers for girls in second-level education has been impressive between 1970 and 1984 (Table 3): globally the number of girls has increased by 66 per cent during the period. The increase has been particularly impressive in developing countries (141 per cent) over the 14-year period. The annual rate of growth of female enrolment has slowed down during the period observed, since it dropped from 9.3 per cent in the early 1970s to 3.5 per cent in the early 1980s, but it remains higher than that of males for the period reviewed.

In developed countries, adjusted gross enrolment ratios, which relate the enrolment to the corresponding population age group,[5] have been slightly higher for girls than for boys since 1975. The growth rate of enrolment of girls in developing countries has been faster than for boys, and the result is that girls represented 38 per cent of the total number of enrolled children in the second level in 1970 and 41 per cent in 1984. This still means, however, that if girls had the same adjusted gross enrolment ratio as boys (i.e., 42.7 per cent instead of 29.7 per cent) in developing countries, there would have been approximately 30 million more girls enrolled at the second level. This could have important implications in the preparation of tomorrow's pool of university students or females in the labour force.

Considerable differences in the enrolment ratios can be observed between areas in the developing regions: the ratio reached 52 per cent in 1984 in Latin America and the Caribbean, 24 per cent in Africa and 30 per cent in Asia. It should be noted that both Africa and the Arab States progressed considerably between 1970 and 1984, since their enrolment ratios more than trebbled during that period.

Besides the inequality observed in the enrolment of girls and boys, the chance for a girl in a developing country being enrolled at the second level is much lower (29.7 per cent) than that of her sister in a developed country (88.4 per cent).

The level of repetition by sex during secondary schooling[6] was higher for boys than girls in 45 of the 71 countries covered. It should be noted that 22 of the 26 countries where the level of repetition was higher among girls than among boys were in Africa (3 were in Asia and 1 was in Latin America).

Interrelationship Between Education and Age at Marriage

Education is usually associated with employment, but it also has crucial effects in other areas, for example fertility levels. The illustration chosen here is age at marriage.

Table 5, which is based on data for developing countries from the *World Fertility Survey*, show that age at marriage increases with the number of years of education received by the woman. The four-to six-year level corresponds to the end of primary school, and it can be observed hat several years of education are necessary before the age of marriage rises significantly. What appears to make the most significant difference is associated with women who have gone on from the primary to the secondary level of education (seven years or more): the difference between the age at marriage of women with no formal education and those who have seven or more years of education is 4.8 years.

TABLE 5:   Age at Marriage by Education in 23 Developing Countries

	Number of years of education			
	0	1-3	4-6	7+
Age by which 50 per cent of women had married	17.6	18.0	19.1	22.4

Source: Fertility Behaviour in the Context of Development (ST/ESA/SER.A/100).

Enrolment of Girls in Third-level education

Third-level education[7] is of particular importance not only for women themselves, but also for the nature of their contribution to development and society. Furthermore, third-level education determines to a great extent the pool of future managers and decision makers at both the national and international level.

Increasing Enrolment of Women in Third-level Education

The changes in female enrolment in third-level education are shown in Table 6.

Between 1970 and 1984, the enrolment of women in third-level education nearly doubled in the developed countries and almost quadrupled in the developing countries. Thus the gap between the two groups of countries is closing rapidly: in 1984 the developed countries had less than twice as many female students as the developing countries.

TABLE 6:   Standardized Total and Female Enrolment in Third-level education in
            1970 and 1984

Region	Total male and female (millions)	Female (millions)	Female (percentage)
World total			
1970	28	11	38
1984	54	23	42
Developed countries			
1970	21	9	41
1984	32	15	48
Developing countries			
1970	7	2	29
1984	23	8	35
Africa			
1970	0.5	0.1	23
1984	2	0.5	28
Asia			
1970	7	2	27
1984	18	6	32
Latin America and the Caribbean			
1970	2	0.6	35
1984	6	3	44

Source: UNESCO, *A summary statistical review of education in the world,
             1970-1984*, UNESCO, Paris, 1986 (ED/BIE/CONFINED 40/Ref.1).
Note: Figures have been rounded.

In 1984, as could be expected, Asia clearly dominated numerically:
there were 11 times as many Asian women students as African ones,
and twice as many as Latin American and Caribbean ones. The
increases in Africa are impressive, since the number of female students
has multiplied by 5 in 14 years; however the region still has a long way
to go to achieve equality in the enrolment of the sexes.

Catching Up With the Male Students?

Table 6 also provide information on the extent to which women's
enrolment is nearing that of men. It is clear that the developed

countries have reached near equality.

The focus, therefore, should shift to the distribution of women students by subjects studied; the impact on career possibilities etc. In the developing countries, the picture is different: in 1984 just over a third of the students were women and although a rapid increase in the number of women students was shown, since there was also a concomitant rise in male students, their progress in closing the gap seems to have been slow. It is important to note that in the developing regions, the Latin American and Caribbean countries stand out as having made remarkable progress and have almost reached parity of enrolment. This contrasts with countries in the African and Asian regions in which less than a third of the students were women in 1984; however, fewer African and Asian women, compared with men, were enrolled in third-level education in 1970, and so there was a larger gap initially between female enrolment in the African and Asian regions than in the Latin American and Caribbean region. Nevertheless, the fact remains that the rate of progress in this latter region was also faster. The changes in the Latin American and the Caribbean countries occurred despite a tradition of machismo and can be expected to have a profound impact on this aspect of their culture. In Asian, where in 1984 there were nearly 12 million male students, the gap between male and female enrolment was of such a dimension that it represented more than the total number of female students. The difference was even greater in Africa, where the number of male students was roughly one and a half times the number of female students.

In considering simultaneously the changes in numbers and percentage of female students in Africa and Asia, it is important to realize the effects over time: although female enrolment is catching up with that of males, the accumulated deficit is such that it will take a considerable time for women to eliminate it since, for example, previous generations of male students will already be occupying the more senior positions when the younger generations of women arrive on the job market and are starting their careers.

Proportion of Young Women Studying

Another question is what proportion of women to men in the same age group are studying at the third level? This information is provided by the adjusted gross enrolment ratio, i.e. the total enrolment at the third level, regardless of the age of the pupils, compared to the population which, according to national regulations, should be enrolled at that level. These ratios are presented in Table 7.

TABLE 7:   Adjusted Gross Enrolment Ratios For Third-level Education, 1970-84
(Percentage)

Region	Males	Females
World total		
1970	10.8	6.7
1984	13.4	10.2
Developed countries		
1970	27.2	19.1
1984	33.3	31.8
Developing countries		
1970	4.3	1.8
1984	8.1	4.4
Africa		
1970	2.4	0.7
1984	5.7	2.2
Arab States		
1970	6.5	2.0
1984	12.1	6.6
Asia		
1970	5.3	2.1
1984	8.3	4.1
Latin America and the Caribbean		
1970	8.0	4.5
1984	16.7	13.2
Northern America		
1970	51.7	37.1
1984	59.4	64.0

Note: Data for the Arab States are also included in those for Africa and Asia.

The increases in the enrolment ratios between 1970 and 1984 are much less impressive for the developing countries than the increases in the absolute number of students; for example, as noted in Table 6, the number of female students in Africa increased approximately five-fold during that period, while the adjusted ratio was multiplied by 3, owing to the rapid increase in population that occurred in Africa then. In the other developing regions, the picture is similar. In the more developed regions, however, the rate of increase in the numbers of female students is not so different from that of the ratio of female students. The result is that the increase in the ratio in the developed regions is much greater than it is in the developing ones: nearly 13 points. These differences imply practical consequences for decision makers, for example, in the investments necessary just to maintain the *status quo* or to close the gap.

These ratios also provide an idea of the human resource potential of a number of regions. If, for example, the developing regions had the same ratio of women students as the developed ones, they could be expected to have had nearly 57 million women students enrolled in 1984 instead of approximately 8 million. Women in different regions thus have unequal opportunities of participating in higher education and that inequality is much greater between women in different regions than it is between women and men in the same region. If the ratio of women students in developing regions had been same as that of men in the same region there could have been over 14 million women students instead of 8 million in 1984. This gives an idea of the importance of the gender factor compared with the development factor. The combination of both these factors constitutes a serious handicap for women in developing regions and prevents them from playing a decisive role in their countries. Another aggravating factor has been identified by the World Bank:[8] the cost per student in higher education as a percentage of per capita GNP varies considerably according to the country's level of development: it is 3.7 times (370 per cent) the per capita GNP in developing countries in general, but 8 times (800 per cent) the per capita GNP in sub-Saharan Africa in particular, whereas in industrial countries it represents only 49 per cent of the per capita GNP.

It should be noted that there are considerable variations in the developed countries also. In Table 7, Northern American countries have by far the highest enrolment ratio and it is even higher for women than it is for men. The Table includes the Arab States since their enrolment ratios are significantly higher than those of the regions to which they belong.

Fields of Study of Women in Higher Education

It is of interest to analyse the major field of study of women in third-level education. Before doing so, however, two preparatory remarks ar necessary. First, if women were equal to men, one could expect roughly equal number of female and male students distributed in a similar manner between the different field of study. Secondly, if all fields of study can enrich the individual and society in a broad sense, some are valued more highly than others by society (i.e., those for which it is willing to provide jobs and prestige). It is attempted to provide some data taken from a study prepared by the United Nations Educational, Scientific and Cultural organization UNESCO[9] to illustrate these points in an indicative way. In view of the objective which is to identify and illustrate certain problems, even if the data are incomplete[10] and a field of study in one country does not correspond rigorously with one carrying the same label in another country, the patterns still appear valid and consistent, at this level of generality. In fact, in view of the importance of the implications of such data for both the advancement of women and national development, national authorities should give greater attention to improving the quality of such data.

In its study, UNESCO regrouped the 20 fields of study in higher education defined by the International Standard Classification of Education into two broad categories, i.e., arts: education (teacher training, etc.) and social sciences; and sciences: natural sciences (engineering, computer science etc.), medical sciences and agriculture.

These distinctions correspond, to a certain extent, to the *traditional* roles of men and women: education and social sciences correspond to women's roles of understanding and caring, and are therefore labelled care-oriented fields; while the others, particularly natural sciences and agriculture, correspond more to men's role of changing the world and are therefore labelled action-oriented fields. Perhaps medical sciences incorporate both roles and thus form an intermediate category.

It is of interest, therefore, to examine the extent to which present-day youth are reproducing the traditional gender roles.

The striking features of Table 8 are the similarity between the distribution in the more developed regions and the less developed regions and the distribution according to traditional roles: two thirds of the female students are in care-oriented fields. Since natural sciences and agriculture account for less than one fifth of the female students, the question arises as to what the potential impact of female graduates will be on the development of their countries over the next decades; for example, in industrialization, rural development or environmental issues. In view of the similarity of distribution between the more developed regions and the less developed regions, the process of development in itself does not appear to be sufficient to correct the distribution. A planned and systematic effort to correct the imbalance of the existing distribution should, therefore, be directed both at girls already in primary school and at their teachers and parents.

TABLE 8:   Distribution of Women by Field of Study in More Developed Regions and Less Developed Regions, 1982

(Percentage)

		More developed regions	Less developed regions
Care-oriented	(Education	16	14
	(Social sciences	50	53
		66	67
	Medical sciences	14	10
Action-oriented fields	(Natural sciences	12	17
	(Agriculture	2	2
		14	19
	Others	7	4

Notes: (i) Based on, *Female Participation in Higher Education: Enrolment Trends, 1975-1982*, Current Surveys and Research in Statistics, UNESCO, Paris, 1985, (CSR-E-50).
        (ii) Numbers have been rounded.

Are There Differences Between the Developing Regions?

TABLE 9:   Distribution of Women by Field of Study and region, 1982

(Percentage)

		Africa	Asia	Latin America
Care-oriented field	(Education	15	14	16
	(Social sciences	56	57	43
		71	71	59
	Medical sciences	12	8	14
Action-oriented fields	(Natural sciences	11	19	14
	(Agriculture	6	2	3
		17	21	17
	Others	0	2	11

As shown in table 9, the regional breakdown of the fields of study for Africa and Asia shows great similarity for the care-oriented fields (around 70 per cent of the total of the female students). However, there appear to be slight differences in the sciences: Asian women appear to dominate in the natural sciences (21 per cent) compared with women from other regions; while Latin American women more frequently choose to study medical sciences and African women, agriculture.

Are There Adequate Numbers of Female Students to Make an Impact on Their Status and on Development?

After noting the similarity in the patterns of choice, the number of students in each field can be related to the size of the population to give an idea of the size of the population among which the students would be working to promote the status of women and to advance national development. This can be done by estimating roughly the rate of students in each field per 100,000 inhabitants, which is an indicator of their case-load, and therefore different from that in Table 7, where an indication was given of the opportunities for girls to study by presenting the adjusted gross enrolment ratios that related them to their peer age groups.

The question that needs to be raised is, if the rates are of the magnitude given in Table 10, what are the possible implications for development and the status of women?

Some might consider that the figures given are deceptive since they imply that only the 1982 group of students will be working among the entire population, whereas students have been trained before the generation and many more will be trained after them. While this argument is true for the more developed regions, the reverse could be true for the less developed regions since the number of female students in third-level education has been very small in the past.

TABLE 10:   Rate of Female Students Per 100,000 Inhabitants According to Different Fields of Study

	Africa	Asia	Latin America and the Caribbean
Education	16	32	83
Social sciences	60	133	228
Medical sciences	13	18	77
Natural sciences	12	44	74
Agriculture	6	4	14
Others	—	3	60

The progress made in Latin America is apparent. What is more important, however, is the contrast between the low rate of women studying agriculture and the fact that in Africa, for example, the population is still rural and most of the food is produced by women. The difference between the rates for women in developing regions and those for their sisters in developed countries is still important, as illustrated in Table 11, which show the number of times the figure is higher for developed regions; for example, the figure of 16 means that the number of women studying education is 16 times higher in more developed regions than it is in Africa.

TABLE 11:   Comparison Between More Developed Regions and Less Developed Regions of the Number of Female Students Per 100,000 inhabitants in Different fields of Study (Multiplier)

	Africa compared with more developed regions	Asia compared with more developed regions	Latin America and the Caribbean compared with more developed regions
Education	16	8	3
Social sciences	14	6	4
Medical sciences	18	13	3
Natural sciences	17	4	3
Agriculture	6	8	2

Note: The multiplier is obtained by dividing the number of female students, in a field of study, per 100,000 inhabitants in more developed regions by the number per 100,000 inhabitants in less developed regions.

Could the Gap Between the Developing and Developed Countries be Closed Rapidly?

In most developed countries, even with high rates of female student enrolment over several decades (i.e., with the expected cumulative or possibly compounding effect), problems still remain in the area of equality between the sexes. The gap between the more developed regions and the less developed regions provides an idea of the magnitude of the investment in human resources that would be necessary to close the gap. Although third-level education is not the only way to resolve the issue of advancement of women, it is also an important factor. The question is whether there are short cuts that could provide not short-term victories, but sustainable advancement.[11]

Are Men and Women Similar in Their Choice of Fields of Study?

The data in Table 12 shows the percentage of students who have reached the third level of education and who have therefore survived the discrimination or selection processes undergone since those students started school. Introducing change, therefore, requires modifications at all stages in a student's school career. While a comparison of the choices made by or for male and female students does not imply a value judgement, it can be assumed the, for the present, it does imply a social judgement.

TABLE 12:   Distribution of Male and Female Students by Field of Study in More Developed Regions and Less Developed Regions, 1982

(Percentage)

		More developed regions		Africa		Asia		Latin America and the Caribbean	
		Male	Female	Male	Female	Male	Female	Male	Female
Care-oriented fields	(Education	5	16	10	15	6	14	8	16
	(Social sciences	40	50	52	56	56	57	36	43
	Medical sciences	9	14	9	12	4	8	10	14
Action-oriented fields	(Natural sciences	36	12	20	11	30	19	38	14
	(Agriculture	4	2	7	6	3	2	6	3
	Others	6	6	1	0	1	2	3	11

Notes: (i) Based on, *Female Participation in Higher Education: Enrolment Trends, 1975-1982*, Current Surveys and Research in Statistics, UNESCO, Paris, 1985, (CSR-E-50).
   (ii) Numbers have been rounded.

Table 12 clearly shows the preference of women for the fields of teaching, social sciences and medical sciences when these preferences are compared with those of men. Such preferences do not necessarily mean that women dominate these fields numerically: this depends also on the enrolment ratios which, as seen in, are usually much lower for women. Table 1 also shows the considerable dominance of men in the fields of natural sciences (for whom they are from two to three times as frequent a choice) and agriculture. Except for Africa, where a ratio of only 1 man in 5 selects natural sciences as a field of study, the ratio in other developing regions is roughly 1 in 3, with nearly 4 in 10 men in

Latin America selecting natural sciences. In contrast, between 1 in 7-9 women choose natural sciences, with the exception of Asia, where the ratio is 1 in 5. Agricultural is not a popular choice for either men or women, which is serious in view of the importance in developing regions of issues related to rural development and food, particularly in Africa and Asia.

Some questions can be raised. Are such differences in distribution desirable from the perspective of the status of women? If not, what could be done to change the distribution, in particular, by the female teachers and social scientists? Should special scholarship be introduced for women to study science or incentives given to parents to encourage their daughters to study agriculture? Are there countries in which certain field of study *de jure or de facto* are not open to such studies? One factor of concern is that the data provided are for 1982 and therefore, cover the present generation of young adults: there seems to be a considerable difficulty in modifying the selection process, which may restrict the future advancement of women for a number of years.

In Which Fields Do Women Students Dominate Numerically?

Table 13 shows the percentage of women in each field of study and is therefore independent of the distribution for each sex, but dependent on the enrolment rates by sex for each field. This means that even in an area of study preferred by women, they can still find themselves in a minority if their enrolment rates in third-level education are much lower than those of men.

TABLE 13: Percentage of Women in Each Field of Study in More Developed Regions and Less Developed Regions, 1982

		More developed regions	Africa	Asia	Latin America and the Caribbean
Care-oriented fields	(Education	69	39	51	59
	(Social sciences	49	32	32	46
	Medical sciences	54	36	47	50
Action-oriented fields	(Natural sciences	21	19	22	21
	(Agriculture	30	25	19	23
	Others	45	4	31	74

Note: Number have been rounded.

Table 13 also shows that, except for Africa (and to some extent Asia), parity has been achieved or is close to being achieved in the fields of education, social sciences and medicine. What will be the impact of the present parity in the future implementation of the acquired skills? For example, will the women social scientists be able, through their study of societies, to influence policies in favour of women? Of course, other factors intervene, such as the funding of research, but the influence of women social scientists should be monitored and women should be encouraged to organize themselves and to articulate issues for the advancement of women. Another issue that will emerge or is emerging in relation to these ratios of students is that of fairness between the sexes in career patterns and decision-making. A word of caution is also necessary, however; in certain cases, an over-feminisation can result in a field being equated with low prestige and becoming a ghetto. This could already be the case in certain countries as far as the field of education is concerned.

If women are to catch up in the field of natural sciences, considerable efforts will be required over a long period of time not only because it is difficult in most cases to select natural sciences at the third level if this field was not already selected at the secondary level, but also because of the high proportion of men in the natural sciences. However, considering the data for agriculture in tables 1 and 2, and given that this field is not popular with men or women, a shift in women's preferences towards agriculture could have a rapid and dramatic impact in developing countries. This issue should perhaps be considered by policy makers, particularly in Africa and Asia: not only could women have an impact in helping to increase food production, but also the introduction of modernization could be expected to take into account the needs of rural women and their status.

Can the World be Changed Through the Advancement of Women?

In Table 14, the combined effects of the enrolment ratios and distribution are illustrated. This means, for example, that out of 100 students of both sexes in the more developed regions, only one women is studying agriculture; the corresponding number for Africa is two and for Asia and Latin America, one. Such figures should be compared with national priorities and estimated needs: conclusions can then be drawn for the future; for example, who will be able, in many developing countries, to improve the situation of rural women?

TABLE 14:   Distribution of Students by Field of Study and Sex in More Developed
              Regions and Less Developed Regions

(Percentage)

		More developed regions		Africa		Asia		Latin America and the Caribbean	
		Male	Female	Male	Female	Male	Female	Male	Female
Care-oriented fields	(Education	3	7	7	5	4	4	5	6
	(Social sciences	23	22	37	17	38	18	21	18
	Medical sciences	5	6	6	3	3	2	6	6
Action-oriented fields	(Natural sciences	20	5	14	3	21	6	22	6
	(Agriculture	2	1	5	2	2	1	4	1
	Others	3	3	1	—	1	—	1	4
Total by sex		56	44	70	30	69	31	59	41
Grand total		100		100		100		100	

Note: Numbers have been rounded.

Similar remarks can be made concerning the field of natural
sciences; however, Table 14 has many possible implications for the
future role of women in decision-making. In so far as decision-making
is not only linked to individuals, but also to the statistical weight and
distribution of various groups, the data in the table could mean that
women might face difficulties in having an influence in important
areas not only for their advancement, but also for development. For
example, what could be their weight in decisions on the future of
industrialization? It is not enough just to have a minister of industry;
women engineers and technicians are also required in the sectors that
influence the conception and the implementation of projects. The same
can be said for rural development, which leads to such questions as:
what would happen to rural women in Africa or Asia if, instead of 7 or
3 per cent of the students choosing to study agriculture, 25 per cent
chose to do so, of which over half were women? Of course, such
changes would entail many policy and programme measures since it
would also be necessary not only to intervene at all levels of education,

but also to promote the provision of employment opportunities corresponding to this field of study.

Note: Reproduced in the hope that this data may be of interest and help to those interested in improving the status of women.

Source: *Data Highlights* prepared by the Division for the Advancement of Women Centre for Social Development and Human Affairs, United Nations Office at Vienna, and published with funds made available to the Centre by the Government.

NOTES

1. Estimates for 1960 are from, *A Summary Statistical Review of Education in the World 1960-1980*, Paris, 1981; estimates for 1985 from, *The Current Literacy Situation in the World*, UNESCO, Paris, 1987, and *Compendium of Statistics on Illiteracy*, UNESCO, Paris, 1988.
2. First-level education is the level of basic instruction, i.e., in elementary schools, primary schools or basic schools; second-level education is in middle schools, secondary schools or high schools.
3. *A Summary Statistical Review of Education in the World, 1970-1984*, UNESCO, Paris, 1986, (ED/BIE/CONFINTED 40/Ref.1).
4. *Evolution of Wastage in Primary Education in the World Between 1970 and 1980*, UNESCO, Paris, (ED/BIE/CONFINTED/39/Ref.2).
5. Unlike the gross enrolment ratio, the adjusted ratio compared the number of pupils enrolled to the total population at the same age level.
6. *Wastage in Primary and General Secondary Education: A Statistical Study of Trends and Patterns in Repetition and Drop-out*, UNESCO, Paris, 1980, (CSR-E-37).
7. Third-level education refers to higher education: universities and equivalent degree-granting institutions; distance learning university institutions and other institutions of higher education, such as teacher training colleges and technical colleges.
8. World Bank, *World Development Report 1988*, Oxford University Press, Oxford, 1988, p. 135.
9. *Female Participation in Higher Education: Enrolment Trends, 1975-1982*, Current surveys and research in statistics, Paris, 1985, (CSR-E-50).
10. The data have been taken from *Female Participation in Higher Education...*, tables A.1.2, A.1.6, A.1.3.2, A.3.4, A.5.2 and A.5.4. A few of the largest countries were not covered by the data; for example, Brazil, China, the United States of America and the Union of Soviet Socialist Republics.
11. Statement by the Division for the Advancement of Women, United Nations Office at Vienna, at the WHO Consultation with International Women's Non-governmental Organizations, Geneva, 21-22 December 1989, p. 3.

CICIL LIST

CONCEPTS IN COMMUNICATION, INFORMATICS & LIBRARIANSHIP

(CICIL)

General Editor: **S.P. AGRAWAL**

CICIL-1   Development of Library Services in India: Social Science Information
S.P. Agrawal Rs. 150

CICIL-2   Development of Documentation in India: Social Science Information
S.P. Agrawal Rs. 250

CICIL-3   UNESCO and Social Sciences: Retrospect and Prospect
S.P. Agrawal and J.C. Aggarwal Rs. 250

CICIL-4   INDIANA : A Bibliography of Bibliographical Sources
M.K. Jain Rs. 200

CICIL-5   Dimensions of Library and Information Science: Kaula Festschrift
V. Venkatappaiah (Eds.) Rs. 600

CICIL-6   Book Numbers: Some Indian Methods
M.P. Satija and S.P. Agrawal Rs. 100

CICIL-7   National Policy for University Libraries in India: Problems and Perspectives
N.B. Inamdar and **L.S. Ramaiah** (Ed.) Rs. 250

CICIL-8   Media Utilisation for the Development of Women and Children
B.S. Thakur and **Binod C. Agrawal** Rs. 150

CICIL-9   Terrorism: An Annotated Bibliography
Susheela Bhan (Ed.) Rs. 275

CICIL-10 Transnational Library Relations: The Indo-American Experience
M.B. Konnur Rs. 175

CICIL-11 Geography of Marketing and Commercial Activities in India (Documentation on Research Information)
R.S. Dixit Rs. 130

CICIL-12 Information India 1988: Global View
S.P. Agrawal and **J.C. Aggarwal** Rs. 200

CICIL-13 Women's Education in India: Historical Review, Present Status and Perspective Plan
S.P. Agrawal and **J.C. Aggarwal** Rs. 360

CICIL-14 Cultural Communication in India: Role and Impact of Phonograms
J.M. Ojha (in press)

CICIL-15 Second Historical Survey of Educational Development in India: Select Documents 1985-1989
S.P. Agrawal and **J.C. Aggarwal** (in press)

CICIL-16 Documentation Encyclopaedia of UNESCO and Education
J.C. Aggarwal and **S.P. Agrawal** Rs. 800 (set of 2 parts)

CICIL-17 Attitude Towards Information: A Study of Post-Graduate Teachers and Researchers in Social Sciences
N.G. Satish (in press)

CICIL-18 Librarianship and Bureaucratic Organisation: A Study in the Sociology of Library Profession in India
P.K. Jayaswal Rs. 175

CICIL-19 Literature Search
K.A. Isaac Rs. 150

CICIL-20 Child Education in India: Index to Scholarly Writings in Indian Educational Journals and Newspapers since independence
S.P. Agrawal and **Naresh Kanta** Rs. 100

CICIL-21 Lok Sabha and Vidhan Sabha Elections in India 1989 & 1990: Process and Results with Comparative Study of Manifestos
S.P. Agrawal and **J.C. Aggarwal** Rs. 250

CICIL-22 Islamic Studies in India: A Survey of Human, Institutional and Documentary Sources
Mohamed Taher Rs. 180

CICIL-23 Panchayati Raj: An Annotated Bibliography
N.B. Inamdar, N.G. Satish and Anil Takalkar (in press)

CICIL-24 Information India 1989-90: Global View
S.P. Agrawal and **J.C. Aggarwal** Rs. 500

CICIL-25 First Handbook of Psychological and Social Instruments
Udai Pareek and **T. Venkateswara Rao** (in press)

CICIL-26 Educational and Social Uplift of Backward Classes: At What Cost and How? Mandal Commission and After
S.P. Agrawal and **J.C. Aggarwal** Rs. 275

CICIL-27 Mass Media and New Horizons: Impact of TV & Video an Urban Milieu **H.R. Trivedi** Rs. 180

CICIL-28 Indian Writings on Education : An Indicator to Indian Educational Journals Grouped by Subject Descriptors 1979 to 1986 (in two volumes) **S.P. Agarwal** and **J.C. Aggarwal** Rs. 900 (per set)

CICIL-29 Nation in Crisis
S.P. Agrawal and **J.C. Aggarwal** Rs. 200